SOFTWARE DESIGN

Dr. Bechoo Lal

Toronto Academic Press

Software Design

Dr. Bechoo Lal

Toronto Academic Press
224 Shoreacres Road
Burlington, ON L7L 2H2
Canada
www.tap-books.com
Email: orders@arclereducation.com

ISBN: 978-1-77469-779-5

ABOUT THE AUTHOR

Bechoo Lal, PhD. became a Member (M) of IAENG: International Association of Engineers, USA with membership (108820) in 2010, a Senior Member (SM) in 2019. I am doctorate PhD in Computer Science, PhD- Information System from University of Mumbai, Master from Banaras Hindu University (BHU), PGP- Data Science from Purdue University, USA. Currently working as a Associate Professor in Department of Computer Science & Engineering, KLEF- KL University Vijayawada Campus Andhra Pradesh, India. His research areas are data science, big data analytics and Machine Learning.

Contents

List of Figures

List of Table

List of Abbreviations

ALU	Arithmetic/Logic Unit
CASE	Computer-Aided Software Engineering
COTS	Commercially Off-the-Shelf
CPU	Central Processing Unit
CU	Control Unit
GUI	Graphical User Interface
JVM	Java Virtual Machine
KFV	Keyword Frequency Vector
SDLC	Software Development Life Cycle
SIMD	Single instruction, Multiple Data
SRA	Software Requirement Analysis

PREFACE

The importance of design in software development cannot be overstated. Software design is complex for a variety of reasons. It is significantly more challenging to teach and learn software design. There have been numerous textbooks created on software design. Most focus on a single program design method, such as object-oriented software development. Few, however, have tackled software design at a higher level of abstraction, such as the methodological level, which is the focus of this subject.

In my experience teaching software design in advanced undergraduate courses and overseeing student dissertation projects, I've discovered that students frequently have misconceptions about software design. One of the most widespread misconceptions about software design is that there is only one correct answer to each design problem. Many software design textbooks provide case studies and examples, but few offer many answers to a single design problem. A prevalent fallacy to software design approaches is that using a well-established design method correctly always results in the correct solution to a design problem.

As a result, many students rush to the implementation stage of their dissertation projects after completing a design without extensively analyzing and assessing it; even fewer thought of creating alternative ideas and comparing them. Few software design textbooks tackle how to analyze a design and compare different software designs. Learning software design techniques might help correct misconceptions about software design methodologies. Theories of software architecture, particularly software architectural styles and architectural design analysis and evaluation, are at the appropriate level of abstraction and are especially useful for correcting students' mistakes.

Another difficulty in teaching and learning software design is that most students have no prior experience with large-scale, complex software systems. The theories of software architecture also provide an appropriate communication medium for students to learn how to design large-scale software systems. It can combine numerous software engineering, development processes, and programming information taught in multiple courses into a well-organized framework. It also considerably broadens students' understanding of software systems.

—Author

CHAPTER 1

INTRODUCTION TO SOFTWARE DESIGN

UNIT INTRODUCTION

Software design refers to the process of envisioning and designing software solutions for one or more types of concerns. The software requirement specification analysis (SRA) is considered one of the most important aspects of the design process for software (SRA). The SRA is a component in the process of developing software that is responsible for listing the software engineering standards. Program design may entail user experience design, which results in the creation of a storyboard to assist in determining those criteria when the software in question is "semi-automated" or user oriented. If the program has no users or user interfaces, then the design of the software can be as basic as a flow diagram or text expressing a predetermined order of events. This is the case when the software is said to be fully automated. Additionally, some ways are considered to be more of a standard, such as Unified Modeling Language with Fundamental modeling ideas. In either scenario, the design process will often result in some sort of record of the strategy. In addition, the accessibility of the technology utilized in the design can determine whether a software design is platform-independent versus platform-specific for such application it is intended for (Littlewood et al., 2001).

The outcome of a software analysis typically consists of several small issues that need to be solved, which is the primary distinction between software design and analysis. Furthermore, the analysis shouldn't be constructed substantially differently amongst various members of the team or different groups of people. In comparison, the design emphasizes capabilities; as a result, more than one solution to the same issue is possible and will in all likelihood be found. Whether it is constructed from dependable frameworks or applied with appropriate design guidelines, the design frequently shifts and changes depending on the context in which it is used. Examples of design may be seen in operating systems, websites, mobile devices, and even the recently developed concept of cloud computing (Sullivan et al., 2001).

The design of software may be thought of as both a method and a model. The schematic design is comprised of a series of processes that gives the designer the ability to explain all parts of the program that is being constructed. A few examples of important success characteristics for a professional design include creative ability, previous expertise, an understanding of what constitutes "excellent" software, as well as an overall dedication to quality. The design phase, on the other hand, is not always an easy method; the design model may be likened to the drawings which an architect creates for a house. It is vital to keep this in mind while discussing the design process. It begins by showing the entirety of the object that is to be produced (for example, a three-dimensional depiction of the home), and then, slowly but surely, the thing is polished to offer advice for creating every detail (e.g., the plumbing lay). Similarly, the design model which is developed for computer software offers several distinct perspectives on the program itself (Thomas et al., 2010).

Learning Objective

At the end of this chapter students will be able to learn:

- Basics of software design;
- Principles of software design;
- Difference between coupling and cohesion;
- Object-oriented design;
- User interface design.

Key Terms

- Software design
- Coupling
- Cohesion
- Pseudo-code
- UI design principles
- Software reliability
- Coding standards

SOFTWARE DESIGN PRINCIPLES

Software design ideas aim to provide methods for effectively handling the complexity of a design process. Effective complexity control may reduce the risk of making errors during design and the labor needed for it (Zhu, 2005).

TIPS

Software design yields three levels of results:

Architectural Design: It is the highest abstract version of the system. It identifies the software as a system with many components interacting with each other. At this level, the designers get the idea of proposed solution domain.

High-Level Design: It breaks the 'single entity-multiple component' concept of architectural design into less-abstracted view of sub-systems and modules and depicts their interaction with each other. High-level design focuses on how the system along with all of its components can be implemented in forms of modules. It recognizes modular structure of each sub-system and their relation and interaction among each other.

Detailed Design: It deals with the implementation part of what is seen as a system and its sub-systems in the previous two designs. It is more detailed towards modules and their

The principles of software design are discussed in subsections (Figure 1.1).

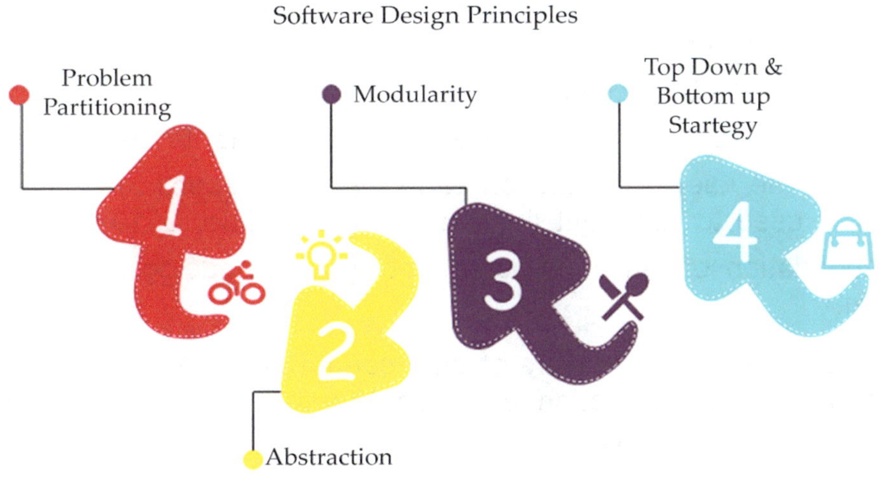

Figure 1.1. Design principles for software.

Source: Image by javapoint.com.

Problem Partitioning

When addressing a minor problem, we could do so at once. Therefore, to manage each problem separately while dealing with a huge issue, we must divide it into smaller concerns. Software design aims to divide the problem into distinct, controllable components (Arató et al., 2003).

Benefits of problem partitioning:

- The software is simple to use;
- Software is made easier;
- Software testing is simple;
- Software is simple to alter;
- Software is simple to update;
- Software may be easily expanded.

Since they work together to build the system, these components cannot be completely independent of one another. To fix the issue, they must collaborate and talk to one another. This interaction increases complexity (Schmidt-Kessen, 2017).

Abstraction

A designer may consider a portion of this type of abstraction without stressing about the details of an application alone thanks to a technique known as abstractions. Abstraction could be advantageous for both already-existing elements as well as newly built ones (Jackson, 2012).

There are two typical abstraction processes shown here:

- Functional Abstraction:
  - A module's mode of operation serves as its specification.
  - The user of a function cannot see the specifics of the algorithm used to carry out the function (Xu & Cao, 2010).

The foundation of function-oriented design methodologies is a functional abstraction.

- **Data Abstraction:** Users of data cannot see the specifics of the data pieces. The foundation of object-oriented design methodologies is database abstraction.

Modularity

Software is divided into discrete modules with distinct addresses and names which are then combined to produce fully functional software. It's the one quality that makes a program mentally understandable. Single large programs are hard to understand and analyze because of the number of forms the matching, control pathways, local variables, etc. (Sullivan et al., 2001).

The desirable properties of a modular system are:

- Every module is a clear system that may be applied to other programs;
- Every module does have a single set of goals;
- Individually compiled modules may be stored inside the library;
- The use of modules must be simpler than their creation;
- The exterior of modules is simpler than the interior (Bate & Kelly, 2003).

1.1.3.1. Advantages and Disadvantages of Modularity

We shall cover several modularity benefits and drawbacks in this topic (Figure 1.2).

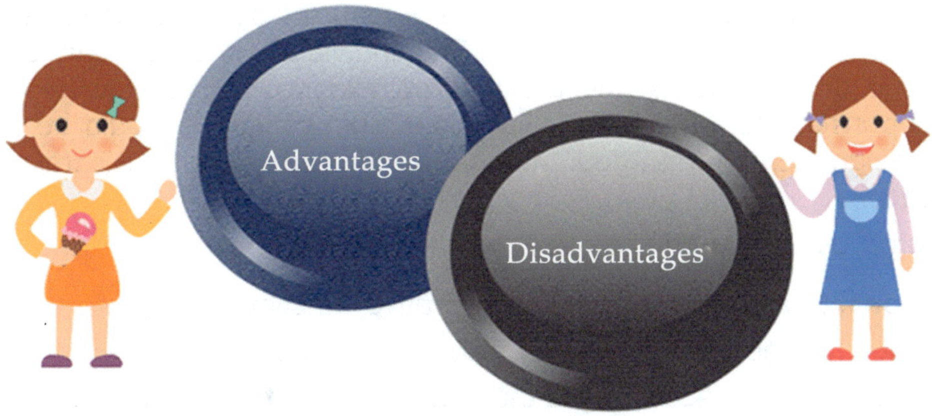

Figure 1.2. Benefits and drawbacks of modularity.

Source: Image by javapoint.com.

Advantages of Modularity: Modularity has several benefits:

- It enables the writing of huge programs by numerous or various authors;
- It streamlines the overlay process of loading a big program into the main storage;
- It offers additional benchmarks to gage development;
- It offers a foundation for comprehensive testing, making testing easier;

- It created understandable and well-designed software (Offermans, 2004).

Disadvantages of Modularity: Modularity has several drawbacks:

- Execution time might be longer, but it's not a guarantee;
- Maybe, but not necessarily, higher storage size;
- There could be a delay in the compilation as well as loading;
- Issues with inter-module communications could get worse;
- More linkage is needed, the run-time could be longer, there are more source lines to write, and there is more documentation to complete (Rajahonka, 2013).

Modular Design

By enabling the parallel creation of different system components, modular design lowers the model complexity and leads to simpler and quicker implementation. In this part, we go into greater detail about a different aspect of modular design (Stone, 1997).

- **Functional Independence:** It is possible to create functions which perform just one type of work and don't interface with some other modules too frequently. Independence is crucial since it facilitates quicker and easier implementation. The individual modules can be utilized in other systems and are less complicated to manage, test, and stop errors from spreading. Functional independence would be a good design element that guarantees the software's quality (Picard et al., 2013).

It is measured using two criteria:

- **Cohesion:** It gages a module's comparative function strength.
- **Coupling:** It gages the degree of module interdependence.
- **Information Hiding:** According to the fundamentals of hiding information, modules could be distinguished from one another by design choices, i.e., modules must be defined so that data contained within a module is accessible to certain other modules which do not require such information. When testing as well as later updating software calls for modifications, using information concealing as a design criterion for modular systems offers the most important advantages. This is due to accidental faults made during updates becoming less likely to spread to multiple locations inside the software so because the majority of data and methods are concealed from other portions of the software (Sullivan et al., 2005).

STRATEGY OF DESIGN

The organization of the software components in some kind of way that makes them simple to develop and, later on, change is a solid system design strategy. Developers can manage the complexity and size of programs with the aid of structured design methodologies. Analysts produce guidelines for developers regarding how to write code and how they should fit parts of code together to create a program (Liedtka, 2000).

Two methods can be used to develop a system:

- **Top-Down Approach:** This method begins by identifying the primary components before breaking them down into their more intricate sub-components (Figure 1.3) (Crespi & Lerman, 2008).

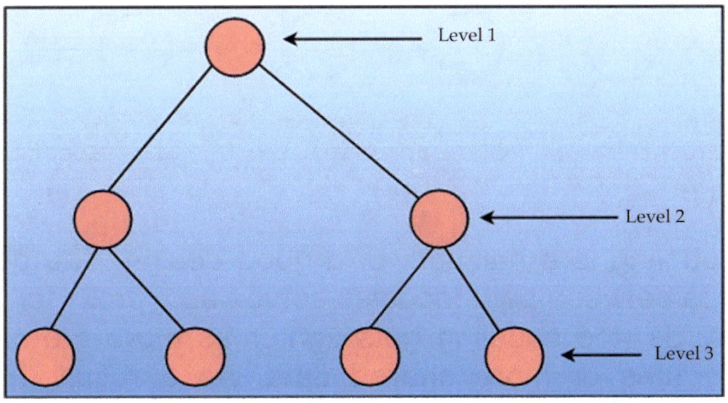

Figure 1.3. Top-down method Source: Image by ecomputernotes. com.

- **Bottom-Up Approach:** As seen in Figure 1.4, a bottom-up strategy starts with the smallest details and works its way up the hierarchy. When a system is already in place, this strategy is appropriate (Marriam et al., 2018).

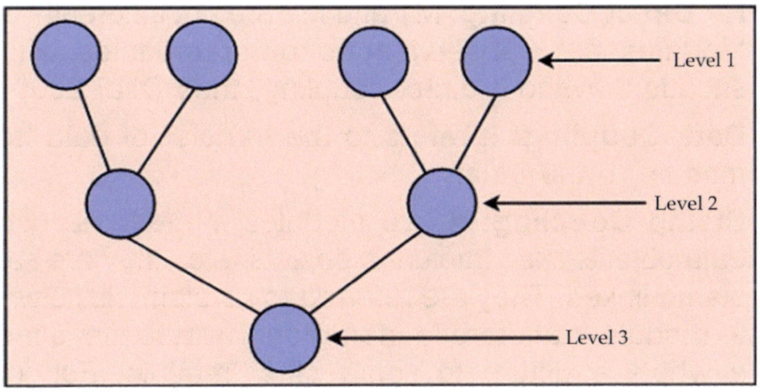

Figure 1.4. Bottom-up method.

Source: Image by ecomputernotes.com.

COUPLING AND COHESION

Module Coupling

The degree of reliance among software modules is referred to as coupling in software development. Two tightly connected modules are highly reliant on one another. Loosely connected modules, however, are independent of one another. Inside uncoupled modules, there is no interdependence (Figure 1.5) (Hall & Munson, 2005).

Module Coupling

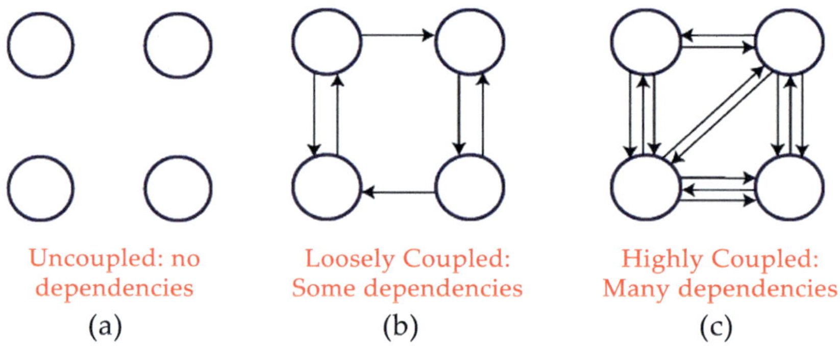

Figure 1.5. Module coupling Source: Image by javapoint.com.

Low coupling is a hallmark of a good design. The quantity of relationships between both modules serves as a proxy for coupling. In other words, the coupling gets tighter as there are more calls among modules or more shared data. As a result, it may be claimed that a high coupling design will contain more faults (Qiu et al., 2018).

Did you Know?

Alan Turing is credited with being the first person to come up with a theory for software in 1935, which led to the two academic fields of computer science and software engineering.

Types of Module Coupling

- **No Direct Coupling:** M1 and M2 are not inherently coupled. Modules are subservient to other modules within this situation. Without direct coupling, thus (Xia, 2000).
- **Data Coupling:** It refers to the transfer of data from one module to the other.
- **Stamp Coupling:** If two modules interact via composite data objects like structures, objects, etc., they are said to be stamp linked. They are referred to as stamp links whenever a module transfers a non-global database schema or a whole structure to some other module. For instance, giving a C++ or C structural variable or item to a module (Razafimahatratra et al., 2017).

- **Control Coupling:** When information through one module is utilized to control how instructions are executed in another, this is known as control coupling between the two modules.
- **External Coupling:** Whenever two modules use the same artificially imposed file formats, communication protocols, as well as device interface, this is referred to as external coupling. Communication with outside devices and devices is relevant here.
- **Common Coupling:** When two modules exchange intelligence through certain global data objects, they are said to be commonly linked (Khavari & Zangeneh, 2020).
- **Content Coupling:** When two modules exchange code, such as when two modules branch into another, then there is content coupling between them (Figure 1.6) (Ribeiro-Neto et al., 2005).

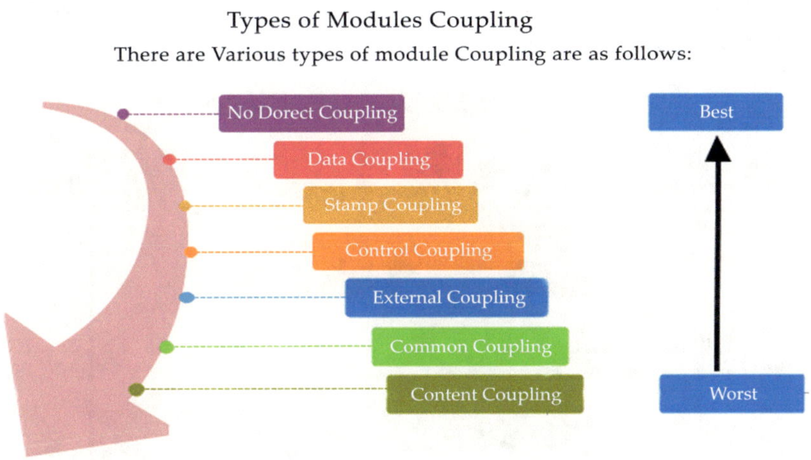

Figure 1.6. Module coupling types.

Source: geeksforgeeks.org.

Module Cohesion

Cohesiveness in computer coding refers to how well-integrated a module's components are. Cohesion, then, gages the quality of connections between functional components inside a specific module. Functionality, for instance, and cohesiveness are closely related. Cohesion is a statistic that can be expressed as either "high cohesion" or "poor cohesion," according to an ordinal scale (Lakhotia, 1993).

1.3.3.1. *Types of Modules Cohesion*

- **Functional Cohesion:** If a module's various components work together to fulfill a single function, then that module is considered to have functional cohesion (Hu & Gao, 2012).
- **Sequential Cohesion:** When a module's components make up a sequence and the outputs from one of those components serve as the input for another, that module is said to have sequential cohesiveness.
- **Communicational Cohesion:** If each of a module's activities updates as well as refer to a common data structure, such as the collection of functions specified on such an array or a stack, then the module is said to possess communicational cohesiveness (Zhao & Xu, 2004).
- **Procedural Cohesion:** A module is said to have procedural coherence if its set of objectives are all components of a process in which a specific order of steps must be followed to accomplish a task, such as an algorithm for message decoding.

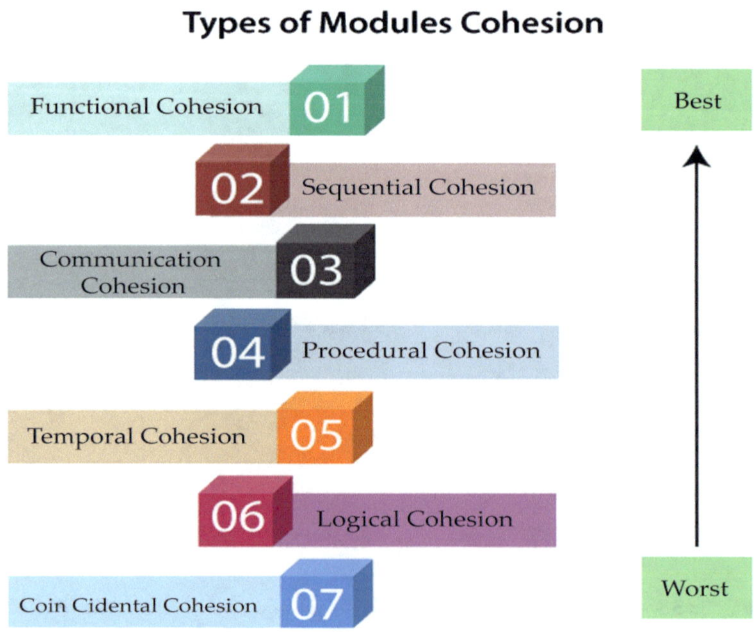

Figure 1.7. Types of module coherence.

Source: geeksforgeeks.org.

- **Temporal Cohesion:** A module is considered to display temporal cohesiveness when it contains functions that are connected by the requirement that each method is run simultaneously.

- **Logical Cohesion:** If every component of a module carries out a similar function, the module is considered to be logically coherent. As an illustration, consider error checking, data input and output, etc. (Al-Dallal, 2010).
- **Coincidental Cohesion:** If a module completes a series of tasks which are only tangentially if at all, related to one another, that module is considered to have coincidental cohesiveness (Figure 1.7) (Dhama, 1995).

DIFFERENTIATE BETWEEN COUPLING AND COHESION

Function Oriented Design

Within the mechanism design approach, the model is broken down into a collection of interconnected pieces or modules, each of which serves a distinct function. As a result, the system is created with functionality in mind (Wang & Gong, 2021).

Remember

"Coupling" describes the relationships between modules, and "cohesion" describes the relationships within them.

Design Notations

Design Notations are utilized to express designs or design choices and are primarily intended for usage throughout the design process. For one function-oriented design, the following could be used as a graphic or mathematical representation of the design (Van Den Berghe et al., 2017).

Data Flow Diagram

Designing a sequence of functional transformations which change system inputs into the necessary outputs is the focus of the data-flow design. Data-flow diagrams are used to model the design. The movement of data throughout a system and the way the output is created from the inputs through a sequence of functional transformations are depicted in these diagrams (Li & Chen, 2009).

Data-flow diagrams are still a practical and understandable technique to explain a system. Without specific training, they are typically understandable, especially if relevant data is left out. They demonstrate the entire process. It is possible to track the processing flow from the point at which data reaches the system to the point at which it departs the system (Ward, 1986).

Many design methodologies include data-flow design, and the majority of CASE tools enable the development of data-flow diagrams. Data-flow diagram elements can be represented in a variety of ways using a variety of icons, but they all convey the same information (Aleryani, 2016).

Data Dictionaries

A data dictionary contains a list of every data element that appears in a program's DFD model. The data products listed include all data flows and all data storage contents as seen through the DFDs of a program's DFD model.

Every data item's goal is listed in a data dictionary, along with every composite data element's description in terms of its constituent data items. For instance, a database structure entry might state that the components regularly with overtime Pay make up the data grossPay (Navathe & Kerschberg, 1986).

grossPay = regularPay + overtimePay

The data dictionary contains the name and kind of the smallest subsets of data components.

Due to the obvious following factors, a data dictionary is crucial to every software development process:

- A data dictionary gives engineers involved in a project a common language for all pertinent information. Since various engineers working on large projects frequently use different names to relate to the same data, this unnecessary confusion can be avoided by using a uniform vocabulary for data items.
- The data dictionary gives the analyst a way to ascertain how different data structures are defined as a result of their constituent parts (Buchanan et al., 2021).

Structured Charts

In simpler terms, a system can be divided into smaller components called block boxes. Each block box is created using a technology that works like a "black box." This means that even though the user knows what the block box does, they are not aware of how it has been designed internally.

A structured chart is a visual depiction that demonstrates:

- System modules are divided up;
- Module component hierarchies;
- How processing modules are related to one another;

- Module-to-module communication;
- Data sent between modules (Aoyama et al., 1989).

Pseudo-Code

It is possible to employ pseudo-code notations in both the conceptual as well as detailed design stages. The system designer uses pseudo-code along with characteristics in the form of short, snappy stages that are organized by keywords like If-Then-Else, While-Do, and End (Oda et al., 2015).

OBJECT-ORIENTED DESIGN

The system is seen as a group of objects when using the object-oriented design approach (i.e., entities). All of the objects share the state, but every item manages its state information. Every library representation, for instance, might be a distinct object inside a library automation software, complete with data and capabilities for manipulating it. The tasks established for one reason are not permitted to refer to or alter the information of other objects. Objects contain internal data that reflects their internal status. A class is created by similar objects. In those other words, every object belongs to a class. Characteristics from the superclass may be inherited by classes (Booch, 1990).

The different terms related to object design are:

- **Objects:** These are also the collective term for all elements engaged in the solution design. People, banks, companies, and users are a few examples of objects. Each entity has certain attributes connected to it, and each attribute does have some procedures to be applied to it (Shaw, 1995).
- **Classes:** A class is a more thorough explanation of an item. A class's instances are objects. All of the characteristics and functions that define the functioning of an object are defined by a class.
- **Messages:** Objects exchange messages to communicate. The targeted object's integrity, the name of the desired operation, as well as any additional steps required to complete the function are all included in messages. It's common to implement notifications as method or function calls (Lilja & Salonen, 2009).
- **Abstraction:** It is used in object-oriented designing to deal with complexity. The act of abstraction involves eliminating the extraneous and amplifying the crucial (Kramer & Hazzan, 2006).
- **Encapsulation:** Information concealing is another name for the notion of encapsulation. Operations as well as data are connected to a single component. Encapsulation limits access to data as well as functions

from the external world in addition to grouping the important information of an entity together (Page-Jones, 1992).

- **Inheritance:** Similar classes may be stacked one on top of the other using OOD, and the bottom or subclasses may import, utilize, and reuse permitted functions and variables within their adjacent superclasses. The term "inheritance" refers to this attribute of OOD. As a result, it is simpler to define a particular class and build generalized categories from particular ones (Taivalsaari, 1996).
- **Polymorphism:** OOD languages have a system that allows methods with similar functions but different arguments to be given the very same name. This is referred to as polymorphism, which enables a single interface to carry out operations for several kinds. The specific section of the code is performed following how the services are invoked (Benlarbi & Melo, 1999).

USER INTERFACE DESIGN

The interface allows a client to engage visually with such a computer application as well as the operating system. It controls how data is shown on the screen and how instructions are given to such computers or software (Thimbleby, 1990).

Types of User Interface

User Interfaces come in two main categories:

Text-Based User Interface (Command Line Interface): The keyboard is usually used in this technique. UNIX is a prime example of this (Stone et al., 2005).

- Advantages:
  - Possibilities for customization are plentiful and simpler;
  - Usually competent to handle more significant responsibilities.
- Disadvantages:
  - Mainly relies on memory rather than familiarity;
  - Navigation is frequently more challenging (Chen & Zhang, 2007).
- **Graphical User Interface (GUI):** It relies on the mouse a lot more. Any edition of the operating system Windows serves as an example of this style of interface (Banerjee et al., 2013).
- Advantages:
  - Use of it requires less specialized knowledge;
  - Simpler to use and allows for rapid guess-and-check browsing of directories;

- The user can easily transition between tasks and can engage with a variety of applications.

- Disadvantages:
  - Typically fewer choices;
  - Less customizable, typically. Utilizing a single button for numerous variations is difficult (Farrugia, 1997).

UI Design Principles

- **Structure:** According to exact, consistent models which are obvious and recognized to people, the design must actively arrange the interface by grouping relevant things again and isolating unconnected things, distinguishing dissimilar things, including making comparable things resembling one another. The general architecture of the user experience is addressed by the structural concept (Ruiz et al., 2020).
- **Simplicity:** By clearly communicating immediately within the user's language and offering useful shortcuts which meaningfully connect to longer processes, the design must make a straightforward, common task simple.
- **Visibility:** A given function's choices and materials must be made visible by the design even without the user being diverted by unnecessary or superfluous information (Fu, 2010).
- **Feedback:** The design must employ simple, unambiguous language which is familiar to users to tell users about actions and interpretations, changes in status or condition, problems or problems that are pertinent as well as of interest to them.
- **Tolerance:** The design must be adaptable and forgiving, lowering the cost of mistakes and abuse by permitting undoing and redoing, and, whenever possible, preventing defects by accepting a variety of inputs and sequencing and by interpreting all legitimate actions (Basu, 2013).

Coding

Coding is a method of transforming a program's design into a specific computer language style. Throughout this stage of software development, software should convert design requirements into

source code. Source code and inner documents are necessary to make it easy to check if the code complies with its requirements (Holton, 2007).

The coding is done by the programmer or programmer(s), who are separate from the designer. Instead of reducing the labor and cost of such a coding phase, the goal is to decrease the expenditure of a subsequent stage. Testing and maintaining good code may be done much less often (Richardson & Urbanke, 2008).

Goals of Coding

- **To Translate the Design of a System into a Computer Language Format:** Coding is the method of translating a system's concept into a computer program that can be utilized by a system to do the tasks that are specified by the design or processes carried out in the design phase.
- **To Reduce the Cost of Later Phases:** Effective code can considerably lower the cost of testing and maintenance (Sudan, 2001).
- **Making the Program More Readable:** The program must be simple to read and comprehend. It improves code comprehension and can result in more maintained software by making accessibility and understandability a distinct goal of the coding activity (Sacheli et al., 2015).

We need a good functional language to translate our idea into code. Further section discusses some qualities that should be present in a programming language.

CHARACTERISTICS OF PROGRAMMING LANGUAGE

The qualities of programming languages are as follows:

- **Readability:** The ability to write programs in some ways that approach a fairly-English explanation of underlying functions with the help of a competent high-level language. It is possible to code in a largely self-documenting manner.
- **Portability:** Since high-level languages are essentially machine-independent, creating portable software must be simple (Wasserman, 1975).
- **Generality:** The majority of high-level programming languages make it unnecessary for programmers to become fluent in a wide range of different languages by enabling the creation of a large number of programs.
- **Brevity:** The algorithm must be easier to implement in a language with little code. Programs written in high-level languages are frequently much shorter than those written in low-level languages.
- **Error Checking:** A programmer is prone to making numerous mistakes when creating computer software. Numerous high-level languages perform a great deal of run-time as well as compile-time bug checking.

- **Cost:** A programming language's total cost depends on a number of its features.
- **Quick Translation:** It ought to make translation quick.
- **Efficiency:** It ought to grant permission for the development of effective object code (Ohashi, 2014).
- **Modularity:** The ability to create programs within language as several independently compiled modules with the proper structure to guarantee self-consistency between these modules is required.
- **Widely Available:** It must be possible to provide translations for all the key devices and all the main operating systems, therefore, languages must be readily accessible. A coding standard outlines several guidelines that must be followed when writing code, including norms for error return codes, variable naming, and code organization (Howatt, 1995).

CODING STANDARDS

Regardless of the programming language that is used, fundamental coding standards when it comes to the way a developer writes code. In this section, we will explore several fundamental standards.

The following are some representative coding standards:

- **Indentation:** For programs to be easily readable and maintained, correct, and consistent spacing is crucial. Use of indentation is advised for:
  - In a control structure, like a loop or even a select statement, emphasis the body;
  - Put more emphasis on a conditional statement's body;
  - Incorporate a new scope block (Boogerd & Moonen, 2008).
- **Inline Comments:** These are that examine how a subroutine works or important elements of an algorithm should be utilized regularly.
- **Rules for Limiting the Use of Global:** These regulations specify which kinds of data can and must not be deemed global.
- **Structured Programming:** Methods of structured (or modular) programming must be employed. Except where specifically permitted by the FORTRAN Standards and Guidelines, "GOTO" statements should not be used since they produce "spaghetti" code, which is difficult to comprehend and maintain.
- **Naming Conventions for Global Variables, Local Variables, and Constant Identifiers:** One proposed naming practice is that constant identifiers are always written in upper case letters, global qualitative variables always start with an uppercase letter, and limited information

regarding names is composed of small characters (Li & Prasad, 2005).

- **Error Return Conventions and Exception Handling System:** The way various computer functions handle error conditions must be uniform across an organization.

For instance, separate activities should consistently return a 0 or 1 when they face an error circumstance (Hunter & Robinson, 1980).

Coding Guidelines

The finest techniques for making programs easier to comprehend and maintain are provided to programmers by general coding principles. The C language syntax is used in the majority of the examples, however, the same principles apply to many languages.

The following are a few typical coding best practices that many software development companies advise (Syed & Nelson, 2015):

- **Line Length:** Keeping source code lines to 80 characters or less is thought to be excellent practice. On certain terminals and tools, lines that are longer than this may not be seen. If a line is longer than 80 columns, certain printers will truncate it.
- **Spacing:** It is possible to make code lines easier to understand by using spaces in the right places.
- **Bad:** cost=price+(price*sales_tax) fprintf(stdout,"The total cost is %5.2f\n,"cost);
- **Better:** cost = price + (price * sales_tax) fprintf (stdout,"The total cost is

%5.2f\n,"cost);

- **The Code should be Well-Documented:** As a general guideline, for every three source lines, there ought to be at least one remark line.
- **The Length of Any Function Should Not Exceed 10 Source Lines:** Due to the possibility that it performs numerous different activities, a long function is typically exceedingly challenging to understand. Long functions may also include an excessively high number of problems for the same reason.
- **Do Not Use Goto Statements:** A program becomes disorganized and highly challenging to understand when goto statements are used.
- **Inline Comments:** Comments within the text encourage reading (De Cremer et al., 2020).
- **Error Messages:** Programming for computers must include error handling. This requires making error signals intelligible as well as including the appropriate functionality to test for them and handle issues.

PROGRAMMING STYLE

The method used to create a computer program's source code is referred to as programming style. The majority of programming paradigms are created to aid programmers in efficiently reading, comprehending, and avoiding mistakes. (Older programming idioms also prioritized screen real estate.) Whereas a poor coding style can undermine the goals of an exceptional language, a good coding style can address the many shortcomings of a first programming language (Oman & Cook, 1988).

Good programming practices aim to provide comprehensible, uncomplicated, and elegant code. The coding standards as well as code conventions of a business or other computing organization, in addition to the preferences of the actual programmer, might influence the programming style utilized in a particular program.

Some general rules or guidelines in respect of programming style:

- **Clarity and Simplicity of Expression:** The programs must be created in a way that makes it obvious what their goals are.
- **Naming:** You must name the module, activities, variables, and other elements of a program. It is important to take care that now the naming scheme is representative and not obscure.
- **For Example:** a = 3.14 * r * r area of circle = 3.14 * radius * radius;
- **Control Constructs:** It is preferable to employ single-entrance and single-exit structures whenever possible (Oman & Cook, 1990).
- **Information Hiding:** Wherever possible, the data structures' protected data should be kept secret first from the system's other components. Module coupling could be reduced and the system could be made more manageable by using information hiding.
- **Nesting:** Deep loop and conditions layering are very bad for a program's static and dynamic behavior. Deep layering should be avoided because it makes the program logic more difficult to grasp.
- **User-Defined Types:** Use user-defined types of data like Enum, class, union, and structure a lot. Your application code is simpler to create and comprehend thanks to these data kinds.
- **Module Size:** This ought to be constant. The module's size shouldn't be excessively large or small. When a module is excessively big, it usually lacks functional coherence. Overheads are created if the module size is insufficient (Oman & Cook, 1989).
- **Module Interface:** The interface of a module must be carefully scrutinized.
- **Side-Effects:** Invoking a module can occasionally have the unintended

consequence of changing the state of the program. Wherever possible, such adverse effects must be avoided (Inamdar, 2004).

STRUCTURED PROGRAMMING

The whole program is broken down into digestible modules in a programming language to make it simpler to understand. The objective of programming language is to linearize the control flow inside a computer program so that it runs in the same sequence also as code. The dynamic and static architecture of the software resembles each other. This enhances the program's capacity to be read, tested, and modified. To manage this linear process of control, the list of authorized applications could be restricted to a single center and single exit forms (Dahl & Hoare, 1972).

Why Do We Use Structured Programming?

Because procedural programming makes it simpler for developers to understand the code, we employ it. It may be difficult to track out an error in a program containing thousands of commands if one does occur. However, the problem may be rapidly identified and resolved with organized programming. That saves so much time (Dijkstra, 1970).

These are the following rules in structured programming:

- **Structured Rule One: Code Block:** The error should be in the block if indeed the exit circumstances are correct but the entering conditions are incorrect. If somehow the execution is permitted to hop into a block, this is not true. Anywhere in the software could contain the problem. Under these conditions, debugging is substantially more difficult.
  - **Rule 1 of Structured Programming:** A code block is structured, as shown in the picture. A box with only one exit point and one entry point is set up in a flow chart fashion. A method for proving the program's validity is structural programming (Castro et al., 2002).
- **Structure Rule Two: Sequence:** The order of blocks is correct if the conditions for entering one block and leaving the next match. Execution enters and exits each block using its entrance point as well as an exit point, accordingly. Consider the whole sequence as a single block with just an entry as well as an exit (Mills, 1986).
  - **Rule 2 of Structured Programming:** The figure 1.7 depicts the structure of two or more code blocks in the sequence (Bowerman & Croft, 2007).
- **Structured Rule Three: Alternation:** Alteration is another name for

the "if-then-else" clause (because there are alternative options). In a programming language, every choice represents a code block. If alternating is set up as shown in the diagram to that same right, there is only one input point (just at the top) and one exit route (at the bottom). The building should be coded such that once the requirements for access are satisfied, the requirements for leaving are likewise met (just like a code block).

- **Rule 3 of Structured Programming:** As seen in the image, the alternating of two code blocks are organized. A signed integer found in register $8 represents an example of an entrance prerequisite for an alternating approach. One alternative exit condition is the exact number of a signed number, which is included in the register at $8. The branching structure satisfies the exit requirement (Juang & Hsieh, 2011).

- **Structured Rule 4: Iteration:** The setup for the whole loop is shown to the right. It has a solitary exit and entry point as well. Both the entrance point as well as the departing point have conditions that must be satisfied. There are not any jumps through into the page from outside of the code.
  - **Rule 4 of Structured Programming:** The graphic depicts the structure of an iteration of a code block (Linger & Witt, 1979).
- **Structured Rule 5: Nested Structures:** Any code block could be stretched into one of the structures when using a flowchart. A section of the flowchart can be condensed into a single code block if it only contains one entrance point and one exit point.
  - **Rule 5 of Structured Programming:** Any building (regardless of size) with such a single entry point and departure will be considered a coding block. For example, we are developing a program to iteratively compute the exact number of every value in a collection of signed numbers. (i) At first, we may consider the program to be one block; (ii) sketch the required amount of iterations; followed by (iii) inserting the specifications of a loop body as shown in the figure 1.7.

The case, do-until, do-while, and control structures are unnecessary. Although they are typically thought of as a component of structured programming, they can occasionally be useful. They don't make things easier in assembly language (Song & Qi, 2020).

SOFTWARE RELIABILITY

Operational reliability is the same as software reliability. It is defined as a system or component's capacity to carry out its essential tasks under constant conditions for a predetermined amount of time. The chance that a software system completes its assigned task in a specific environment for a predetermined number of input cases, providing that the hardware, as well as the input, is error-free, is another definition of software reliability (Pham, 2000).

Software reliability, together with functionality, usability, efficiency, serviceability, capacity, installability, ease of maintenance, and documentation, is a crucial component of software quality. Software reliability is challenging to accomplish because of how complicated software has become. System developers frequently push complex nature into the software layer due to the quick increase in system size as well as the ease of achieving this by upgrading the software, even though any system with a high degree of difficulty that contains software would be difficult to achieve a specific level of reliability (Lyu, 1996).

For example, the forthcoming International Space Station will also have more than 2 million lines of software on board more than 10 million lines of ground support software, large next-generation aircraft will include more than 1 million origin lines of software on board, upcoming air traffic management processes will still have for between as well as 2 million lines, and several substantial life- critical defense systems will include more than 5 million source lines. Software complexity has an inverse relationship with program reliability, but a direct relationship with other important aspects of software quality, such as functionality and capability, etc. (Wood, 1996).

SUMMARY

Software design is the process of imagining and specifying software solutions to one or more sets of issues. Software requirement analysis (SRA) is a critical component of software design. SRA is a component of the software development process that lists software engineering standards. If the program is "semi-automated" or user-centered, user experience design may result in a storyboard to help decide those parameters. A software design can be as simple as a flow chart or text expressing a planned sequence of events if the product is automated (no user or user interface). Unified Modeling Language and Fundamental modeling ideas are two semi-standard methodologies. In either scenario, some plan documentation is usually the result of the design. Furthermore, depending on the availability of the technology used for the design, a software design may be platform-independent or platform- specific.

The critical distinction between software analysis and design is that software analysis produces more minor problems to address. Furthermore, the analysis should not be designed significantly differently for different team members or groups. On the other hand, the design concentrates on capabilities, which means that several designs for the same problem can and will exist. The design often differs depending on the environment, whether generated from dependable frameworks or executed using appropriate design patterns. The design includes operating systems, websites, mobile devices, and the emerging cloud computing paradigm.

REVIEW QUESTIONS

1. Describe briefly the principles of software design.
2. What are the strategies of design?
3. What is the difference between coupling and cohesion?
4. What is the difference between object-oriented design and user interface design?

MULTIPLE CHOICE QUESTIONS

1. What is the first step in the software development lifecycle?

a. System design
b. Coding
c. System testing
d. Preliminary investigation and analysis

2. What does the study of an existing system refer to?

a. Details of DFD
b. Feasibility study

c. System analysis

d. System planning

3. Which of the following is involved in the system planning and designing phase of the software development life cycle (SDLC)?

a. Sizing

b. Parallel run

c. Specification freeze

d. All of the above

4. What does RAD stand for?

a. Rapid application document

b. Rapid application development

c. Relative application development

d. None of the above

5. Which of the following prototypes does not associated with prototyping model?

a. Domain prototype

b. Vertical prototype

c. Horizontal prototype

d. Diagonal prototype

Answers to Multiple Choice Questions

1. (d) 2. (c) 3. (d) 4. (b) 5. (d)

REFERENCES

1. Al Dallal, J., (2010). Mathematical validation of object-oriented class cohesion metrics. *International Journal of Computers, 4*(2), 45–52.
2. Aleryani, A. Y., (2016). Comparative study between data flow diagram and use case diagram. *International Journal of Scientific and Research Publications, 6*(3), 124–126.
3. Aoyama, M., Miyamoto, K., Murakami, N., Nagano, H., & Oki, Y., (1989). Design specification in Japan: Tree-structured charts. *IEEE Software, 6*(2), 31–37.
4. Arató, P., Juhász, S., Mann, Z. Á., Orbán, A., & Papp, D., (2003). Hardware-software partitioning in embedded system design. In: *IEEE International Symposium on Intelligent Signal Processing, 2003* (pp. 197–202). IEEE.
5. Banerjee, I., Nguyen, B., Garousi, V., & Memon, A., (2013). Graphical user interface (GUI) testing: Systematic mapping and repository. *Information and Software Technology, 55*(10), 1679–1694.

6. Basu, S., (2013). Modern UI design. In: *Real World Windows 8 Development* (pp. 11–24). A press, Berkeley, CA.
7. Bate, I., & Kelly, T., (2003). Architectural considerations in the certification of modular systems. *Reliability Engineering & System Safety, 81*(3), 303–324.
8. Benlarbi, S., & Melo, W. L., (1999). Polymorphism measures for early risk prediction. In: *Proceedings of the 21st International Conference on Software Engineering* (pp. 334–344).
9. Booch, G., (1982). Object-oriented design. *ACM SIGAda Ada Letters, 1*(3), 64–76.
10. Booch, G., (1990). *Object Oriented Design with Applications*. Benjamin-Cummings Publishing Co., Inc.
11. Boogerd, C., & Moonen, L., (2008). Assessing the value of coding standards: An empirical study. In: *2008 IEEE International Conference on Software Maintenance* (pp. 277–286). IEEE. Bowerman, M., & Croft, W., (2007). The acquisition of the English causative alternation. In: *Crosslinguistic Perspectives on Argument Structure* (pp. 287–316). Routledge.
12. Buchanan, E. M., Crain, S. E., Cunningham, A. L., Johnson, H. R., Stash, H., Papadatou-Pastou, M., & Aczel, B., (2021). Getting started creating data dictionaries: How to create a shareable data set. *Advances in Methods and Practices in Psychological Science, 4*(1), 2515245920928007.
13. Castro, M., Druschel, P., Kermarrec, A. M., & Rowstron, A., (2002). One ring to rule them all: Service discovery and binding in structured peer-to-peer overlay networks. In: *Proceedings of the 10th Workshop on ACM SIGOPS European Workshop* (pp. 140–145).
14. Chen, J. W., & Zhang, J., (2007). Comparing text-based and graphic user interfaces for novice and expert users. In: *AMIA Annual Symposium Proceedings* (Vol. 2007, p. 125). American Medical Informatics Association.
15. Crespi, V., Galstyan, A., & Lerman, K., (2008). Top-down vs bottom-up methodologies in multi-agent system design. *Autonomous Robots, 24*(3), 303–313.
16. Dahl, O. J., Dijkstra, E. W., & Hoare, C. A. R., (1972). *Structured Programming*. Academic Press Ltd. De Cremer, P., Desmet, N., Madou, M., & De Sutter, B., (2020). Sensei: Enforcing secure coding guidelines in the integrated development environment. *Software: Practice and Experience, 50*(9), 1682–1718.
17. Dhama, H., (1995). Quantitative models of cohesion and coupling in software. *Journal of Systems and Software, 29*(1), 65–74.
18. Dijkstra, E. W., (1970). *Notes on Structured Programming.*(Vol. 1, pp. 07–11).
19. Djunaedy, E., (2005). *External Coupling Between Building Energy Simulation and Computational Fluid Dynamics.* (Vol. 1, pp. 1–7).
20. Farrugia, L. J., (1997). ORTEP-3 for windows-a version of ORTEP-III with a graphical user interface (GUI). *Journal of Applied Crystallography, 30*(5), 565–566.
21. Fu, X., (2010). Mobile phone UI design principles in the design of human-machine

interaction design. In: *2010 IEEE 11th International Conference on Computer-Aided Industrial Design & Conceptual Design 1* (Vol. 1, pp. 697–701). IEEE.

22. Hall, G. A., Tao, W., & Munson, J. C., (2005). Measurement and validation of module coupling attributes. *Software Quality Journal, 13*(3), 281–296.
23. Holton, J. A., (2007). The coding process and its challenges. *The Sage Handbook of Grounded Theory, 3*, 265–289.
24. Howatt, J., (1995). A project-based approach to programming language evaluation. *ACM SIGPLAn Notices, 30*(7), 37–40.
25. Hu, J., & Gao, Z., (2012). Modules identification in gene positive networks of hepatocellular carcinoma using Pearson agglomerative method and Pearson cohesion coupling modularity. *Journal of Applied Mathematics, 2012*.
26. Hunter, R., & Robinson, A. H., (1980). International digital facsimile coding standards. *Proceedings of the IEEE, 68*(7), 854–867.
27. Inamdar, S. L., (2004). *VHDL Coding Style Guidelines and Synthesis: A Comparative Approach*. .(Vol. 1, pp. 1–10).
28. Jackson, M., (2012). Aspects of abstraction in software development. *Software & Systems Modeling, 11*(4), 495–511.
29. Juang, C. F., & Hsieh, C. D., (2011). A fuzzy system constructed by rule generation and iterative linear SVR for antecedent and consequent parameter optimization. *IEEE Transactions on Fuzzy Systems, 20*(2), 372–384.
30. Kagami, S., Nishiwaki, K., Kuffner, J. J., Kuniyoshi, Y., Inaba, M., & Inoue, H., (2002). Online 3D vision, motion planning and bipedal locomotion control coupling system of humanoid robot: H7. In: *IEEE/RSJ International Conference on Intelligent Robots and Systems* (Vol. 3, pp. 2557–2562). IEEE.
31. Kästner, D., Mauborgne, L., Wilhelm, S., Mallon, C., & Ferdinand, C., (2022). Static data and control coupling analysis. In: *11th Embedded Real Time Systems European Congress (ERTS2022)*.
32. Khavari, F., Badri, A., & Zangeneh, A., (2020). Energy management in multi-microgrids considering point of common coupling constraint. *International Journal of Electrical Power & Energy Systems, 115*, 105465.
33. Kramer, J., & Hazzan, O., (2006). The role of abstraction in software engineering. *ACM SIGSOFT Software Engineering Notes, 31*(6), 38, 39.
34. Lakhotia, A., (1993). Rule-based approach to computing module cohesion. In: *Proceedings of 1993 15th International Conference on Software Engineering* (pp. 35–44). IEEE.
35. Li, Q., & Chen, Y. L., (2009). Data flow diagram. In: *Modeling and Analysis of Enterprise and Information Systems* (pp. 85–97). Springer, Berlin, Heidelberg.
36. Li, X., & Prasad, C., (2005). Effectively teaching coding standards in programming. In: *Proceedings of the 6th Conference on Information Technology Education* (pp. 239–244).

37. Liedtka, J., (2000). In defense of strategy as design. *California Management Review, 42*(3), 8–30. Lilja, J., & Salonen, P., (2009). Textile material characterization for softwear antennas. In: *MILCOM 2009–2009 IEEE Military Communications Conference* (pp. 1–7). IEEE.

38. Linger, R. C., Mills, H. D., & Witt, B. I., (1979). *Structured Programming: Theory and Practice.*.(Vol. 1, pp. 1–22).

39. Littlewood, B., Popov, P., & Strigini, L., (2001). Modeling software design diversity: A review. *ACM Computing Surveys (CSUR), 33*(2), 177–208.

40. Lu, M. H., & Sturm, J. C., (2002). Optimization of external coupling and light emission in organic light- emitting devices: Modeling and experiment. *Journal of Applied Physics, 91*(2), 595–604.

41. Lyu, M. R., (1996). *Handbook of Software Reliability Engineering* (Vol. 222). Los Alamitos: IEEE computer society press.

42. Marriam, I., Wang, X., Tebyetekerwa, M., Chen, G., Zabihi, F., Pionteck, J., & Zhu, M., (2018). A bottom-up approach to design wearable and stretchable smart fibers with organic vapor sensing behaviors and energy storage properties. *Journal of Materials Chemistry A, 6*(28), 13633– 13643.

43. Mills, H. D., (1986). *Structured Programming-Retrospect and Prospect.* .(Vol. 1, pp. 1–25).

44. Navathe, S. B., & Kerschberg, L., (1986). Role of data dictionaries in information resource management. *Information & Management, 10*(1), 21–46.

45. Oda, Y., Fudaba, H., Neubig, G., Hata, H., Sakti, S., Toda, T., & Nakamura, S., (2015). Learning to generate pseudo-code from source code using statistical machine translation. In: *2015 30th IEEE/ACM International Conference on Automated Software Engineering (ASE)* (pp. 574– 584). IEEE.

46. Offermans, D., (2004). Advantages of modularity. In: *Proceedings from the 2nd Seminar on Development of Modular Products* (p. 67).

47. Ohashi, Y., (2014). Characteristics of programming education in elementary, junior high and high schools in Japan. In: *Inted2014 Proceedings* (pp. 3889–3892). IATED.

48. Oman, P. W., & Cook, C. R., (1988). A paradigm for programming style research. *ACM SIGPLAN Notices, 23*(12), 69–78.

49. Oman, P. W., & Cook, C. R., (1989). Programming style authorship analysis. In: *Proceedings of the 17th Conference on ACM Annual Computer Science Conference* (pp. 320–326).

50. Oman, P. W., & Cook, C. R., (1990). A taxonomy for programming style. In: *Proceedings of the 1990 ACM Annual Conference on Cooperation* (pp. 244–250).

51. Page-Jones, M., (1992). Comparing techniques by means of encapsulation and connascence. *Communications of the ACM, 35*(9), 147–151.

52. Pham, H., (2000). *Software Reliability*. Springer Science & Business Media.

53. Picard, L., Mayor-Dubois, C., Maeder, P., Kalenzaga, S., Abram, M., Duval, C., &

Piolino, P., (2013). Functional independence within the self-memory system: New insights from two cases of developmental amnesia. *Cortex, 49*(6), 1463–1481.

54. Qiu, Q., Xiao, L., Zhang, Z., Jing, L., Liu, Q., Zhang, G., & Xia, D., (2018). Design and test of 10 kV/400 a flux-coupling-type superconducting fault current limiting module. *IEEE Transactions on Applied Superconductivity, 28*(3), 1–6.
55. Rajahonka, M., (2013). Views of logistics service providers on modularity in logistics services. *International Journal of Logistics Research and Applications, 16*(1), 34–50.
56. Razafimahatratra, H., Mahatody, T., Razafimandimby, J. P., & Simionescu, S. M., (2017). Automatic detection of coupling type in the UML sequence diagram. In: *2017 21st International Conference on System Theory, Control and Computing (ICSTCC)* (pp. 635–640). IEEE.
57. Ribeiro-Neto, B., Cristo, M., Golgher, P. B., & Silva De, M. E., (2005). Impedance coupling in content- targeted advertising. In: *Proceedings of the 28th Annual International ACM SIGIR Conference on Research and Development in Information Retrieval* (pp. 496–503).
58. Richardson, T., & Urbanke, R., (2008). *Modern Coding Theory*. Cambridge University Press.
59. Ruiz, J., Asensio, E. S., & Snoeck, M., (2020). Learning UI functional design principles through simulation with feedback. *IEEE Transactions on Learning Technologies, 13*(4), 833–846.
60. Sacheli, L. M., Candidi, M., Era, V., & Aglioti, S. M., (2015). Causative role of left aIPS in coding shared goals during human–avatar complementary joint actions. *Nature Communications, 6*(1), 1–11.
61. Schmidt-Kessen, M. J., (2017). EU digital single market strategy, digital content and geo-blocking: Costs and benefits of partitioning EU's internal market. *Colum. J. Eur. L., 24*, 561.
62. Shaw, M., (1995). Beyond objects: A software design paradigm based on process control. *ACM SIGSOFT Software Engineering Notes, 20*(1), 27–38.
63. Song, Q., Qin, M., Wang, R., & Qi, Y., (2020). How does the nested structure affect policy innovation?: Empirical research on China's low carbon pilot cities. *Energy Policy, 144*, 111695.
64. Stone, D., Jarrett, C., Woodroffe, M., & Minocha, S., (2005). *User Interface Design and Evaluation*. Elsevier.
65. Stone, R. B., (1997). *Towards a Theory of Modular Design*. The University of Texas at Austin. Sudan, M., (2001). Coding theory: Tutorial & survey. In: *Proceedings 42nd IEEE Symposium on Foundations of Computer Science* (pp. 36–53). IEEE.
66. Sullivan, K. J., Griswold, W. G., Cai, Y., & Hallen, B., (2001). The structure and value of modularity in software design. *ACM SIGSOFT Software Engineering Notes, 26*(5), 99–108.
67. Sullivan, K., Griswold, W. G., Song, Y., Cai, Y., Shonle, M., Tewari, N., & Rajan,

H., (2005). Information hiding interfaces for aspect-oriented design. *ACM SIGSOFT Software Engineering Notes, 30*(5), 166–175.

68. Syed, M., & Nelson, S. C., (2015). Guidelines for establishing reliability when coding narrative data. *Emerging Adulthood, 3*(6), 375–387.
69. Taivalsaari, A., (1996). On the notion of inheritance. *ACM Computing Surveys (CSUR), 28*(3), 438– 479. Thimbleby, H., (1990). *User Interface Design*. ACM.
70. Thomas, L., Buckland, S. T., Rexstad, E. A., Laake, J. L., Strindberg, S., Hedley, S. L., & Burnham, K. P., (2010). Distance software: Design and analysis of distance sampling surveys for estimating population size. *Journal of Applied Ecology, 47*(1), 5–14.
71. Van, D. B. A., Scandariato, R., Yskout, K., & Joosen, W., (2017). Design notations for secure software: A systematic literature review. *Software & Systems Modeling, 16*(3), 809–831.
72. Von, H. E., (1990). Task partitioning: An innovation process variable. *Research Policy, 19*(5), 407– 418.
73. Wang, D., & Gong, X. Q., (2021). Function-oriented design of robust metal cocatalyst for photocatalytic hydrogen evolution on metal/titania composites. *Nature Communications, 12*(1), 1–6.
74. Ward, P. T., (1986). The transformation schema: An extension of the data flow diagram to represent control and timing. *IEEE Transactions on Software Engineering*, (2), 198–210.
75. Wasserman, A. I., (1975). Issues in programming language design: An overview. *ACM SIGPLAN Notices, 10*(7), 10–12.
76. Wood, A., (1996). Predicting software reliability. *Computer, 29*(11), 69–77.
77. Xia, F., (2000). On the concept of coupling, its modeling and measurement. *Journal of Systems and Software, 50*(1), 75–84.
78. Xu, C. D., Hu, C. S., & Cao, X. B., (2010). The study on framework and functions of integrated design environments for preliminary design. In: *Advanced Materials Research* (Vol. 139, pp. 1105– 1108). Trans Tech Publications Ltd.
79. Xu, W., & Liu, Y., (2000). A method for determining customer and utility harmonic contributions at the point of common coupling. *IEEE Transactions on Power Delivery, 15*(2), 804–811.
80. Zeh, C. M., (2006). *Softwear: A Flexible Design Framework for Electronic Textile Systems.* Doctoral dissertation, Virginia Tech.
81. Zhao, J., & Xu, B., (2004). Measuring aspect cohesion. In: *International Conference on Fundamental Approaches to Software Engineering* (pp. 54–68). Springer, Berlin, Heidelberg.
82. Zhu, H., (2005). *Software Design Methodology: From Principles to Architectural Styles*. Elsevier.

CHAPTER 2

SOFTWARE DESIGN PROCESS

UNIT INTRODUCTION

Software Design is the method of transforming user requirements into a format appropriate that facilitates software development and implementation by the programmer. During the software design phase, the design document has been generated depending upon the SRS document's consumer demands. This phase's objective is to convert the SRS document into a design document (Curtis et al., 1988).

- During the design process, the following elements are created and documented (Sonnentag, 1998):
- Various modules are necessary;
- Control the relationships between modules;
- The interface between various modules;
- The data structure of the various modules;
- Algorithms are needed for implementation amongst the various modules.

Learning Objective

At the end of this chapter students will be able to learn:

- What is software;

- Building models of software;
- Processes of software design.

Key Terms

- Software design process
- Software
- Building models
- Design knowledge
- Design decision

WHAT IS SOFTWARE?

This chapter would focus on evaluating how software design fits into this larger pattern and outlining any potential differences between the process of designing software and the task of creating other types of artifacts. Therefore, since the first question in the earlier chapter was "what is design?" this is fair to start this chapter by thinking about the same subject (Ralph, 2010; Boehm, 1999).

The such topic had been probably never posed when individuals 1st started creating computer-based applications that had been deemed significant enough to require an explicit design phase. The software had been thought to include any processes that produced "executable binary code" that had been meant to be executed on a single machine, at least till the middle of the 1970s. This presumption had been practically implicit throughout all earlier software design thought (Göransson et al., 2003; Hazzan & Hadar, 2008). Because the structure of these systems had been mainly established at compile time (also known as "compile-time binding"), the designer(s)' thoughts were focused on creating a single monolithic piece of binary code. Although "source code" and the final binary code may both be referred to be "software" at various periods, the tight relationship between both usually made the distinction irrelevant (Card & Agresti, 1988).

By the 1970s, the idea of distributing computing tasks among several computers and having the ability to dynamically change the connections between those machines had already been introduced. Even though this change may mostly be viewed as a variation in the specifics of implementation, it undoubtedly affected the way such system designers thought (Brooks, 1996). When deciding how to split or share functionality and data amongst machines, what kind of communication channels to use, and how such decisions would likely affect performance, the designers of the system now had to take such extra considerations into account (Guindon & Curtis, 1988).

The advent of the Internet, particularly throughout the 1990s, introduced various new factors to the process of having a range of different forms of implementation. The possibility of using runtime binding to determine the ultimate structure of a system has been significantly broadened thanks to several ideas concerning distribution (terms like "client-server" are now common, while not being especially clearly defined) (Adelson & Soloway, 1986). Our ideas about the forms that "software" might take have also been

Did you Know?

The software design process can be divided into the following three levels of phases of design:

1. Interface design;
2. Architectural design; and
3. Detailed design.

enlarged as a result of the inclusion of "scripting" forms to static representation notations such as XML and HTML. These notations allow for the creation of programs. By the 1970s, the idea of distributing computing tasks among several computers and having the ability to dynamically change the connections between those machines had already been introduced (Yau & Tsai, 1986).

In certain aspects, the impact of such innovations on design thinking has likely been below anticipated (and possibly less than would be appropriate). Solely on a single level, concepts like *architectural style* have contributed to the classification of the vast variety of implementation forms.

Thus, it is less of a fundamental change like the design stage than it is a matter of considering the topic of implementation type early in the design phase (Curtis et al., 1987).

The one aspect that such advancements have drawn attention to in specific and that current design techniques, several of which are discussed in this book, have had the least success addressing, has been the ongoing need for speedier system delivery. Although this is an issue, the idea of "internet time" is the one that most directly contradicts the necessity for a reflective design stage (Geyer, 2012; Osterloh & Rota, 2007). This occurs in part because we may modify and expand our notions about what systems must accomplish far faster than we may create solutions that specify how they are to do it. Given the proper care to maintain its structure, a system may be expanded and modified without impairing other qualities like response time, reliability, and uniformity, which is one trait of good design. Therefore, without putting in a lot of work, this is doubtful that such a feature will be attained. It's unclear if this would be possible for many "web-based" solutions (Brereton et al., 1998).

By utilizing a higher level of abstraction for what we regard to be software, it will be possible to increase the rate at which new systems may be delivered to customers. This was achieved in the 1970s by shifting away from writing programs in machine-specific assembly code and toward using "high-order languages." That liberated them from reliance upon a specific brand and model of machine and also accelerated code output. Prioritizing the manipulation of existing 'things' and 'components' rather than the creation of new ones is a strategy that offers the possibility of a comparable phase in the design phase (Picco et al., 2014).

While we focus on the impact of selecting particular types of execution where this can dramatically change design decisions, for the most part, we take a fairly abstract and general perspective of what could constitute "software" because that is the main focus of this book. Since it may be argued that a system's design must still represent a set of coherent principles and concepts regardless of the type(s) of software utilized to execute it, our premise is one of unification (Alegría & Bastarrica, 2012; Beller et al., 2015).

BUILDING MODELS

It has long been understood that developing software-based systems is challenging. Software development processes appear to have advanced in a sequence of relatively tiny steps, in contrast to seemingly related technologies like hardware design and production, which have advanced rapidly whereas acquiring orders of magnitude in efficiency and equally decreasing size and price (Zanni et al., 2017). Numerous explanations are given for this, and Fred Brooks has identified a number of the main factors contributing to this comparatively slow progress in his broadly praised study "No silver bullet: Essence and accidents of software engineering" (Brooks, 1987). According to Brooks, the following characteristics of software are particularly important influences on its development (Brooks et al., 1987).

- **Complexity:** This is considered to be an important characteristic of software, wherein no 2 components are identical, and a system can hold a large number of states during execution. This sort of complexity is likewise unpredictable, because the designer, not the problem, decides how difficult it should be.
- **Conformity:** Software is required to conform to the standards established by other components, such as hardware, external organizations, or even other software, due to the "pliable" nature of software.
- **Changeability:** Software constantly has to be updated, in part because of how simple it seems to do so (and relatively inadequate methods for assessing them).
- **Invisibility:** As software is "hidden," any representations used to explain this would lack a visual link that provides a clearly understood association between the depiction and the system, in contrast to, say, a building design, which may be immediately associated with the visible characteristics of the building.

This makes it difficult for us to conceive software's qualities and makes it difficult for individuals working on it to communicate with one another. For the reasons listed above (and particularly the final one), even though the process of developing software typically exhibits the same fundamental traits, it also involves numerous additional issues for the designer. As a consequence of this, we will begin this chapter by contemplating the essential component of design known as model-building, which is utilized by a designer to propose a solution (Bersson et al., 2012).

Exploring different design concepts with the help of a "model" of some kind is not a particularly innovative practice. Shipbuilders in the 17th century had constructed spectacular scale models of sailing ships as a planning tool and, more importantly, as a means of communicating such ideas to the shipyard workers who would be constructing the vessel (Wang et al., 2020). These models were immensely valuable in both of these capacities. The question now is, what exactly is a model? The following is an illustration of a typical definition found in dictionaries:

It is a very physical viewpoint, but models can be more abstract and have concerns beyond simple creation. The mathematical model seems to be an illustration of such an abstract form. It may be used to forecast stresses in metal bridge elements, describe the life expectancies of insurance policyholders, and describe traffic flow at intersections, among other things. These kinds of models may be utilized to forecast how a system will act in a particular situation or environment, which is significantly in line with the requirements of a software designer (Pelzer et al., 2014).

To create software, we frequently require models that are less accurate than those utilized by mathematicians, more abstract as compared to those by shipbuilders, and most definitely not 3D in the physical sense! Their function is still to depict the intentions of the creator in a certain way. Software models are typically abstract (limited to only the characteristics that directly pertain to the problem at hand), which also aids in addressing the problem of how we manage scale. We'll look at a few of the shapes that a model may take subsequently (Kim et al., 2013).

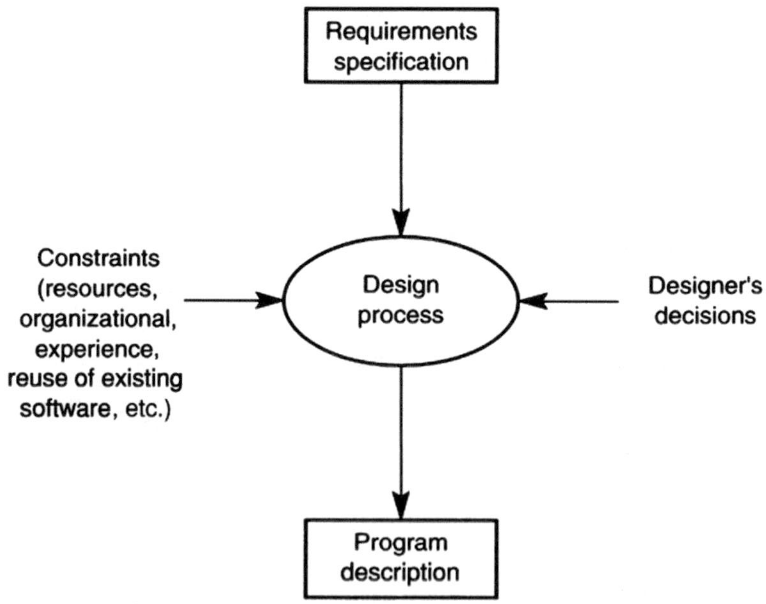

Figure 2.1. A basic illustration of the software development process.

Source: Image by enwikipedia.org.

Making a model of a suggested solution enables the designer to evaluate the solution's structure and behavior and to examine any potential constraints. In light of this, the designer was required to construct just extremely basic models for the first two case studies to carry out an analysis of the "solution space." In contrast to the models that are necessary to support the software design process, this one is quite straightforward (Lin & Chen, 2002). In this section, an attempt will be made to determine the fundamental characteristics and characteristics of the models that are applied in the process of developing software (Fruchter et al., 1996). Figure 2.1 illustrates a "model" of the software development process that is extremely general in scope. The specifications documents serve as the process' input, and the outputs ought to be a set of in-depth specifications that outline the shape of the final program elements. (Of course, we are aware that it is an ideal and perfect account from our examination of the traits of difficulties) (Borrmann et al., 2009).

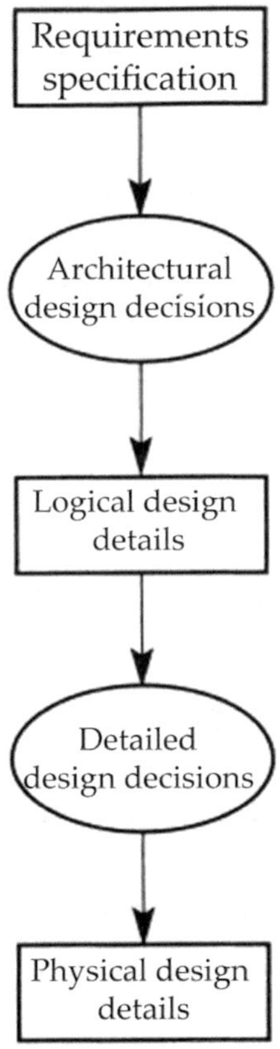

Figure 2.2. The principal stages of the software development process.

Source: Image by javapoint.com.

As seen in Figure 2.2, the design process is sometimes broken up into two distinct stages, which is especially common when creating larger systems. The first thing a designer does is develop an extremely abstract representation of a resolution, which is referred to as either the "architectural" or the "logical" design. This representation only comprises the surface properties of the model parts (Sangiovanni-Vincentelli & Martin, 2001). Therefore, the primary focus of this first black-box division of the problem is on the nature and shape of the problem itself, and it is less strongly affected by the eventual solution form. The abstract 'chunks' of the problem that were found in the previous phase are transferred onto technologically-based components (the specific' or 'physical' design) in the second step, converting the black box into a white box in the process. Where implementation and design are different tasks, the outcome of this step gives programmers specifications (Arrighi et al., 2015).

Once more, this is an idealized depiction, but it still has some conceptual value, even in cases where it is impractical to retain the tasks of the two stages separate (like when attempting to recycle existing elements, for instance.). In the subsequent chapters, as we study several approaches to software design, we shall employ this one. Instead of focusing on the precise shapes that the models and changes would take for different design techniques, we would focus for the time being mostly on the basic role of model-building during design (de Hoog et al., 1994). An early "architectural model" is typically very abstract and describes the planned form that a system would take. In a fascinating investigation of the methods used by software designers, Adelson & Soloway looked at how this is created during the designing process (1985). In its research, it looked at how experienced and novice designers approached the task of creating their models in response to a variety of different issues (Adelson & Soloway, 1985). The tests had been depending upon scenarios that asked a designer:

- A recognizable issue;
- An unknown issue in-depth, yet from a familiar domain; and
- An unknown issue in every sense.

The study's breadth was constrained because it focused on a specific specialized problem domain and only examined a limited number of individuals. Furthermore, the issues themselves were of a manageable size for practical purposes. Such outcomes do, however, appear to show more widespread knowledge of the software design phase (Shaw, 1995).

Following had been certain significant findings from such a study (Hinostroza & Mellar, 2001):

- The designer's utilization of fictitious "mental models" to replicate the dynamic behavior of the final system that would result from the design. Retaining design aspects at the same level of accuracy as they are produced, gradually adding to the detail of a model. This then makes the simulation process easier.

- When tackling a new challenge, it's important to be as explicit as possible about any restrictions that affect the design.
- Reusing earlier design plans. This occurs when a previously created structure or design object may be used to tackle a portion of an issue. Instead of articulating the strategy in depth at that time, designers can employ a "label" to describe the plan in these situations.
- Making notes on future (specific) plans to help a design be expanded systematically. The final point is much less directly related to how a model is created and used, but it illustrates how a skilled designer eliminates the trap of focusing on one aspect of a design in excessive detail. (Fixing the specifics of one part of a design at the initial stage could substantially and unjustly limit the designer's options later) (Kuhn, 1998).

The activities associated with software design from the perspective of the actions of the designer are only briefly investigated in a small number of empirical studies of software designers performed in a regulated experimental setting. Moreover, other researchers have carried out certain comparable investigations of design activity in more conventional working settings (Curtis et al., 1988; Visser & Hoc, 1990). Even though the focus of this work was on researching the procedure for software design rather than programming, several programmers would realize that several of the observed strategies are also utilized for the more intricate design activities that programmers undertake whenever they "program in the little." For example, when creating conditional loop structures, several programmers likely simulate by running mental simulations of the relevant portions of their programs (Taylor et al., 2007). This entails replicating the exit/entry circumstances that emerge during the initial execution of the loop and verifying that the loop would then conclude as planned when the simulation was completed. In this respect, the concept of simulation is well-known, and its significance at all levels of abstraction is without a doubt unquestionable (Penuel et al., 2007).

If we scrutinize various software design methodologies, we will then see that several offer quite comprehensive types of assistance for a designer in constructing preliminary abstract models to explore concepts. To return to the large-scale design problems (like those that arise for the kind of issue that we term "programming in the large"), this is something we would discover. In "systematic" methods, the forms of the models are graphical, whereas, in more "formal" methods, the forms are dependent upon mathematics (Parnas & Clements, 1985). In every situation, using an abstract model typically enables the designer to forecast the most probable system behavior for various scenarios. The models may also be employed to assist in the systematic development of the designer's original concepts into a comprehensive design specification (Kautz, 2011).

The initial design stages' models have been mostly focused on helping with the issue's evaluation or definition (or with both because they are frequently intertwined) (Adelson & Soloway, 1985).

Therefore, in many ways, the numerous strategies for assisting and organizing the software design procedure that we would discuss in this book are mostly focused on the different methods for defining, creating, and refining models. The expertise required to create and evaluate these models may be seen as a key component of the designer's portfolio. Thus, we will look more closely at this knowledge transfer problem and find certain additional aspects that can be implicated in it in succeeding section (Visser & Hoc, 1990; Squires, 1999).

TRANSFERRING DESIGN KNOWLEDGE

Designing isn't dependent upon an analytical approach that seeks to pinpoint the one real solution to an issue as established by physical principles (Lehman et al., 1984). Rather, it's an extremely creative procedure that is extremely unlikely to produce just one answer to any given issue. As may be anticipated, certain individuals are better designers than others, according to experimental research on software designers and associated methods (Curtis et al., 1988). Nevertheless, because there are so few truly outstanding designers, we must look for ways to effectively impart design knowledge to a larger population (Hsiao & Chen, 2018).

Excellent designers had been found to have 3 key traits by Curtis et al. (1988). These are shown in Figure 2.3.

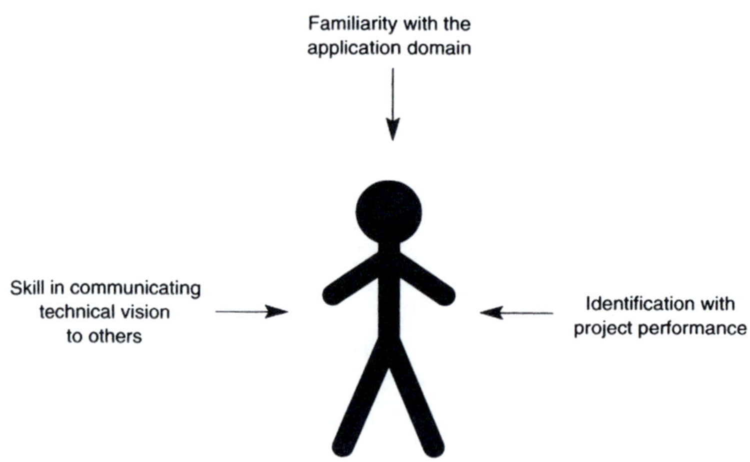

Figure 2.3. The qualities of an excellent designer.

Source: Image by geeksforgeeks.org.

- **Ability to effectively convey the technical vision to certain other project participants:** This had been found to have such a big effect that a lot of the design work had been frequently done in group settings.
- **Familiarity having the application domain:** It allows them to easily map among issue and solution structures. (In this context, a domain could be anything from data processing to real-time telecommunications systems).
- **Identification with the success of the project:** To the point where they were seen taking on important management duties to guarantee technical advancement. It's interesting to note, however, that the top designers in the study frequently lacked strong programming abilities.

Others have recognized the value of the designer's subject-matter expertise in the creation of successful designs (Adelson & Soloway, 1985), and it is possible that this component can only be obtained through the accumulation of experience in a certain issue domain. Having said that, it is possible to gain this knowledge more expediently and efficiently.

There have been additional aspects to take into account in addition to those that were mentioned in the preceding section when examining how effective designers operate. Opportunistic is the term utilized by Visser & Hoc (1990) to characterize their findings of software design activities. Even when designers strive to adhere to a technique like "top-down," which involves gradually breaking down the explanation of the solution into ever-smaller activities, they can veer off course (Visser & Hoc (1990):

- If the essential data isn't yet accessible at this design level, the choice may need to be delayed; alternatively;
- It may be processed to define modules using the data which is presently accessible in anticipation of future design advances.

This type of opportunistic design effort isn't unstructured; rather, it's more likely to demonstrate the designer's background and subject matter expertise. One significant implication is that creators of software design toolkits shouldn't provide an interface that prevents designers from acting in this way (Caine & Gordon, 1975).

There can still be advantages to trying to formalize design techniques in a certain way, although strict processes for carrying out the transitions among a designer's model's phases can't be developed. Due to their significant subject experience and

Remember

Software design process is a high-rank, technology-independent concept that describes a system that will be able to accomplish the established tasks in the requirement analysis phase.

knowledge, experienced designers may employ opportunistic tactics to their advantage. Where these traits are absent, although, these procedures are insufficient, raising the dilemma of how they are to be acquired (Sullivan et al., 2001; Filieri et al., 2015). A collection of design techniques that may be connected to a specific field can be learned, as may a certain level of experience and domain knowledge. These procedures emphasize the need of basing choices on the essential traits of the subject area. Utilizing design methodologies is one technique to master such procedures (Gomaa, 1984). Design approaches are a concept that was developed in the 1970s to address this requirement for the transfer of knowledge, and in certain respects, its usage and forms do seem to be unique to the software development industry. As a result, we might consider the goal of a software design approach to be to offer the framework necessary for a designer to construct and develop a design methodically (Kruchten, 2005; Xue & Zhu, 2009).

Not all domain information can be formalized through design approaches; more recently, the concept of design patterns has provided a less "procedural" method for doing so (Gamma et al., 1995). However, because the use of design approaches is so ingrained in the software industry and consequently in how we think of software design, we would concentrate on their function in knowledge transmission in this chapter and return to the idea of the pattern later (Yu & Mylopoulos, 1994). For our objectives, a software design methodology can be thought of as offering a framework that is supportive and comprises two key elements (as depicted in Figure 2.4).

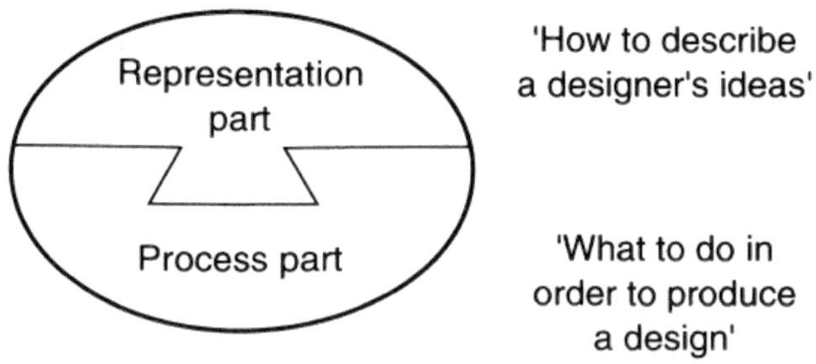

Figure 2.4. The two basic elements of a software design approach.

Source: Image by tutorialspoint.org.

- The depiction section offers a collection of detailed types that the designer may utilize to create both white box and black box models of the issue and their proposed solutions, as well as to explain the solution's structural elements to those who will execute them.

- The processing element is concerned with outlining the organization of the required transitions between the depiction forms and any necessary elaboration of their specifics.

Many design methodologies also include the following element. A set of heuristics may be applied to offer recommendations on how the actions specified in the process component may be arranged for specific problem classes. These are typically depending upon knowledge gained through using the technique in a specific domain or for a specific type of structure in the past (Cossentino et al., 2010).

These might help in building the subject knowledge that a designer needs, even though they can't always offer it. Both forms that may be utilized to model the issue and forms that depict the key structural elements of the execution media are typically included in the depiction portion of a design process. The latter type uses drawings to depict a garden shed's plan, elevation, and end view as well as to demonstrate how essential joints should be put together (Mills, 1980). When defining software, someone would often employ precise design forms that outline the subunits of the program's structure, their connections to one another, and their connections to other system entities. Therefore, representational forms typically reflect the characteristics of the designed objects (Carvajal et al., 2013).

Types that explain the complex architecture could concentrate on very particular features, such as the calling hierarchy, complex data structures, the number of arguments, and so on. On the other hand, the problem modeling forms will be the two most important components of a software design process that will be centered on the more general characteristics of the problem objects as well as any potential relationships between these (Burge & Brown, 2004). This method, which is typically constructed on concepts that are somewhat abstract, such as operations and data flow, is the one that comes the closest to giving a designer the "domain knowledge" component they require because it emphasizes the domain characteristics that have been thought to be of the utmost significance (Kellner et al., 1990).

The process component of the design is more challenging to quantify and categorize. Its structure can come from rather general theory, particular "principles," or heuristics (the idea that something previously done that way worked well). It will most likely show a combination of each one of these. Current design methodologies generally lack solid theoretical foundations, and even the guiding concepts may be largely empirical. Although, we may still pinpoint some of the demands we have on a design method's procedure, which would involve offering some assistance for the following duties (Guindon, 1990; Yu et al., 2008):

- The recognition of the design actions that need to be carried out;

- The utilization of the representation types;
- The methods for making transformations among depictions;
- Quality measures to assist in the decision-making process;
- The identification of specific constraints that need to be taken into consideration;
- The validation and verification processes.

The majority of design methodologies focus more on providing the designer with specific guidance than they do on providing particular answers to problems. This is due, in large part, to the fact that many of the decisions that a designer must make are problem-oriented (Kim et al., 1991). The role of the technique is to assist the designer in identifying the options that are available to them and in evaluating such options in terms of the potential outcomes that they will have. Akin (1990) proposed that 3 'classic' characteristics are followed in creative activities like design. One of these prerequisites is that the creative act must be original (Akin, 1990). Which include:

- The moment of recognition is often known as the "Aha!" reaction. This ability allows the designer to spot a problem that has existed all along. (Though when we eventually come to investigate the conception of the design pattern, we would discover that efficient application of patterns does base on a sort of recognition step, this type of creative activity is likely more typical of scientific development than of design progress).
- The problem restructures stage results in significant advancement in a problem's resolution when the perspective utilized to explain or model an issue is changed. As an illustration, the designer may choose to keep the information as an array to solve a particular problem. This decision might then necessitate a very complicated collection of algorithms, and the developer might later recognize that switching from an array to a linked list will produce far simpler algorithms.
- The acquisition of procedural knowledge regarding the most effective ways to approach these issues enables the designer to engage in a variety of creative activities within a domain. (Again, Akin points out that this is applicable across a wide range of human endeavors).

The process phase of a design approach contains several important components, one of which is the organization of the design alterations. The sequence that is depicted in the "process diagram" that is used in Figure 2.2 is, of course, still fairly abstract, and it does not provide any particular regarding the repetitions that would frequently take place while a designer analyzes and evaluates the design alternatives. The heuristics aren't "officially" included either because they are substantially method- specific to be considered general enough for inclusion (Mihnev & Zafirova-Malcheva, 2015).

Further examination of the modification steps themselves reveals that for every step, a broad structure of the type depicted in Figure 2.5 may be identified. Every change necessitates (Meehan & Richardson, 2002):

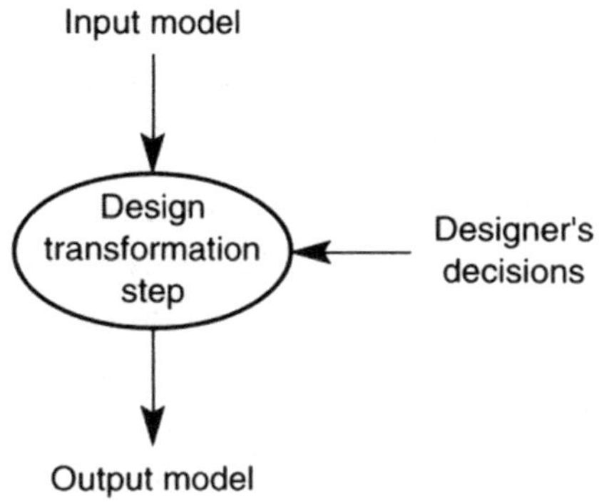

Figure 2.5. Model for modification in design work.

Source: Image by Linda C. Schmidt.

- An input model that can be represented in an appropriate way, such as through text, graphics, or mathematics;
- An ultimate model, which once more may take any of these shapes;
- Design inputs are how the designer provides the model with new data. Additionally, we may distinguish between two major types of design modification, each of which involves:
  - The elaboration (or refinement) of structures, where the model's output and input types are identical however additional detail is included; and
  - The shift of perspective can bring forth a new representational form or a new way of interpreting an existing one.

Generally, refinement transformations tend to keep the depiction form while introducing additional detail, whereas perspective transformations introduce both judgments and a change in the layout of the design model (Ball et al., 2010). By making more choices and options in the first scenario, the designer has been primarily concerned with narrowing the potential "solution space," while in the second scenario, the designer can be adding details regarding novel connections between design components. The idea that design is a succession of changes is researched and applied in a variety of contexts (Lehman et al., 1984; Friel & Budgen, 1997). Because it is such an effective generic model for model-based structuring, the chapters that examine individual design methods will make use of it for the reason that they are discussing those methods. As was said before, design approaches have been an integral part of the framework upon which software designers have been building their careers since the 1970s. Furthermore, even as they offer this support, their shape and nature may also act as a barrier to innovation (Budgen, 1999), as well as certain aspects of "traditional" design behavior that they are ill-suited to facilitate, most obviously the recycling of effectively employed part-solutions (Budgen, 1999).

Two further methods to aid in the transfer of design and technical knowledge had been created in the 1990s, in part due to the necessity to solve this issue as well as for other reasons. According to Shaw & Garlan (1996), the idea of software architecture is more structural and less procedural in its technique for understanding how a design might be produced (Shaw & Garlan, 1996). Similarly, to this, the design pattern concept (Gamma et al., 1995) centered on classifying solution structures that could be applied to many issues.

Some compromises need to be made for their implementation to be successful, as is the case whenever design problems are being considered (Royce, 1987). Whereas both such methods offer greater scope for repurposing brilliant ideas than "traditional" software design approaches, their lack of a procedural component can create them less available to novices, and there are concerns about the scalability of design patterns (how several models seem to be helpful and available in a particular context?).

In subsequent chapters, we would investigate these two strategies in further detail. Its key focus in the undertaking of transmitting design and subject matter expertise is, in several respects, exemplified by the provision of tactics that are complementary to those utilized in design processes (Franks et al., 1995). However, as is regrettably typical in the field of software development, the search for methods that may successfully combine the positive aspects of a variety of methodologies is likely to prove fruitless.

CONSTRAINTS WITH THE DESIGN PROCESS AND PRODUCT

Because every design activity is performed inside a certain context, there are limited opportunities to create a system having complete freedom in practice. As a result, the design's shape and perhaps even its production process would be subject to some restrictions. This was demonstrated in the case studies of designing a garden shed and changing houses (Saeki et al., 1989; Capra et al., 2008). The limitations in the moving house instance included both practical ones (blocking outlets and windows) and cosmetic ones (style or color clashes, placing a bed in the dining room, etc.).

These elements have a significant impact on the shape of the answer that must be given (or products in such a situation). In terms of the layout of garden sheds, the most significant constraints were once again associated with the design of the product itself (Miller et al., 1996; Oduor et al., 2014). These constraints had been brought about as a result of the requirement to provide a method for constructing sheds using easily accessible prefabricated components. In a manner comparable to how we can quickly notice numerous limits placed on the form of the product, the situation of software design presents us with the same opportunity (Alshayeb & Li, 2005). Some may be influenced by the final run-time environment (arrangement of file structures; the look and feel of the consumer interface), while others may have to do with the requirement to follow norms set out by a particular architectural style (JavaBeans; options for remote access; decision amongst processes or objects, etc.). When it is also anticipated that existing software elements would be used to build the final system, this could place additional restrictions on the "acceptable" architectural designs that the elements can have as well as the challenge of dividing functionality among them (Garlan et al., 1995).

The eventual type of execution is likely among the most important limitations on the creative project and the type of the design itself. Before even starting on the actual design process, the majority of software development projects have long taken the method of purchasing the hardware and choosing the key software components (operating system, programming language). Whereas awareness can (very slowly) be spreading, the selection of programming language remains more likely to be affected by outside factors like the knowledge and abilities of the programmer than by the characteristics of the issue itself (Adelson & Soloway, 1985).

The primary tool used in software development is still the imperative types of programming languages (ALGOL, COBOL, Ada, FORTRAN, C, C, Modula-2, Java, and scripting languages like JavaScript, etc.). Practically every design technique currently in utilize implicitly uses imperative language constructs, hence this is believed throughout this book that this is the case. The design procedure does not, however, require the usage of imperative types, and the design ideas discussed here are undoubtedly not limited to the imperative paradigm (Card & Agresti, 1988; Alam et al., 2013). The limitations of the design procedure are more challenging to pinpoint. They might be worried about the expertise and skills of the designer (experience with a specific method), or about the requirement to adhere to a specific "architectural style" of design to facilitate future repairs. Sometimes a limitation on the process results from a limitation on the outcome, like in the scenario in which the output form must be compatible with the type typically generated by a specific design method (Adelson & Soloway, 1986; Frese, 1987). Limitations, in whatever shape they take, may be thought of as defining a set of boundaries around the "solution space." The consequences of the limitations can restrict the amount of potential deviation that would be tolerable in specific circumstances, even though the design process won't always converge on one solution to a specific issue. Numerous restrictions would be noted in the preliminary specification documents; however, this isn't always the case for restrictions connected to assumptions of reuse. Regardless of its origin, limitations effectively reduce the range of options open to the designer, therefore reducing the overall solution space (Sonnentag, 1998; Kim & Evans, 2009). (Although, there has been the chance that inconsistent specifications will prevent a solution from being found.) Certain constraints are more relevant to the proposed solution, whereas others are more pertinent to the proposed problem (like the degree of user capabilities that must be anticipated for a new application). Even if they can't readily be accommodated into any standard design approach, the influence of problem-specific limits must be taken into account at each level of the design process (like a design method). One way to find out what the limits are and keep track of them is to conduct regular design reviews. These reviews, which may also be tasked with the obligation of ensuring that an audit trail has been maintained, are one method (Dickove et al., 1977).

RECORDING DESIGN DECISIONS

From the perspective of the design task directly, as well as from the perspective of the maintenance staff, who may require modifying and enhance the design in the future, it's crucial to document the decisions made by the design engineer (or, for bigger projects, the design team). Regrettably, whereas designers can meticulously note the key decisions, this is considerably less common to record the reasoning behind the ultimate conclusion. (Experience indicates that this isn't only a software engineering issue; it also appears to affect several other engineering practice fields) (Juristo et al., 2007).

If the design procedure involves any kind of design audit, the documenting of rationale, starting with the initial task of design, is almost certainly recommended. Peer evaluation of the designer's concepts can make up such an audit, or the project manager can perform a more official audit. No matter the format, audits would be conducted more methodically and effectively if the justifications for judgments are documented (Taylor & Van der Hoek, 2007; Ball et al., 2010). The duty of system maintenance has a greater demand than before (It is estimated to need between 50% and 80% of the programming and design effort). The maintenance designers of a system need to have the capability of recapturing the original models that were utilized by the system designers to be able to modify or extend a design. They won't be able to decide with any degree of certainty how to implement their adjustments most efficiently unless they have a model that's sufficiently complete (Littman et al., 1987). It is helpful to have some record of the reasons for the existing structure to assist with recreating this model as well as evaluate the effects of any changes that may be implemented. The reasons for the modification, in turn, need to be added to the records held by the maintainers so that a consistent and comprehensive history of the system design can be maintained (Floyd et al., 1989).

Therefore, quality control is a key driver for documenting the justification for all design decisions, both during the design phase and much later, while maintaining. We may only hope to completely comprehend a design if we possess a full picture, and this is a crucial aspect of creating a good, dependable design (Walz et al., 1993; Wegerif et al., 1998). However, software design approaches are frequently poorer on process issues, like recording the reasoning for the decision, even though they normally offer adequate types of assistance for documenting decisions regarding product problems, mainly through charts or other notation. Although it is reasonably simple to incorporate the documentation of decisions and their justifications into design practice, this is challenging to enforce without a robust quality control mechanism in place (Zhang & Budgen, 2011; Egyed, 2010).

TIPS

The principles of a good software design are:

- Modularity;
- Coupling;
- Abstraction;
- Anticipation of change;
- Simplicity;
- Sufficiency and completeness.

The design approach used has some bearing on how design decisions are recorded. There has been certain research done on how to model this design discussion process using the "Potts and Bruns model" (Lee, 2000), and it has been used to demonstrate the JSD technique. However, there is little to no universal tool support available right now that may be utilized for this task.

Parnas & Clements (1986) have brought up a significant issue about the importance of documenting design decisions (Parnas & Clements, 1986). They have noted that even if a design was not generated through a rational design procedure, the final documentation should nonetheless give the impression that it was. To put it another way, the documentation must be written like the "ideal" design approach used. They contend that because the design is never a rational procedure (as we have seen during this chapter and the one before it), any documentation created must always "fake" this impression of rationality (Hinostroza & Mellar, 2001).

The key advantages of this strategy are that new team members must be capable to learn about the project more quickly and that the chore of sustaining the system would also be made simpler in the long run. Even with a scientific document like a mathematical proof, Clements & Parnas note that the published version seldom corresponds to the original derivation because, as knowledge increases, simplifications are frequently possible (Franks et al., 1995). Because readers are more concerned about the validity of the theorem than with the method of discovery, they need shorter proof. In a similar vein, the architecture of a design rather than how it was created is what counts to a new team member or maintainer (Griswold et al., 2006).

Before wrapping up this chapter, we must also briefly discuss the birth of open-source software, among the most intriguing social and technological trends of the 1980s and 1990s. These pieces of software have been typically freely distributed and the voluntary labor of several developers. The Linux operating system seems to be arguably the most well-known instance of this kind of software product, although there have been several others (this served as the foundation for the creation of this new edition.). In this part, we must highlight that documentation and version control are crucial components in managing the activities of several volunteers. We would return to examine how the development of this software is structured in the following chapter (Wu & Lin, 2001). Curiously, though, there hasn't been much academic research done to date on how the methods used in creating open-source software vary from those used in the more "conventional" modes of development discussed in the previous sections (Guindon & Curtis, 1988).

DESIGNING WITH OTHERS

Whereas the construction of a sound design is vital for all software development activities, this is required for large-scale programming, when a design team seems to be more involved than a designer (Wan-Kadir & Loucopoulos, 2004). Due to the nature of the design phase, this is unsurprising that creating as a team brings additional complexities, several of which take the shape of additional limits on the process and, consequently, on the product's form. (For medium-sized systems, sometimes it seems as though there is a universal "rule" of design dictating that the number of design modules must equal the amount of design team members!) (Gorschek et al., 2014; Rossmann et al., 1975).

Numerous extremely successful and 'exciting' software systems are the product of one or a small number of 'excellent designers.' To illustrate this argument, Brooks (1987) contrasts the 'excitement' of Unix, Modula, Pascal, and similar systems having the 'boringness' of PL/1, COBOL, MVS/370, and MS-DOS. (A more contemporary comparison would be Linux vs Windows XX!) (Brooks & Bullet, 1987). In the absence of exceptional designers, constructing a system via a team introduces two significant difficulties that must be addressed inside the selected design process. These include:

- How to divide up the design effort among the team and figure out the connections between the pieces; and

- How to divide up the design effort among the team and figure out the connections between the pieces.

The growing trend toward modular designs, which is a topic that will be covered later, is one factor that helps alleviate at least some of the initial effects of these problems (Baker & van der Hoek, 2010). For the time being, it is essential to observe that this method helps in resolving the challenge of dividing design operations across a team, while it is required to establish a fair balance of work, as required (Figure 2.6) (Coplien, 1998; Jackson & Damon, 1996).

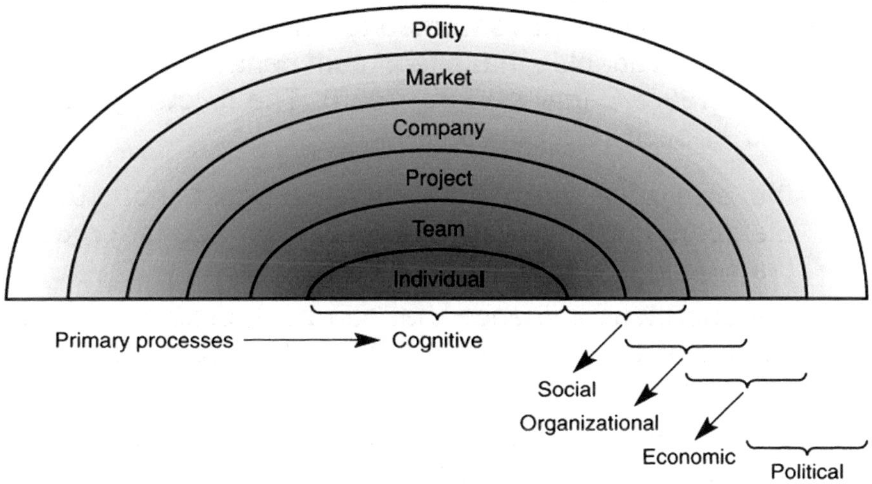

Figure 2.6. Influencing aspects of the software design procedure.

Source: Image by Murat Yilmaz.

Again, putting a design together and the associated talks include a mix of technological and managerial challenges. Even though a negotiation procedure could be appropriate and required, the integrity of the overall design shouldn't be compromised. The psychology of computer programming (Weinberg, 1971), a classic work by Gerald Weinberg, describes some of the early studies on how teams do programming (and consequently designing). In this, he studied the results of various forms of group structure, from those that functioned as an "egoless" set of peers (wherein various group members may assume the lead for particular tasks) to those that were very hierarchical form (Feichtinger et al., 2011; Squires, 1999).

The proponents of the "head programmer" school once favored a more hierarchical structure (Baker, 1972; Brooks, 1975). The chief programmer acts in a very restricted position as the chief designer within the context of the design, while the other members of the team carry out tasks that are only intended to help her or his activity. The surgical team is frequently used as a point of comparison, which raises the question of why the latter group has such a radically different objective. Members of the team may take on specialized roles such as administrator, librarian, or documentation specialist. Additionally, the primary programmer is supported by a backup who acts as the technical deputy (Thomas et al., 2010).

ACTIVITY 2.1.

Consider a recent item of software that you may have written. Thinking about how you developed it, are you aware of any way in which you might have reused experience from previous programs in deciding upon particular structures or algorithms?

Perhaps because there aren't many outstanding designers who may take on the extremely demanding central role it necessitates, few design teams appear to operate along these lines in practice. Additionally, researchers have worked to comprehend and simulate the psychological variables that affect team behavior when creating (Curtis et al., 1988; Curtis & Walz, 1990). The following elements are covered in such references:

- the size of a team (indications suggest that 10 to 12 members has been likely the maximum size for productive teamwork);
- the enormous influence that can be exercised by a small subset of team members with better application domain expertise;
- the impact of internal organizational problems in a corporation (and specifically the requirement to maintain a connection between the designers and the consumer).

SUMMARY

This chapter has enlarged upon the issues raised in Chapter 1 by considering how they apply to the particular domain of software design. Major points from this chapter are:

- The widening interpretation of what consists of' software;
- the complexity of the model-building processes for software systems, with their need to consider static forms, as well as the dynamic behavior of the eventual system;
- the influence of the invisible nature of software upon any attempts to describe it;
- the need for domain knowledge on the part of the designer;

REVIEW QUESTIONS

1. Explain the software design process in detail.
2. What do you understand by the term "software"?
3. Explain briefly the building models.

MULTIPLE CHOICE QUESTIONS

1. — is a set of computer programs and associated documentation and data.

a. Software

b. Building Models

c. Both (a) and (b)

d. None of above

2. Which of the following is the element of building model?

a. Complexity

b. Conformity

c. Changeability

d. All of above

3. Software Design consists of ____________

a. Software Product Design

b. Software Engineering Design

c. Software Product & Engineering Design

d. None of the mentioned

4. Which of the following is true?

a. Analysis – Solving problem

b. Design – Understanding problem

c. Analysis & Design

d. None of the mentioned

5. What is true about generic software product design process?

a. It begins with SRS

b. It ends with Product Design Problem

c. Analysis is done and end product is project mission statement

d. None of the mentioned

Answers to Multiple Choice Questions

1. (a) 2. (d) 3. (c) 4. (d) 5. (d)

REFERENCES

1. Adelson, B., & Soloway, E., (1985). The role of domain expenence in software design. *IEEE Transactions on Software Engineering,* (11), 1351–1360.
2. Adelson, B., & Soloway, E., (1986). A model of software design. *International Journal of Intelligent Systems, 1*(3), 195–213.
3. Akin, Ö., (1990). Modelling human machine interaction: Techniques for prediction of performance. In: *Empirical Foundations of Information and Software Science V* (Vol. 1, pp. 231–235). Springer, Boston, MA.
4. Alam, O., Kienzle, J., & Mussbacher, G., (2013). Concern-oriented software design. In: *International Conference on Model Driven Engineering Languages and Systems* (pp. 604–621). Springer, Berlin, Heidelberg.
5. Alegría, J. A. H., & Bastarrica, M. C., (2012). Building software process lines with CASPER. In: *2012 International Conference on Software and System Process (ICSSP)* (Vol. 1, pp. 170–179). IEEE.
6. Alshayeb, M., & Li, W., (2005). An empirical study of system design instability metric and design evolution in an agile software process. *Journal of Systems and Software, 74*(3), 269–274.
7. Arrighi, P. A., Le Masson, P., & Weil, B., (2015). Addressing constraints creatively: How new design software helps solve the dilemma of originality and feasibility. *Creativity and Innovation Management, 24*(2), 247–260.
8. Baker, A., & Van, D. H. A., (2010). Ideas, subjects, and cycles as lenses for

understanding the software design process. *Design Studies, 31*(6), 590–613.

9. Ball, L. J., Onarheim, B., & Christensen, B. T., (2010). Design requirements, epistemic uncertainty and solution development strategies in software design. *Design Studies, 31*(6), 567–589.
10. Beller, M., Gousios, G., & Zaidman, A., (2015). How (much) do developers test? In: *2015 IEEE/ACM 37th IEEE International Conference on Software Engineering* (Vol. 2, pp. 559–562). IEEE.
11. Bersson, T. F., Mazzuchi, T., & Sarkani, S., (2012). A framework for application of system engineering process models to sustainable design of high performance buildings. *Journal of Green Building, 7*(3), 171–192.
12. Boehm, B., (1999). Escaping the software tar pit: Model clashes and how to avoid them. *ACM SIGSOFT Software Engineering Notes, 24*(1), 36–48.
13. Borrmann, A., Hyvärinen, J., & Rank, E., (2009). Spatial constraints in collaborative design processes. In: *Proceedings of the International Conference on Intelligent Computing in Engineering (ICE09)* (Vol. 1, pp. 1–8). Berlin, Germany.
14. Brereton, P., Lees, S., Gumbley, M., Boldyreff, C., Drummond, S., Layzell, P., & Young, R., (1998). Distributed group working in software engineering education. *Information and Software Technology, 40*(4), 221–227.
15. Brooks, F. P., & Bullet, N. S., (1987). Essence and accidents of software engineering. *IEEE computer, 20*(4), 10–19.
16. Brooks, J., (1996). CSCW as form of organizational memory: Implications for organizational learning. *ACM SIGOIS Bulletin, 17*(3), 39–42.
17. Budgen, D., (1999). Software design methods: Life belt or leg iron? *IEEE Software, 16*(5), 136–135.
18. Burge, J. E., & Brown, D. C., (2004). An integrated approach for software design checking using design rationale. In: *Design Computing and Cognition'04* (Vol. 1, pp. 557–575). Springer, Dordrecht.
19. Caine, S. H., & Gordon, E. K., (1975). PDL: A tool for software design. In: *Proceedings of the* May 19–22, 1975, *National Computer Conference and Exposition* (Vol. 1, pp. 271–276).
20. Capra, E., Francalanci, C., & Merlo, F., (2008). An empirical study on the relationship between software design quality, development effort and governance in open-source projects. *IEEE Transactions on Software Engineering, 34*(6), 765–782.
21. Card, D. N., & Agresti, W. W., (1988). Measuring software design complexity. *Journal of Systems and Software, 8*(3), 185–197.
22. Carvajal, L., Moreno, A. M., Sanchez-Segura, M. I., & Seffah, A., (2013). Usability through software design. *IEEE Transactions on Software Engineering, 39*(11), 1582–1596.
23. Coplien, J. O., (1998). Software design patterns: Common questions and answers. *The Patterns Handbook: Techniques, Strategies, and Applications, 13*(1), 311.

24. Cossentino, M., Gaud, N., Hilaire, V., Galland, S., & Koukam, A., (2010). ASPECS: An agent-oriented software process for engineering complex systems. *Autonomous Agents and Multi-Agent Systems, 20*(2), 260–304.
25. Curtis, B., Krasner, H., & Iscoe, N., (1988). A field study of the software design process for large systems. *Communications of the ACM, 31*(11), 1268–1287.
26. Curtis, W., Krasner, H., Shen, V., & Iscoe, N., (1987). On building software process models under the lamppost. In: *Proceedings of the 9th International Conference on Software Engineering* (Vol. 1, pp. 96–103).
27. De Hoog, R., De Jong, T., & De Vries, F., (1994). Constraint-driven software design: An escape from the waterfall model. *Performance Improvement Quarterly, 7*(3), 48–63.
28. Dickover, M. E., McGowan, C. L., & Ross, D. T., (1977). Software design using: SADT. In: *Proceedings of the 1977 Annual Conference* (Vol. 1, pp. 125–133).
29. Egyed, A., (2010). Automatically detecting and tracking inconsistencies in software design models. *IEEE Transactions on Software Engineering, 37*(2), 188–204.
30. Feichtinger, C., Donath, S., Köstler, H., Götz, J., & Rüde, U., (2011). WaLBerla: HPC software design for computational engineering simulations. *Journal of Computational Science, 2*(2), 105–112.
31. Filieri, A., Hoffmann, H., & Maggio, M., (2015). Automated multi-objective control for self-adaptive software design. In: *Proceedings of the 2015 10th Joint Meeting on Foundations of Software Engineering* (Vol. 1, pp. 13–24).
32. Floyd, C., Mehl, W. M., Resin, F. M., Schmidt, G., & Wolf, G., (1989). Out of Scandinavia: Alternative approaches to software design and system development. *Human–computer Interaction, 4*(4), 253–350.
33. Franks, G., Hubbard, A., Majumdar, S., Neilson, J., Petriu, D., Rolia, J., & Woodside, M., (1995). A toolset for performance engineering and software design of client-server systems. *Performance Evaluation, 24*(1, 2), 117–136.
34. Frese, M., (1987). A theory of control and complexity: Implications for software design and integration of computer systems into the work place. *Psychological Issues of Human Computer Interaction in the Work Place, 1,* 313–337.
35. Friel, G., & Budgen, D., (1997). Design transformation and prototyping using multiple viewpoints. *Information and Software Technology, 39*(2), 91–105.
36. Fruchter, R., Clayton, M. J., Krawinkler, H., Kunz, J., & Teicholz, P., (1996). Interdisciplinary communication medium for collaborative conceptual building design. *Advances in Engineering Software, 25*(2, 3), 89–101.
37. Garlan, D., (1996). Style-based refinement for software architecture. In: *Joint Proceedings of the Second International Software Architecture Workshop (ISAW-2) and International Workshop on Multiple Perspectives in Software Development (Viewpoints' 96) on SIGSOFT'96 Workshops* (Vol. 1, pp. 72–75).
38. Geyer, P., (2012). Systems modelling for sustainable building design. *Advanced Engineering Informatics, 26*(4), 656–668.

39. Gomaa, H., (1984). A software design method for real-time systems. *Communications of the ACM, 27*(9), 938–949.

40. Göransson, B., Gulliksen, J., & Boivie, I., (2003). The usability design process–integrating user- centered systems design in the software development process. *Software Process: Improvement and Practice, 8*(2), 111–131.

41. Gorschek, T., Tempero, E., & Angelis, L., (2014). On the use of software design models in software development practice: An empirical investigation. *Journal of Systems and Software, 95*(1), 176–193.

42. Griswold, W. G., Sullivan, K., Song, Y., Shonle, M., Tewari, N., Cai, Y., & Rajan, H., (2006). Modular software design with crosscutting interfaces. *IEEE Software, 23*(1), 51.

43. Guindon, R., & Curtis, B., (1988). Control of cognitive processes during software design: What tools are needed? In: *Proceedings of the SIGCHI Conference on Human Factors in Computing Systems* (Vol. 1, pp. 263–268).

44. Guindon, R., (1990). Knowledge exploited by experts during software system design. *International Journal of Man-Machine Studies, 33*(3), 279–304.

45. Hazzan, O., & Hadar, I., (2008). Why and how can human-related measures support software development processes? *Journal of Systems and Software, 81*(7), 1248–1252.

46. Hinostroza, J. E., & Mellar, H., (2001). Pedagogy embedded in educational software design: Report of a case study. *Computers & Education, 37*(1), 27–40.

47. Hsiao, K. L., & Chen, C. C., (2018). What drives smartwatch purchase intention? Perspectives from hardware, software, design, and value. *Telematics and Informatics, 35*(1), 103–113.

48. Jackson, D., & Damon, C. A., (1996). Elements of style: Analyzing a software design feature with a counterexample detector. *IEEE Transactions on Software Engineering, 22*(7), 484–495.

49. Juristo, N., Moreno, A. M., & Sanchez-Segura, M. I., (2007). Analyzing the impact of usability on software design. *Journal of Systems and Software, 80*(9), 1506–1516.

50. Kautz, K., (2011). Investigating the design process: Participatory design in agile software development. *Information Technology & People, 24*(3), 217–235.

51. Kellner, M. I., Feiler, P. H., Finkelstein, A., Katayama, T., Osterweil, L. J., Penedo, M. H., & Rombach, H. D., (1990). Software process modeling example problem. In: *Proceedings of the 6th International Software Process Workshop 'Support for the Software Process'* (Vol. 1, pp. 19– 20). IEEE Computer Society.

52. Kim, S. J., Suh, N. P., & Kim, S. G., (1991). Design of software systems based on axiomatic design. *Robotics and Computer-Integrated Manufacturing, 8*(4), 243–255.

53. Kim, S., Coffeen, R. C., & Sanguinetti, P., (2013). Interoperability building information modeling and acoustical analysis software-A demonstration of a performing arts hall design process. In: *Proceedings of Meetings on Acoustics ICA2013* (Vol. 19, No. 1, p. 015136). Acoustical Society of America.

54. Kim, Y., & Evans, R. G., (2009). Software design for wireless sensor-based site-specific irrigation. *Computers and Electronics in Agriculture, 66*(2), 159–165.
55. Kruchten, P., (2005). Casting software design in the function-behavior-structure framework. *IEEE Software, 22*(2), 52–58.
56. Kuhn, S., (1998). The software design studio: An exploration. *IEEE Software, 15*(2), 65–71. Lee, P. G., (2000). Process control and artificial intelligence software for aquaculture. *Aquacultural Engineering, 23*(1–3), 13–36.
57. Lehman, M. M., Stenning, V., & Turski, W. M., (1984). Another look at software design methodology. *ACM SIGSOFT Software Engineering Notes, 9*(2), 38–53.
58. Lin, L., & Chen, L. C., (2002). Constraints modelling in product design. *Journal of Engineering Design, 13*(3), 205–214.
59. Meehan, B., & Richardson, I., (2002). Identification of software process knowledge management. *Software Process: Improvement and Practice, 7*(2), 47–55.
60. Mihnev, P., & Zafirova-Malcheva, T., (2015). A general model for educational software design and development. In: *EDULEARN15 Proceedings* (Vol. 1, pp. 4079–4089). IATED.
61. Miller, L., Chaika, M., & Groppe, L., (1996). Girls' preferences in software design: Insights from a focus group. *Interpersonal Computing and Technology, 4*(2), 27–36.
62. Mills, H. D., (1980). The management of software engineering, Part I: Principles of software engineering. *IBM Systems Journal, 19*(4), 414–420.
63. Oduor, M., Alahäivälä, T., & Oinas-Kukkonen, H., (2014). Persuasive software design patterns for social influence. *Personal and Ubiquitous Computing, 18*(7), 1689–1704.
64. Osterloh, M., & Rota, S., (2007). Open-source software development—Just another case of collective invention? *Research Policy, 36*(2), 157–171.
65. Parnas, D. L., & Clements, P. C., (1985). A rational design process: How and why to fake it. In: *International Joint Conference on Theory and Practice of Software Development* (Vol. 1, pp. 80–100). Springer, Berlin, Heidelberg.
66. Parnas, D. L., & Clements, P. C., (1986). A rational design process: How and why to fake it. *IEEE Transactions on Software Engineering*, (2), 251–257.
67. Pelzer, S., Aspöck, L., Schröder, D., & Vorländer, M., (2014). Integrating real-time room acoustics simulation into a cad modeling software to enhance the architectural design process. *Buildings, 4*(2), 113–138.
68. Penuel, W. R., Roschelle, J., & Shechtman, N., (2007). Designing formative assessment software with teachers: An analysis of the co-design process. *Research and Practice in Technology Enhanced Learning, 2*(01), 51–74.
69. Picco, M., Lollini, R., & Marengo, M., (2014). Towards energy performance evaluation in early stage building design: A simplification methodology for commercial building models. *Energy and Buildings, 76*(1), 497–505.
70. Ralph, P., (2010). Comparing two software design process theories. In: *International*

Conference on Design Science Research in Information Systems (Vol. 1, pp. 139–153). Springer, Berlin, Heidelberg.

71. Rossmann, G. E., Flynn, M. J., Fuller, S. H., Bell, C. G., Brooks, F. P., & Hellerman, H., (1975). A course of study in computer hardware architecture. *Computer, 8*(12), 44–63.
72. Royce, W. W., (1987). Managing the development of large software systems: Concepts and techniques. In: *Proceedings of the 9th International Conference on Software Engineering* (Vol. 1, pp. 328– 338).
73. Saeki, M., Horai, H., & Enomoto, H., (1989). Software development process from natural language specification. In: *Proceedings of the 11th International Conference on Software Engineering* (Vol. 1, pp. 64–73).
74. Sangiovanni-Vincentelli, A., & Martin, G., (2001). Platform-based design and software design methodology for embedded systems. *IEEE Design & Test of Computers, 18*(6), 23–33.
75. Shaw, M., & Garlan, D., (1996). *Software Architecture: Perspectives on an Emerging Discipline* (Vol. 1, pp. 4–9). Prentice-Hall, Inc.
76. Shaw, M., (1995). Beyond objects: A software design paradigm based on process control. *ACM SIGSOFT Software Engineering Notes, 20*(1), 27–38.
77. Sonnentag, S., (1998). Expertise in professional software design: A process study. *Journal of Applied Psychology, 83*(5), 703.
78. Squires, D., (1999). Usability and educational software design: Special issue of interacting with computers. *Interacting with Computers, 11*(5), 463–466.
79. Sullivan, K. J., Griswold, W. G., Cai, Y., & Hallen, B., (2001). The structure and value of modularity in software design. *ACM SIGSOFT Software Engineering Notes, 26*(5), 99–108.
80. Taylor, R. N., & Van, D. H. A., (2007). Software design and architecture the once and future focus of software engineering. In: *Future of Software Engineering (FOSE'07)* (Vol. 1, pp. 226–243). IEEE.
81. Thomas, L., Buckland, S. T., Rexstad, E. A., Laake, J. L., Strindberg, S., Hedley, S. L., & Burnham, K. P., (2010). Distance software: Design and analysis of distance sampling surveys for estimating population size. *Journal of Applied Ecology, 47*(1), 5–14.
82. Visser, W., & Hoc, J. M., (1990). Expert software design strategies. In: *Psychology of Programming* (Vol. 1, pp. 235–249). Academic Press.
83. Walz, D. B., Elam, J. J., & Curtis, B., (1993). Inside a software design team: Knowledge acquisition, sharing, and integration. *Communications of the ACM, 36*(10), 63–77.
84. Wang, R., Lu, S., & Feng, W., (2020). Impact of adjustment strategies on building design process in different climates oriented by multiple performance. *Applied Energy, 266*(1), 114822.

85. Wan-Kadir, W. M., & Loucopoulos, P., (2004). Relating evolving business rules to software design. *Journal of Systems Architecture, 50*(7), 367–382.
86. Wegerif, R., Mercer, N., & Dawes, L., (1998). Software design to support discussion in the primary curriculum. *Journal of Computer Assisted Learning, 14*(3), 199–211.
87. Xue, M., & Zhu, C., (2009). The socket programming and software design for communication based on client/server. In: *2009 Pacific-Asia Conference on Circuits, Communications and Systems* (Vol. 1, pp. 775–777). *IEEE.*
88. Yau, S. S., & Tsai, J. J. P., (1986). A survey of software design techniques. *IEEE Transactions on Software Engineering*, (6), 713–721.
89. Yu, E. S., & Mylopoulos, J., (1994). Understanding "why" in software process modelling, analysis, and design. In: *Proceedings of 16th International Conference on Software Engineering* (Vol. 1, pp. 159–168). IEEE.
90. Yu, Y., Lapouchnian, A., Liaskos, S., Mylopoulos, J., & Leite, J. C., (2008). From goals to high- variability software design. In: *International Symposium on Methodologies for Intelligent Systems* (Vol. 1, pp. 1–16). Springer, Berlin, Heidelberg.
91. Zanni, M. A., Soetanto, R., & Ruikar, K., (2017). Towards a BIM-enabled sustainable building design process: Roles, responsibilities, and requirements. *Architectural Engineering and Design Management, 13*(2), 101–129.
92. Zhang, C., & Budgen, D., (2011). What do we know about the effectiveness of software design patterns? *IEEE Transactions on Software Engineering, 38*(5), 1213–1231.

CHAPTER 3

DESIGN QUALITIES

UNIT INTRODUCTION

The principle of excellence is well-known; however, we frequently link it with qualities that result from construction instead of design tasks. Many individuals tend to name well-made connections on a piece of furniture, the caliber of the paintings on an expensive vehicle, or the composition of a synthetic fabric when asked for instances of "excellent" quality. These are all examples of premium manufacturing instead of high-quality design, even though both are necessary to produce a high-quality result. To attain high-quality standards in product designs, one must pursue high standards of quality during the design phase (Oinas-Kukkonen & Harjumaa, 2009).

Unsurprisingly, quality is a principle that is infrequently tied to absolute fact. Including manufactured products, concepts about quality are frequently impossible to measure in a useful way on any absolute basis. The most we can typically manage is to place things on an ordinal scale, like when we state that we think this coffee table's construction is superior to another one in terms of the products used and the level of craftsmanship it demonstrates (Cheng & Tang, 2010). However, there is no way for us to quantify how much better one is than the other. The issue is, if anything, more excellent when evaluating design as opposed to construction. As we evaluate the quality of typography, furniture, and clothing, esthetic qualities are frequently linked to design excellence (Khalighy et al., 2015). We often equate elegance with better design, but this association does not define our thinking. Moreover, it is more likely to have transitory elements since it may be heavily impacted by our perceptions of fashion, which would serve to contextualize excellence. (For instance, a radio from the 1930s would fit right in in a room that is decorated in that era, but it might look out of place in a 1980s-styled home.)

Software is an abstract commodity that may be less likely to be impacted by fashion (dubious statement, maybe, especially in connection to interface design by user). Still, it should be no surprise that the definition of excellence is challenging for software. Many qualities can be measured either way, and the measurements we do must have varying degrees of value. Moreover, the notion of quality as it pertains to software is at least partially a massive issue by nature; therefore, it is surely not ensured by applying a specific design form (Park et al., 2006).

It can be challenging to distinguish thoughts about the quality of design from thoughts about implementation quality when discussing software while comparing it to other objects. No matter how well-designed something is, if it is poorly assembled, we need not regard it to be of high quality. In the same way, if its design is flawed, no degree of skillful manufacturing would be able to cover up its underlying flaws. (Even if the door is well constructed and closes securely, we would still find it uncomfortable to use if it is placed so that our knuckles are scraped whenever it opened) (Becker et al., 2015).

When considering how to evaluate software's quality, we again run into the dual aspect (static & Dynamic) of software. Any collection of metrics we may create should aim to evaluate both of these aspects of software and should take into account the possibility of interfering with one another. (A software may be very effective at satisfying real-time requirements, but its internal organization may be so disorganized that any modifications are practically impossible. Similarly, a program's structure could be excellent, but its operating performance might be terrible!) (Hissam et al., 2002).

It is feasible to find certain very broad quality measurements that are fundamental and can be used in software, even though the nature of the designed object itself may primarily determine our conceptions of quality measures. Regarding these goals, the most important criterion for any system should typically be its suitability for the intended use because the finished result must be suitable to carry out the work given. For instance, a chair's design must still satisfy the fundamental necessity that we can sit on it, preferably in a comfortable way. This is true regardless of how lovely the chair may be. As a result, the function (purpose) of the technology being created will be considered when choosing and weighing the quality indicators to be utilized for this assessment (Hofmeister et al., 2007).

This serves as an illustration that it should never take precedence over function while pursuing elegance of any form. In light of this, it is reasonable to assume that software systems will function as intended in all necessary circumstances when they are finally implemented. It must complete the necessary duties in the designated manner and within the parameters of the designated resources. (Again, the implementation of a design is the only way to determine its final success) (Weyns, 2012). Because comparisons are being made with intentions as stated in the requirement analysis, this approach is connected to the concepts of validation & verification that were discussed in the previous chapter. However, as a practical means, it can only be evaluated by any secondary method (Blomkvist, 2005). As a result, it could be preferable to see purpose-based fitness as the ultimate goal and search for ways to evaluate it by identifying a group of related traits and then certain system qualities that offer assessments of these. The first thing we'll deal with in the following section is the structure or framework that allows us to pinpoint a few system characteristics that correspond to our overarching concepts about quality (Alebrahim et al., 2016).

Learning Objective

At the end of this chapter, students will be able to learn the following:

- What are design qualities;
- Evaluation of design quality;
- Design features.

Key Terms

- Design qualities
- Ilities
- Design features
- Design phase

EVALUATION OF DESIGN QUALITY

"You know anything about what you are talking about when you can quantify and represent it in numbers, but your understanding is of a scant and inadequate kind when you are unable to measure it and represent it in numbers." the Lord Kelvin

An Evaluating Framework

Although Lord Kelvin's maxim is frequently cited, it is simple to forget the framework in which it was said. A society of engineers & scientists that sought to record concepts about physical characteristics like velocity, length, mass, etc., where scales for measurements could be more easily established and disseminated, is where concepts about measurement first emerged (Abreu et al., 1995). We can be certain that when measuring the attribute of length in units (centimeters), something with a length value of 8 will be twice as long as something with a length value of 4 since the scales used in these characteristics are ratio scales with well-defined durations and a zero point (Cebi, 2013).

Even if the concept of measuring is still significant outside of this framework, we frequently have to settle for a less extensive understanding than what Lord Kelvin sought. When it comes to the issue of evaluating design qualities, a number of the traits that are important to humans are more likely to be "measured" by using an ordinal scale (in which items can be ordered, but the magnitude of the distances in between elements could not be defined). (We will have to handle numerical numbers for qualities that relate to concepts about quality of design carefully even when we do receive them. Assigning any property a numerical value does not imply that it was evaluated on a ratio scale) (Venable et al., 2016).

In light of Fenton & Pfleeger's (1997) observation that "measurement is associated with collecting information regarding qualities of objects," it is helpful to further explore the connections between our conceptions of quality and those of measurement at this point. An early array of mappings that could be built to connect these concepts is shown in Figure 3.1. The underlying principles apply to the primary concepts used in the figure.

- **Quality Concepts:** These are the conceptual notions we have about what makes for "excellent" and "poor" aspects of a system, which the designer will need to evaluate while making decisions about design.
- **Design Attributes:** These offer a collection of quantifiable (or, at the very least, distinguishable) qualities of the design elements, serving as a bridge between the conceptual notion of a property and the numerical characteristics of an actual design (as a result, efficiently comparable to the comprehensive idea of a metric).
- **Counts:** It require determining the linguistic features of an illustration that

must be tallied to arrive at some quantities for the metrics because they aim to achieve the design parameters.

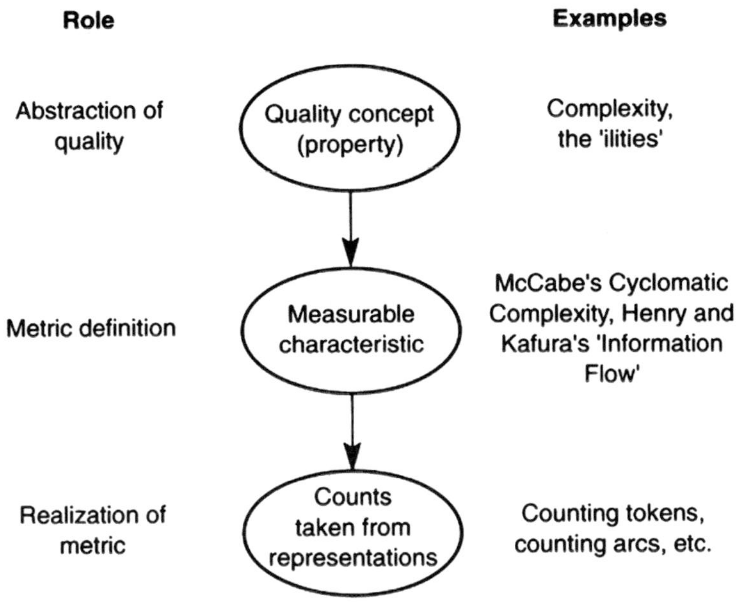

Figure 3.1. Connecting metrics to quality ideas.

Source: Image by easymatrics.com.

The value of program code is frequently thought to be connected to its substrate specificity, which serves as an example of a frequently used statistic suited to this concept (Verschuren & Hartog, 2005). As determined by McCabe's Cyclomatic Complexity measure, the variety of possible control routes present within a program unit is one quantifiable attribute that may be employed to evaluate this intricacy (McCabe, 1976). This is calculated by counting linguistic tokens in the source code, with the number of tokens utilized depending on the language implementation, including IF & WHILE.

It basically involves transforming from a quantifiable characteristic to a collection of accurate and precise counting rules to be utilized with a certain language implementation. However, it takes much more understanding to translate a quality notion into a collection of quantifiable criteria. (This topic is frequently overlooked in code metrics literature (Clifford et al., 2012). McCabe's metric is a notable example of the concept presented above—that a numerical value doesn't always indicate a ratio scale. It is unlikely that anyone would contest that anything with a cyclomatic complexity rating of six is twice as complex as something with a value of three.) We require a more comprehensive model to find the mappings necessary to aid this understanding. Figure 3.2 displays the framework presented in

Figure 3.1 in an enlarged format. Here, the concept of quality has been enlarged into three additional levels, where use determines the goal of measurements (and thereby sharply distinguishes between assessing static attributes of a design and evaluating dynamic behavioral attributes) (Bansiya & Davis, 2002):

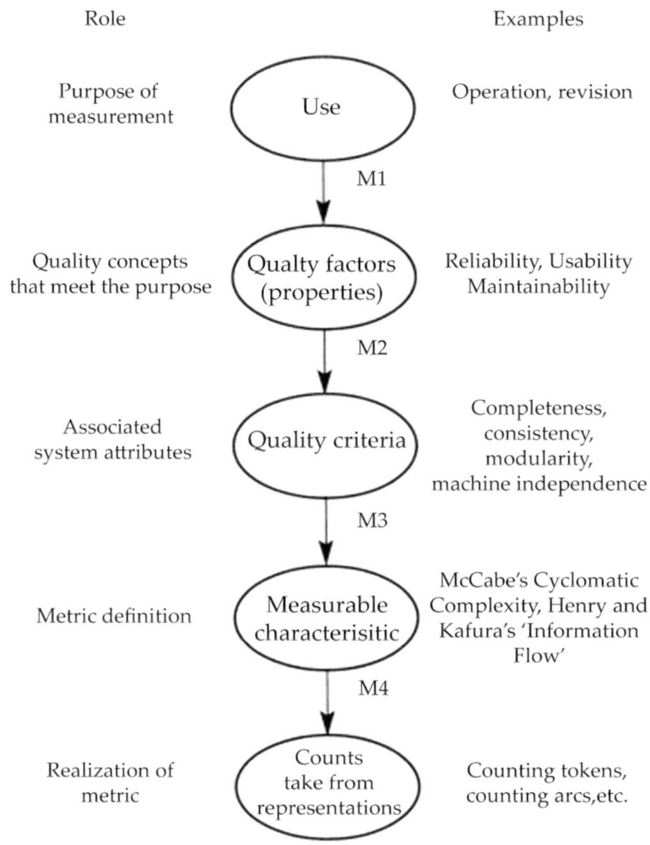

Figure 3.2. A more thorough mapping of quality ideas to design aspects that can be counted.

Source: Image by zapier.com.

- The quality ideas that are connected to the purpose are determined by quality variables (these things are frequently called "ilities");
- Quality criteria correspond the solution-based characteristics of a design to the requirements-based characteristics of the planned system (the 'ilities'), which are then projected onto a selected number of metrics.

It does not lessen the required understanding level, but it makes the connection between the demand for quality evaluations and the forms utilized. Figure 3.3 illustrates an example of the corresponding mappings (M1 & M2) from Figure 3.2, depending on the requirements that were determined to be important for a real-time system and, for reference, those that were determined to be important for a compiler. The nature of an issue and its context must be recognized by any evaluation that incorporates the ultimate objective of fitness for a reason, as was noted in the preceding section. The distributions we assign to the uses represent this balance; therefore, the decision of weightings for the "ilities" is directly tied to both the problem's nature and its context. For an integrated control system, for instance, efficiency might be more important than usability. For an airframe autopilot, stability may be considered one of the most critical components (Venable et al., 2012).

When we apply these concepts, we discover that the demands of a designer and any measuring method unavoidably tend to generate forces that drive in different directions (Tremblay et al., 2010). As was noted in Chapter 2, skilled designers usually attempt to maintain a somewhat constant abstraction level in their arguments at any given point of the construction process and refrain from delving too deeply into detail very early. Abstractions, however, are challenging to measure; thus, metrics analysis methods aim to have as much information about a design at their disposal as feasible (Tremblay et al., 2010).

Specifying qualities and assessing them can be challenging, requiring the thorough declaration of any measuring principles to be applied, including for program code, which has well-defined semantics and syntax (Kitchenham et al., 1997; Conte et al., 1986). The comparatively poor syntax of most optimized design expressions makes the issue worse for design representation forms. The meaning of almost all charts and graphs must be made explicit by carefully using the free-text element because there are very few design compositions that seem to be noticeable.

Therefore, despite several studies to derive various statistics from system engineering abstractions, the automatic interpretation of design notations to derive measures of certain qualities has not had a particularly substantial influence to date (Troy & Zweben, 1981; Hall & Preiser, 1984). Although CASE (computer-aided software engineering) tools can be used to describe designs and, in some situations, help with code creation, most notations still have issues with poor semantics and syntax that necessitate a careful understanding of any written components (Fan et al., 2005).

Another issue with the analysis of metrics processes is that they have, up until this point, focused almost exclusively on evaluating static characteristics of a design, as they may at least be immediately derived from any notation using some form of asset counting. Making behavioral inferences from the static data presented and making assertions more about performance traits of any potential implementation are both necessary for attempts to retrieve information more about the dynamic features (Friel & Budgen, 1997).

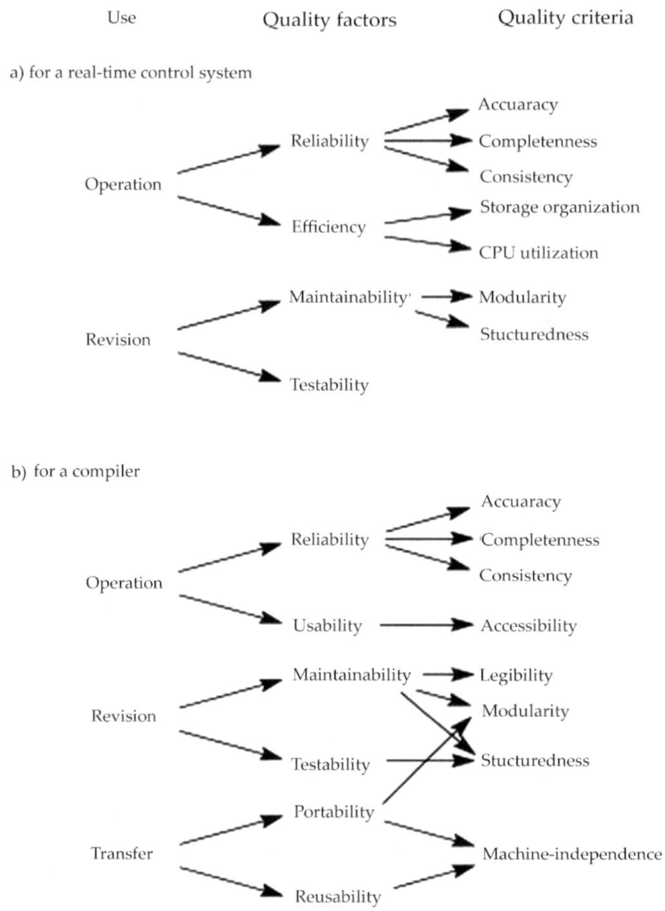

Figure 3.3. Mapping quality criteria to quality variables.

Source: Image by nature.com.

Evaluating static features is inadequate when trying to determine the ultimate criterion of purpose suitability since, as Figure 3.3 illustrates, the characteristics that the designer deems to be particularly significant may well correspond most closely to dynamic attributes (Bosch & Molin, 1999). We can compare musical notation to show why this is the case. In that a static notation is used to express something that requires to be "executed," and as a result, has a comparable combination of static & dynamic traits, music shares some characteristics with software. (Once more, it is quite simple to draw a general difference between the high and low quality in music, but extremely difficult to measure that disparity) (Tu & Xia, 2008).

Figure 3.4 piece of a musical score demonstrates how basic properties, like the count of beats in one bar, should be checked using some analysis criteria that can be specified. We could also create rules to examine chords and sequences, determine note intervals, and listen for specific dissonances. If we had sufficient musical understanding, this could reveal a lot about the composition it depicts, but hearing it performed live is the actual test. We won't know whether we like it or whether it will work for a specific purpose until that point. (The "mental" approach also applies here since anyone with enough expertise will probably "play" the score in their brain to judge its merits!) (Kolokotsa et al., 2001).

Figure 3.4. A musical score notation is an example.

Source: Image by Zengfu Wang.

The 'Ilities'

When evaluating the quality of a design, the "ilities" are a set of quality aspects that must be considered. Since there are numerous ilities, we will only cover the ones that are seen to be the most broadly relevant in this area, namely (Cleven et al., 2009):

- Reliability;
- Efficiency;
- Maintainability;
- Usability.

(The purposes of the other ilities, like reusability, portability, testability, and so forth, are somewhat more specialized) (Boehm et al., 1976).

Reliability

This element primarily addresses the dynamic properties of the final system, requiring the designer to forecast potential behavioral problems. For design purposes, we are particularly interested in approaches to assess whether the ultimate system will be (Suzuki et al., 2002):

- **Complete:** In the extent that it can manage any symmetries of systems & events states.
- **Consistent:** This meaning that irrespective of the system's load capacity at any given time, its behavior will be predictable and repeatable;
- **Resilient:** In the face of mechanical fault or other similar conflicts (for instance, if the data-logging printer in a chemical process-control plant malfunction for any reason, this shouldn't be able to "hang" the entire system, however, it should be treated according to w the philosophy encapsulated in the aspect "graceful degradation").

The challenges of assuring reliability will grow as systems get more extensive and more complicated. Diverse strategies have been devised to overcome various limits in the development and execution procedures for security systems, in which this element is crucial (Chau, 2007; Ma et al., 2015). For instance, the execution will involve several computers, each of whom will have been programmed by a different team for development and monitored independently. This system will be employed in "fly-by- wire" aircraft, where the control surfaces are handled by computer connections rather than by immediate hydraulic controls. Any operating request made to the control system is then analyzed concurrently by every computer, and the desired operation is only carried out when all of the computers are approved (Jin & Chen, 2001).

Efficiency

Utilization of resources, including Computing time, ram, web access, resources, disk usage, and other resources, can be used to gage a system's efficiency. It's a relative and multi-variate construct because there is no unique level to define an ideal efficiency. However, one system can be more effective than another concerning a metric like a processor (Chaudhry et al., 2006). Efficiency was regarded as a critical criterion in the beginnings of computers when there were simple programs and computer time was valuable and was primarily assessed in terms of processor & memory usage. Systems that were put into place. Although the concepts in question have been chiefly expressed using HCI vocabulary and the more visually appealing parts of systems, they still have much to contribute to the process of design in general. Therefore, we quickly discuss some of the more practically pertinent dimensions in this chapter and make suggestions as to when they might be able to provide particularly insightful information (Karathanassis et al., 2017).

Impetuous Commitment (and Imposed Look Ahead)

This occurred when an initial choice for design was made without the correct information, which has the consequence of limiting a later choice. It may be inevitable (data may not be accessible in a realistic amount of time). Still, it might also result from operational design techniques, including methods that support a specific ordering of decisions. (A straightforward illustration of this tendency is found in spoken telephone selection systems, particularly those that employ a hierarchical menu options (Zeng, 2020).

Every set of options is provided in an order, and the user must choose without knowing all the options that will be displayed in the future.) For our intentions, this notion may serve as a "quality measure" of the design phase instead of the design outcome. However, undoubtedly the implications are more likely to be presented in the latter. This concept is meant to be a "measure" used in HCI designs. A design process that acknowledges the necessity for repeated versions through the decision- making processes and a life cycle that enables design choices to be reviewed may be helpful (Sharma & Suryanarayana, 2016).

Hidden Dependencies

This idea depicts a connection between two elements where the connection is not entirely obvious, even though one depends on the other. This focuses on one of the design-related issues that we shall discuss later when looking at design annotation. Notations frequently only mention certain types of dependencies (such as component A calls component B) and leave out others, such as that A & B are aware of specific types of data and structures (Benlarbi & Melo, 1999). However, the designer will have to take into account each of these connections while formulating their solution. Modifying a design is expected to be considerably more challenging if the designer only has a portion of the essential knowledge regarding dependencies to facilitate access to them, a fact that is particularly well shown in the study presented by Littman et al. The problem becomes potentially a lot more severe when a design has been adjusted during renovations (1987). (This attribute is also especially important for maintaining websites) (Littman et al., 1987).

Secondary Notation

This dimension refers to extra information or data communicated outside the "official syntax." The usage of local design standards by designers when employing certain design notations is a prime illustration of this topic. Still, we will only quickly hit on it here because we shall go into more detail in the subsequent chapters. While these may be common knowledge to the designers who came up with the idea, they might not be as obvious to new team members or those who will eventually have to maintain the system (Vanciu & Rajlich, 2010).

Viscosity

In this, the idea of "resistance to change" is explained. This may occur as a result of early commitment during a design creation process, and it may substantially impact the "quality" of design throughout maintenance. Standard programs and websites both feature a variety of methods that, particularly at the more intricate levels of execution, can quickly lead to excessive viscosity (Freitas et al., 2011). (We can use the application of internal mathematical constants rather than specifying symbolic forms to illustrate this dimension inside the framework of computer code. One all-too-common example of this approach is using the value 17.5 at different points in the code instead of specifying a constant rate, including a VAT rate of 17.5 at the beginning of the program. Instead of only altering the value specified for the constant, it will be required to find every instance of the VAT rate when it is later needed to change its value. Far worse, certain values can even be modified accidentally since 17.5 might appear in a certain program for some other factors (for instance, within 217.53) (Latorre et al., 2015).

Even though viscosity is not a characteristic that is easily quantifiable concerning design, it's a feature that is more easily observable at a range of abstraction levels. A design might illustrate the degree of interdependence between modules and the discrepancies between the "conceptual" aspect of a solution and the one that comes about during the system design (Mann & Wong, 1996). Bowman et al. (1999), which examines the "architectural framework" of the software that comprises the Linux operating system, provide an intriguing example of this. The study's findings undoubtedly offer examples of various cognitive domains!) (Bowman et al., 1999).

When considering the quality of design and what it might entail for software, the intellectual dimensions present some intriguing concepts. Later, we will discuss some of the concepts they represent in more detail. But now that we have looked at some of the quality criteria that designers want to be able to evaluate while making decisions, it's time to think about the quality metrics that are really at our disposal during the design process. After that, we may think about how well they can be used to determine how effectively a design satisfies the aforementioned criteria (Wróblewska et al., 2021).

FEATURES OF THE QUALITY DESIGN PRODUCT

After examining a variety of ideas concerning design quality, it is evident that the two main challenges they pose for assessment are (Franceschini & Rossetto, 1997):

- Identifying many design characteristics that are associated with these properties; and

- Figuring out how to extract information about these characteristics from the various design documents available.

A brief explanation of one of the methods by which these might be retrieved follows a description of various features and parameters frequently used for designing an assessment at the beginning of this section (Lin, 2007).

Some Design Features

Simplicity

In whichever field they are generated, ideal designs almost always have a fundamental simplicity. A successful design achieves its goals and lacks extraneous flourishes that distract from it (Lazard et al., 2016). This may be why numerous dual-purpose objects fall short of meeting both goals clearly and effectively. One instance that arises to mind is a rucksack that attempted to grow into a tent but failed since it was far more practical to carry a quality rucksack as well as a decent tent as distinct objects. The majority of us probably have similar instances of inappropriate brilliance in our minds) (Resnick & Montania, 2003).

The commonly referenced Albert Einstein adage, "A proposal should be as simple as feasible, but no simpler," is far more complex than it initially appears (Sarkis, 1998). This is the counterargument to the one against needless decoration; it cautions against trying to exaggerate since the result will be a component that is unable to perform its function. An abstraction is a vital tool for simplification, but to be useful in problem resolution, it must keep the pertinent properties (Abdulkareem et al., 2020).

Though simplicity cannot be easily measured, complexities opposite feature can indeed be tried to quantify. These have been created to be used with software and measure several types of complexity, including (Nowlis & Simonson, 1996):

- Control flow complexity (McCabe, 1976) is associated with the variety of control routes that may be followed during the implementation of a program system;
- The structure's complexity as it relates to the system's ability to move information around (Henry & Kafura, 1984; Kitchenham et al., 1990; Shepperd & Ince, 1993);
- The degree of comprehension difficulty is shown by the variety of descriptors and processors (Halstead, 1977);
- The complexity of the structure as it relates to the connections between system components (mainly object-oriented types), with the metrics given in Chidamber & Kemerer (1994) receiving a lot of attention, but they are by no means the only choices (Briand et al., 2000).

All of them might be used in extensive design documenting forms, but sadly only the last one scaled up easily for usage in design. Other than for object-based forms, there are presently no predefined measures that can be used to help in evaluating the structural complexity of a certain design. Regarding the design quality ideas, supportability, trial ability, dependability, and perhaps efficiency are all directly correlated with simplicity (Bertini et al., 2009; Lee et al., 2015).

Modularity

When a suitable modular architecture is used, it is possible to break down a given problem into many discrete components (Duffey et al., 2008). Again, modularity is not limited to software; other branches of engineering have long recognized its value. The concept of replacing one device with another by simply disconnecting the old one and putting in the new one, especially in electronics, has made maintaining and updating electronic and electrical devices a comparatively simple operation (Agrawal et al., 2013).

This is typically only feasible in a clear range of interface standards. This is typically accomplished for electronic components using a "backplane" that acts as a data expressway and the requisite signal lines. Software may also achieve this module connection (as shown by the presence of libraries containing subprograms), but the level of interface standardization is much lower. Despite this, the idea of the software system is still crucial (Antonio et al., 2007; Rodriguez-Toro et al., 2003).

One must employ a design technique based on the segregation of interests to own a modular structure effectively. It is not sufficient to define interfaces; instead, a designer must arrange functions inside modules to reduce their dependencies. When modules are grouped this way, the interface to the module becomes less complicated. In the context of hardware, it might simply mean that fewer connections are needed; while in the instance of the software, however, we must find additional metrics to assess this factor (Antonio et al., 2009).

Locating a suitable modularity strategy to implement while tackling a particular problem has at least the following advantages when seen generally and also from the perspective of software:

- It is easy to replace the module;
- Each module isolates a particular aspect of an issue, which aids comprehension (and subsequently maintenance) and offers a framework for collaborative creation;
- A fine-structured module is simple to repurpose for a different issue.

The effective use of modularity should therefore be tied to such quality notions as manageability, trial ability, and (potentially) to accessibility and dependability as well in terms of the design features that we are pursuing (Remery et al., 2012; Hockings, 1998).

"Coupling" and "cohesion" are two helpful quality metrics that have been employed for a long time to gage the degree of modular design in software. Following the observations of the issues that arise when creating massive systems, these terms were developed in the early 1970s (Stevens et al., 1974; Yourdon & Constantine, 1979), and they were used to describe how complicated a system was in terms of the structure and interdependence of its constituent modules (Stevens et al., 1974; Yourdon & Constantine, 1979). Although the basic unit of modularity in the original concept was supposed to be the sub-program unit, those principles are still applicable to other modules like Modula-2 "module," Ada "package," and Java "class."

To determine the types of interactions in different modules and their "strength," Coupling, a unit of inter-module connection, must be used.

Generally speaking, modules depending on the process or subprogram are perhaps more favorably treated in the forms of Coupling indicated than types depending on the class. The various methods of calling processes and the use of various parameter-passing techniques are often related to the measurements of coupling. The "uses" hierarchy (Parnas, 1979), which deals with the packaging of relevant data, may also be implemented into the notion. As a result, it can serve as a tool for making decisions about designs at various abstraction levels (Göçer et al., 2015).

The difficulty of rigorously measuring cohesion & coupling is one issue with the fundamental ideas involved. As there is only truly room to detect their existence during design and defining their extent is rarely feasible, this is less of a problem for the system design than for evaluating program structures. Even yet, the usefulness of any such metrics is somewhat constrained. With coupling, it is at least possible to carry out such activities as counting ties, analyzing the sizes of database systems transferred, and so forth. We can use the situation of coordinating control coupling, often known as "switch coupling," as an illustration of the idea that the presence of specific forms is more important in design evaluation than the degree of coupling (Markelj et al., 2014).

This form often appears when one of a procedure's parameters is utilized to specify how the procedure should carry out its work. This can also happen when a program is called from several software sections. It is discovered relatively late that the function it completes may vary slightly depending on the area. Then, the' switch' option is introduced to allow the invoking function to specify which version of the task requires to be executed (Forza, 2002; Khan & Yairi, 2018). To put it another way, it fixes a design flaw! (Writing any cross-program, like an assembler, translator, or link editor, is a typical illustration of a scenario within which this may happen. These all include a series of apparently simple activities that must be repeated but which, upon closer examination, reveal slight variations with each pass.) Therefore, this type of connection is probably the result of inadequately handling the design development duties. Therefore, it is necessary to recognize its presence in any design evaluation. Any idea of its "extent" is difficult to pin down, even if it has dubious value (Nam & Smith-Jackson, 2007).

In turn, cohesion offers a measurement of how closely the elements of a module can be said to be "functionally connected." The optimal module is where each component may be viewed as serving just one function. A stack type with a set of public methods for evaluating the stack and the information structures for the stack itself could serve as an instance of functional connectedness in a situation where the Java class serves as the foundation for the modular structure. Since every component of such a class exists to provide a stacking capability, it can be said to demonstrate functional cohesiveness (Markelj et al., 2014).

Procedural connection, which is heavily focused on the order of actions and hence less naturally matches with the packing notion, may be the main exemption to this rule. (This version was later added in Yourdon & Constantine (1979) and was not on the previous list by Stevens et al., 1974) (Yourdon & Constantine, 1979; Stevens et al., 1974). Our beliefs regarding the priority order of the more desired forms may require some change as a result of redefining these within a framework of packaging subunits, such as the class, instead of operational ones, like the subprogram or procedure. However, the general contrast between pleasant and unpleasant remains the same. The main question is whether the communicational association should now be given a higher ranking than sequential affiliation because it uses the class mechanism's features better. Although the point is very unimportant, it does show how our perceptions of quality may vary as implementation structures develop (Bieman & Kang, 1998).

Although cohesion is perhaps even harder to evaluate than coupling, it offers a metric that may aid the designer in weighing the comparative merits of various solutions. Metrics scholars have therefore shown a great deal of interest in the problem of discovering methods of assessing its presence in a respectably objective manner (Bieman & Kang, 1998).

Though coupling & cohesion are covered in practically every mainstream software engineering textbook, the "structured design" style of textbooks typically has more in-depth treatments. The ones offered in Yourdon & Constantine (1979); and Page-Jones (1988) are most likely two of the more comprehensive ones (Yourdon & Constantine, 1979; Page-Jones, 1988).

Information Hiding

This theory is connected to the idea of modularity, yet it also includes different ideas regarding information management in a system. The fundamental idea urges the designer to guarantee that data more about precise shapes of objects like data structures and device interfaces remains inside a module or unit and is not made "visible" outside of that unit (Parnas, 1972). Like the notions before, it was initially identified via an observational procedure (Parnas, 1999).

When this concept is followed, all other application programs that might use a module are left in the dark regarding the precise structure of any data types within the module (Shull et al., 2000). Many "access procedures" may also grant regulated connectivity to the module's "customers." The result is a "scope wall" that surrounds information and prevents immediate access. The construction of a module that offers an integer stack feature to facilitate a range of reverse Polish computations using numerals is one application of this approach. By using the information-hiding concept, one might try to hide the stack's implementation form and give a variety of access mechanisms, like as (Budgen & Marashi, 1988):

- Add a number to the stack;
- Remove a number from the stack;
- Analyze an empty stack. Illustrated in Figure 3.5 schematically.

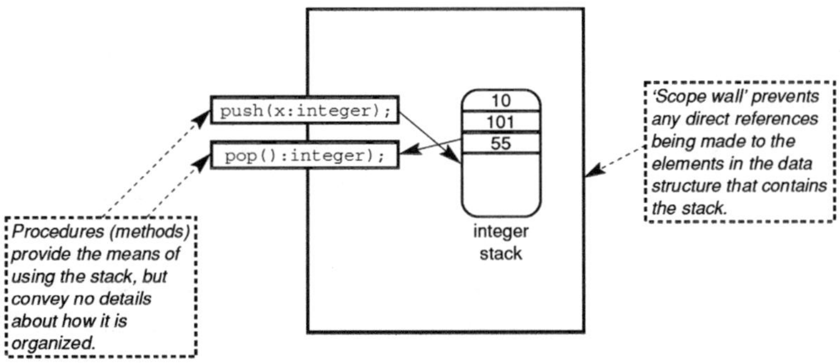

Figure 3.5. An instance of information-hiding employed with a module that gives a number or integer stack.

Source: Image by enwikipedia.org.

The following interface hides the specific design choices made about the stack's implementation, which helps to maintain the stack's stability by avoiding "short-cut" accessibility from other programming units. Additionally, it enables the particular form of execution to be changed without impacting, for example, any of the units using this stack (Cresswell & Sheikh, 2013).

Even though the idea is strong, it is challenging to apply it to any design procedure, and it is also challenging to develop several tests to determine its application. It is, without a doubt, connected to dependability and ease of maintenance in system quality elements. It is sometimes likely to run afoul of efficiency principles in terms of memory & processor consumption, as using a hierarchy of accessing processes may result in poor run-time performance (Kopyscinski et al., 2010).

Although the principals involved are typically highly tractable, the specific ways these traits present them in software applications are difficult to pin down. Examining a design for indications of those characteristics that suggest a design might lose certain traits is a helpful tool for determining the amount of their existence in the design. To do this, a sufficient set of characteristics must be found that match traits opposite to the ones described above. Any of the above traits can be anticipated to make it challenging to read and comprehend the designer's objectives and to adjust the resulting system (Banaee et al., 2013).

Finding characteristics that are the exact opposite of those mentioned above is a considerable challenge. Therefore, the following unfavorable traits of a design might be thought of as being caused by the existence of the inverse attributes (Bardram et al., 2013).

- Dispersing numerous copies of "state" data throughout the system. This makes information updating more difficult and could result in inconsistent system behavior.
- Making use of too complicated interfaces. These are typically described in programming terms by methods with excessive variables, a few of which might not even be required. They are far more easily recognized in terms of their design by the level of information stream they have (Nidhra & Dondeti, 2012).
- The employment of overly complex control mechanisms. This could hint that the designer selected an inappropriate interface and information structure for certain design components.
- Unnecessary information about replication. This can also be seen in module interfaces, where procedures might pass an entire parameter record even though just one field is crucial to how they operate.
- Making use of 'functionally weak' modules. Program units of this kind are not particularly purpose-focused and may participate in this study for use on various tasks.

Since implementation characteristics are more well-known and can be measured more efficiently, these traits have primarily been described in terms of them. Moreover, they can also be evaluated for design explanations, even though any automatic analysis makes it more difficult to retrieve the data (Rising & Callis, 1994).

EVALUATING THE DESIGN PHASE OR PROCESS

Any design project results from some design phase, no matter how organized or unorganized. Therefore, even while no level of quality management can genuinely guarantee a certain level of product quality, the quality of the design phase is undoubtedly an important component that must be taken into account when attempting to comprehend design quality challenges (Nam & Smith-Jackson, 2007).

Our research into the structure of a design process thus far has revealed that it often entails the designer creating a "model" of the intended system before looking into ways to make that model a reality (Jones & Shrauger, 1970). According to Visser & Hoc (1990), opportunistic design strategies are frequently employed for these tasks even when organized design layouts are also in practice. Therefore, it would be reasonable to assume that the innovative aspect of this stage of software development would make it difficult to establish any precise standards of quality (Visser & Hoc, 1990). Experience would indicate that this is the case and that the current measurements of quality and efficiency are somewhat constrained, even for the more measurable operations associated with the development of software, including coding & testing. Watts Humphrey has compiled a valuable overview of quality concerns relevant to processes of software development in his book "Managing the Software Process" (Humphrey, 1991). He explicitly outlines five stages of maturity in the procedures that an organization utilizes to produce software applications in his "software process maturity model" (Humphrey et al., 1991):

- **Initial:** The software development process is described as improvised and sometimes chaotic. The success of a project relies on each individual's effort because very few processes are established.
- **Repeated:** The establishment of fundamental project management procedures and their usage in monitoring expense, timeframe, and performance to replicate previous accomplishments on projects with related applications, the required process consistency is in place.
- **Defined:** The software program is structured, documented, and incorporated into an organization-wide software system for engineering and management tasks. The organization's software development and maintenance process is used in all projects according to an outlined and accepted version.
- **Managed:** The software development process and product quality are measured in great detail. The software development process and its end products are statistically understood and carefully monitored.
- **Optimizing:** Quantitative feedback from the system and from evaluating novel concepts and technology enables continuous improvement in processing.

The information presented in the previous parts and chapters will have made it evident why the proposed solution created for a system will be considerably more strongly problem-oriented than, for example, the coding structuring methods or testing that might be employed. This does not negate the need to find quality standards for the design phase; however, it does highlight the difficulty in making the design phase consistent, even at the highest levels that the whole project development may reach. Finding strategies to include feedback in the designing phase that can accomplish the following is significant to raise the caliber of the design process (Howard et al., 2008):

- Domain expertise regarding the nature of the problem at hand and significant elements of any implementation aspects;
- Methodological expertise that facilitates comprehension of any applied design techniques;
- Any accessible experience from similar projects.

Three methods are frequently used to provide this input data to the design phase or process (Bushnell, 1990).

The utilization of technical reviews, described in the section before, enables the design team to learn from others' experiences and, in particular, from any domain and knowledge about the method they may hold. Even while the main goal of this type of feedback is to improve the design result, it can also substantially impact the design process by pointing up helpful methods or notations that may be appropriate to a specific issue (Xu et al., 2011).

The main goals of management reviews are to create and improve project-wide estimates of manpower and timeframes, as well as to collect any data that may be required for such predictions. Since it needs the use of both to produce the necessary projections, the work of estimating largely relies on both knowledge and experience domains (Yin et al., 2014).

Gaining knowledge domain and some types of experience concerning a specific issue are both possible through prototyping. (In this perspective, prototyping may be seen as serving what Floyd (1984) has referred to as the "experimental" or "exploratory" function.) Therefore, augmenting the design and management team's expertise and experience might be viable by building appropriate prototypes (Barlas & Heavey, 2016).

Of the three, performance management probably entails evaluating how a design has been produced in some way and may offer a foundation for utilizing the other two. The usage of tracking and reporting tools will be crucial for keeping track of quality problems and ensuring they are handled during reviews (Sancar Tokmak et al., 2013). Once more, developing a high-quality process through reusing experience heavily depends on the design documentation quality (and, in larger projects, the quality of any customization and control techniques used for managing this documentation) (Soller et al., 2005). Although the use of standardized design annotation and particular design practices cannot guarantee the quality of the design phase or the design outcome, it should be evident by this point that their usage is likely to have a significant impact. Consequently, we are now in a strong position to start looking at their functions in the context of the more technical challenges impacting software design in the following chapter (Jones- Farmer et al., 2014).

ACTIVITY 3.1.

Given the four 'ilities' reliability, usability, maintainability, reusability, consider how you would rank them in order of importance for each of the following systems:

- A process control system for a chemical plant that produces toxic insecticides.
- A bank auto teller network used to issue cash and short statements describing accounts.
- An interactive database used for stock control at each branch of a chain of stores that sells electrical goods.

SUMMARY

The following points are particularly significant in examining ideas about 'good' design.

- Software quality concepts assess the eventual system's static structure and dynamic behavior.
- The ultimate goal of quality must be fit for purpose, although the criteria for determining whether this is achieved will be problem-dependent and domain-dependent.
- While the use of abstraction is an essential tool for the designer, it makes it difficult to make direct product measurements during the design process.
- Technical design reviews can provide a valuable means of obtaining and using domain knowledge to assess the design product and method knowledge to aid with determining the design process.

REVIEW QUESTIONS

1. Explain the importance of design qualities.
2. How can we evaluate the quality of design?
3. What do you understand by the term "ilities"?

MULTIPLE CHOICE QUESTIONS

1. The activity that distributes estimated effort across the planned project duration by allocating the effort to specific software developing tasks is ____________

a. Project scheduling

b. Detailed schedule

c. Macroscopic schedule

d. None of the mentioned

2. Why do bugs and failures occur in software?

a. Because of Developers

b. Because of companies

c. Because of both companies and Developers

d. None of the mentioned

3. Degree to which design specifications are followed in manufacturing the product is called

a. Quality Control

b. Quality of conformance

c. Quality Assurance

d. None of the mentioned

4. Attributes of good software is ___________

a. Development

b. Functionality

c. Maintainability & functionality

d. Maintainability

5. Quality also can be looked at in terms of user satisfaction which includes

a. A compliant product

b. Good quality output

c. Delivery within budget and schedule

d. All of the mentioned

Answers to Multiple Choice Questions

1. (a) 2. (c) 3. (b) 4. (c) 5. (d)

REFERENCES

1. Abdulkareem, A., Erturun, U., & Mossi, K., (2020). Non-destructive evaluation device for monitoring fluid viscosity. *Sensors, 20*(6), 1657.
2. Abreu, F. B., Goulão, M., & Esteves, R., (1995). Toward the design quality evaluation of object- oriented software systems. In: *Proceedings of the 5th International Conference on Software Quality* (Vol. 1, pp. 44–57). Austin, Texas, USA.
3. Agrawal, T., Sao, A., Fernandes, K. J., Tiwari, M. K., & Kim, D. Y., (2013). A hybrid model of component sharing and platform modularity for optimal product family design. *International Journal of Production Research, 51*(2), 614–625.
4. Alebrahim, A., Faßbender, S., Filipczyk, M., Goedicke, M., Heisel, M., & Zdun, U., (2016). Variability for qualities in software architecture. *ACM SIGSOFT Software Engineering Notes, 41*(1), 32– 35.
5. Antonio, K. L., Richard, C. Y., & Tang, E., (2009). The complementarity of internal integration and product modularity: An empirical study of their interaction effect on competitive capabilities. *Journal of Engineering and Technology Management, 26*(4), 305–326.

6. Antonio, K. L., Yam, R. C., & Tang, E., (2007). The impacts of product modularity on competitive capabilities and performance: An empirical study. *International Journal of Production Economics, 105*(1), 1–20.
7. Banaee, H., Ahmed, M. U., & Loutfi, A., (2013). Data mining for wearable sensors in health monitoring systems: A review of recent trends and challenges. *Sensors, 13*(12), 17472–17500.
8. Bansiya, J., & Davis, C. G., (2002). A hierarchical model for object-oriented design quality assessment. *IEEE Transactions on Software Engineering, 28*(1), 4–17.
9. Bardram, J. E., Frost, M., Szántó, K., Faurholt-Jepsen, M., Vinberg, M., & Kessing, L. V., (2013). Designing mobile health technology for bipolar disorder: A field trial of the monarca system. In: *Proceedings of the SIGCHI Conference on Human Factors in Computing Systems* (Vol. 1, pp. 2627–2636).
10. Barlas, P., & Heavey, C., (2016). Automation of input data to discrete event simulation for manufacturing: A review. *International Journal of Modeling, Simulation, and Scientific Computing, 7*(01), 1630001.
11. Becker, C., Chitchyan, R., Duboc, L., Easterbrook, S., Penzenstadler, B., Seyff, N., & Venters, C. C., (2015). Sustainability design and software: The Karlskrona manifesto. In: *2015 IEEE/ACM 37th IEEE International Conference on Software Engineering* (Vol. 2, pp. 467–476). IEEE.
12. Benlarbi, S., & Melo, W. L., (1999). Polymorphism measures for early risk prediction. In: *Proceedings of the 21st International Conference on Software Engineering* (Vol. 1, pp. 334–344).
13. Bertini, M., Ofek, E., & Ariely, D., (2009). The impact of add-on features on consumer product evaluations. *Journal of Consumer Research, 36*(1), 17–28.
14. Bieman, J. M., & Kang, B. K., (1998). Measuring design-level cohesion. *IEEE Transactions on Software Engineering, 24*(2), 111–124.
15. Blomkvist, S., (2005). Towards a model for bridging agile development and user-centered design. In: *Human-Centered Software Engineering—Integrating Usability in the Software Development Lifecycle* (Vol. 1, pp. 219–244). Springer, Dordrecht.
16. Boehm, B. W., Brown, J. R., & Lipow, M., (1976). Quantitative evaluation of software quality. In: *Proceedings of the 2nd International Conference on Software Engineering* (Vol. 1, pp. 592– 605).
17. Bosch, J., & Molin, P., (1999). Software architecture design: Evaluation and transformation. In: *Proceedings ECBS'99; IEEE Conference and Workshop on Engineering of Computer-Based Systems* (Vol. 1, pp. 4–10). IEEE.
18. Bosmans, A., Vanderreydt, I., Geysen, D., & Helsen, L., (2013). The crucial role of waste-to-energy technologies in enhanced landfill mining: A technology review. *Journal of Cleaner Production, 55*(1), 10–23.
19. Bowman, D., Minehart, D., & Rabin, M., (1999). Loss aversion in a consumption–savings model.

20. *Journal of Economic Behavior & Organization, 38*(2), 155–178.
21. Budgen, D., & Marashi, M., (1988). MDSE advisor: Knowledge-based techniques applied to software design assessment. *Knowledge-Based Systems, 1*(4), 235–239.
22. Bushnell, D. S., (1990). Input, process, output: A model for evaluating training. *Training & Development Journal, 44*(3), 41–44.
23. Cebi, S., (2013). A quality evaluation model for the design quality of online shopping websites. *Electronic Commerce Research and Applications, 12*(2), 124–135.
24. Chau, K. W., (2007). Reliability and performance-based design by artificial neural network. *Advances in Engineering Software, 38*(3), 145–149.
25. Chaudhry, B., Wang, J., Wu, S., Maglione, M., Mojica, W., Roth, E., & Shekelle, P. G., (2006). Systematic review: Impact of health information technology on quality, efficiency, and costs of medical care. *Annals of Internal Medicine, 144*(10), 742–752.
26. Cheng, H. K., & Tang, Q. C., (2010). Free trial or no free trial: Optimal software product design with network effects. *European Journal of Operational Research, 205*(2), 437–447.
27. Cleven, A., Gubler, P., & Hüner, K. M., (2009). Design alternatives for the evaluation of design science research artifacts. In: *Proceedings of the 4th International Conference on Design Science Research in Information Systems and Technology* (Vol. 1, pp. 1–8).
28. Clifford, M., Behrstock-Sherratt, E., & Fetters, J., (2012). *The Ripple Effect: A Synthesis of Research on Principal Influence to Inform Performance Evaluation Design. A Quality School Leadership Issue Brief* (Vol. 1, pp. 2–8). American Institutes for Research.
29. Conte, H. R., Plutchik, R., Wild, K. V., & Karasu, T. B., (1986). Combined psychotherapy and pharmacotherapy for depression: A systematic analysis of the evidence. *Archives of General Psychiatry, 43*(5), 471–479.
30. Cresswell, K., & Sheikh, A., (2013). Organizational issues in the implementation and adoption of health information technology innovations: An interpretative review. *International Journal of Medical Informatics, 82*(5), e73–e86.
31. Duffey, R. B., Pioro, I. L., & Kuran, S., (2008). Advanced concepts for pressure-channel reactors: Modularity, performance and safety. *Journal of Power and Energy Systems, 2*(1), 112–121.
32. Fan, M., Tan, Y., & Whinston, A. B., (2005). Evaluation and design of online cooperative feedback mechanisms for reputation management. *IEEE Transactions on Knowledge and Data Engineering, 17*(2), 244–254.
33. Forza, C., (2002). Survey research in operations management: A process-based perspective. *International Journal Of Operations & Production Management, 1*, 2–9.
34. Franceschini, F., & Rossetto, S., (1997). Design for quality: Selecting a product's technical features. *Quality Engineering, 9*(4), 681–688.

35. Freitas, S. V., Pratas, M. J., Ceriani, R., Lima, A. S., & Coutinho, J. A., (2011). Evaluation of predictive models for the viscosity of biodiesel. *Energy & Fuels, 25*(1), 352–358.
36. Friel, G., & Budgen, D., (1997). Design transformation and prototyping using multiple viewpoints. *Information and Software Technology, 39*(2), 91–105.
37. Göçer, Ö., Hua, Y., & Göçer, K., (2015). Completing the missing link in building design process: Enhancing post-occupancy evaluation method for effective feedback for building performance. *Building and Environment, 89*, 14–27.
38. Hall, N. R., & Preiser, S., (1984). Combined network complexity measures. *IBM Journal of Research and Development, 28*(1), 15–27.
39. Hissam, S. A., Seacord, R. C., & Lewis, G. A., (2002). Building systems from commercial components. In: *Proceedings of the 24th International Conference on Software Engineering. ICSE 2002* (Vol. 1, pp. 679–680). IEEE.
40. Hockings, M., (1998). Evaluating management of protected areas: Integrating planning and evaluation. *Environmental Management, 22*(3), 337–345.
41. Hofmeister, C., Kruchten, P., Nord, R. L., Obbink, H., Ran, A., & America, P., (2007). A general model of software architecture design derived from five industrial approaches. *Journal of Systems and Software, 80*(1), 106–126.
42. Howard, T. J., Culley, S. J., & Dekoninck, E., (2008). Describing the creative design process by the integration of engineering design and cognitive psychology literature. *Design Studies, 29*(2), 160–180.
43. Hulscher, M. E. J. L., Laurant, M. G. H., & Grol, R. P. T. M., (2003). Process evaluation on quality improvement interventions. *BMJ Quality & Safety, 12*(1), 40–46.
44. Humphrey, W. S., Snyder, T. R., & Willis, R. R., (1991). Software process improvement at Hughes aircraft. *IEEE Software, 8*(4), 11–23.
45. Jin, J., & Chen, Y., (2001). Quality and reliability information integration for design evaluation of fixture system reliability. *Quality and Reliability Engineering International, 17*(5), 355–372.
46. Jones, S. C., & Shrauger, J. S., (1970). Reputation and self-evaluation as determinants of attractiveness. *Sociometry, 1*, 276–286.
47. Jones-Farmer, L. A., Woodall, W. H., Steiner, S. H., & Champ, C. W., (2014). An overview of phase I analysis for process improvement and monitoring. *Journal of Quality Technology, 46*(3), 265– 280.
48. Kang, B. K., & Bieman, J. M., (1998). Using design abstractions to visualize, quantify, and restructure software. *Journal of Systems and Software, 42*(2), 175–187.
49. Karathanassis, I. K., Papanicolaou, E., Belessiotis, V., & Bergeles, G. C., (2017). Design and experimental evaluation of a parabolic-trough concentrating photovoltaic/thermal (CPVT) system with high-efficiency cooling. *Renewable Energy, 101*, 467–483.
50. Khalighy, S., Green, G., Scheepers, C., & Whittet, C., (2015). Quantifying the qualities

of aesthetics in product design using eye-tracking technology. *International Journal of Industrial Ergonomics, 49*, 31–43.

51. Khan, S., & Yairi, T., (2018). A review on the application of deep learning in system health management. *Mechanical Systems and Signal Processing, 107*, 241–265.
52. Kitchenham, B., Pfleeger, S. L., & Fenton, N., (1997). Reply to: Comments on "towards A framework of software measurement validation." *IEEE Transactions on Software Engineering, 23*(3), 189– 90.
53. Kolokotsa, D., Tsiavos, D., Stavrakakis, G. S., Kalaitzakis, K., & Antonidakis, E., (2001). Advanced fuzzy logic controllers design and evaluation for buildings' occupants thermal–visual comfort and indoor air quality satisfaction. *Energy and Buildings, 33*(6), 531–543.
54. Kopyscinski, J., Schildhauer, T. J., & Biollaz, S. M., (2010). Production of synthetic natural gas (SNG) from coal and dry biomass–a technology review from 1950 to 2009. *Fuel, 89*(8), 1763–1783.
55. Latorre, J. D., Hernandez-Velasco, X., Bielke, L. R., Vicente, J. L., Wolfenden, R., Menconi, A., & Tellez, G., (2015). Evaluation of a *Bacillus* direct-fed microbial candidate on digesta viscosity, bacterial translocation, microbiota composition and bone mineralization in broiler chickens fed on a rye-based diet. *British Poultry Science, 56*(6), 723–732.
56. Lazard, A. J., Watkins, I., Mackert, M. S., Xie, B., Stephens, K. K., & Shalev, H., (2016). Design simplicity influences patient portal use: The role of aesthetic evaluations for technology acceptance. *Journal of the American Medical Informatics Association, 23*(e1), e157–e161.
57. Lee, D., Moon, J., Kim, Y. J., & Mun, Y. Y., (2015). Antecedents and consequences of mobile phone usability: Linking simplicity and interactivity to satisfaction, trust, and brand loyalty. *Information & Management, 52*(3), 295–304.
58. Lin, R. T., (2007). Transforming Taiwan aboriginal cultural features into modern product design: A case study of a cross-cultural product design model. *International Journal of Design, 1*(2), 4– 9.
59. Littman, D. C., Pinto, J., Letovsky, S., & Soloway, E., (1987). Mental models and software maintenance. *Journal of Systems and Software, 7*(4), 341–355.
60. Ma, K., Zhou, D., & Blaabjerg, F., (2015). Evaluation and design tools for the reliability of wind power converter system. *Journal of Power Electronics, 15*(5), 1149–1157.
61. Mann, L. L., & Wong, K., (1996). Development of an objective method for assessing viscosity of formulated foods and beverages for the dysphagic diet. *Journal of the American Dietetic Association, 96*(6), 585–588.
62. Markelj, J., Kitek, K. M., Grošelj, P., & Zbašnik-Senegačnik, M., (2014). A simplified method for evaluating building sustainability in the early design phase for architects. *Sustainability, 6*(12), 8775–8795.

63. Nam, C. S., & Smith-Jackson, T. L., (2007). Web-based learning environment: A theory-based design process for development and evaluation. *Journal of Information Technology Education: Research, 6*(1), 23–43.

64. Nidhra, S., & Dondeti, J., (2012). Black box and white box testing techniques-a literature review. *International Journal of Embedded Systems and Applications (IJESA), 2*(2), 29–50.

65. Nowlis, S. M., & Simonson, I., (1996). The effect of new product features on brand choice. *Journal of Marketing Research, 33*(1), 36–46.

66. Oinas-Kukkonen, H., & Harjumaa, M., (2009). Persuasive systems design: Key issues, process model, and system features. *Communications of the Association for Information Systems, 24*(1), 28.

67. Page-Jones, M., (1988). *The Practical Guide to Structured Systems Design* (Vol. 1, pp. 5–8). Yourdon Press.

68. Park, D., Kang, S., & Lee, J., (2006). Design phase analysis of software qualities using aspect-oriented programming. In: *Seventh ACIS International Conference on Software Engineering, Artificial Intelligence, Networking, and Parallel/Distributed Computing (SNPD'06)* (Vol. 1, pp. 29–34). IEEE.

69. Parnas, D. L., (1972). On the criteria to be used in decomposing systems into modules. In: *Pioneers and Their Contributions to Software Engineering* (Vol. 1, pp. 479–498). Springer, Berlin, Heidelberg.

70. Remery, M., Mascle, C., & Agard, B., (2012). A new method for evaluating the best product end-of- life strategy during the early design phase. *Journal of Engineering Design, 23*(6), 419–441.

71. Resnick, M. L., & Montania, R., (2003). Perceptions of customer service, information privacy, and product quality from semiotic design features in an online web store. *International Journal of Human-Computer Interaction, 16*(2), 211–234.

72. Rodriguez-Toro, C. A., Tate, S. J., Jared, G. E. M., & Swift, K. G., (2003). Complexity metrics for design (simplicity+ simplicity= complexity). *Proceedings of the Institution of Mechanical Engineers, Part B: Journal of Engineering Manufacture, 217*(5), 721–725.

73. Sancar, T. H., Baturay, H. M., & Fadde, P., (2013). Applying the context, input, process, product evaluation model for evaluation, research, and redesign of an online master's program. *International Review of Research in Open and Distributed Learning, 14*(3), 273–293.

74. Sarkis, J., (1998). Evaluating environmentally conscious business practices. *European Journal of Operational Research, 107*(1), 159–174.

75. Sharma, T., & Suryanarayana, G., (2016). Augur: Incorporating hidden dependencies and variable granularity in change impact analysis. In: *2016 IEEE 16th International Working Conference on Source Code Analysis and Manipulation (SCAM)* (Vol. 1, pp. 73–78). IEEE.

76. Shull, F., Rus, I., & Basili, V., (2000). How perspective-based reading can improve requirements inspections. *Computer, 33*(7), 73–79.

77. Soller, A., Martinez, A., Jermann, P., & Muehlenbrock, M., (2005). From mirroring to guiding: A review of state-of-the-art technology for supporting collaborative learning. *International Journal of Artificial Intelligence in Education, 15*(4), 261–290.

78. Stevens, W. P., Myers, G. J., & Constantine, L. L., (1974). Structured design. *IBM Systems Journal, 13*(2), 115–139.

79. Suzuki, T., Ohashi, T., & Asano, M., (2002). Assembly reliability evaluation method (AREM). In: *ASME International Mechanical Engineering Congress and Exposition* (Vol. 36282, pp. 657– 662).

80. Tremblay, M. C., Hevner, A. R., & Berndt, D. J., (2010). Focus groups for artifact refinement and evaluation in design research. *Communications of the Association for Information Systems, 26*(1), 27.

81. Troy, D. A., & Zweben, S. H., (1981). Measuring the quality of structured designs. *Journal of Systems and Software, 2*(2), 113–120.

82. Tu, J., & Xia, Z. G., (2008). Examining spatially varying relationships between land use and water quality using geographically weighted regression I: Model design and evaluation. *Science of the Total Environment, 407*(1), 358–378.

83. Vanciu, R., & Rajlich, V., (2010). Hidden dependencies in software systems. In: *2010 IEEE International Conference on Software Maintenance* (Vol. 1, pp. 1–10). IEEE.

84. Venable, J., Pries-Heje, J., & Baskerville, R., (2012). A comprehensive framework for evaluation in design science research. In: *International Conference on Design Science Research in Information Systems* (Vol. 1, pp. 423–438). Springer, Berlin, Heidelberg.

85. Venable, J., Pries-Heje, J., & Baskerville, R., (2016). FEDS: A framework for evaluation in design science research. *European Journal of Information Systems, 25*(1), 77–89.

86. Verschuren, P., & Hartog, R., (2005). Evaluation in design-oriented research. *Quality and Quantity, 39*(6), 733–762.

87. Visser, W., & Hoc, J. M., (1990). Expert software design strategies. In: *Psychology of Programming* (Vol. 1, pp. 235–249). Academic Press.

88. Weyns, D., (2012). Towards an integrated approach for validating qualities of self-adaptive systems. In: *Proceedings of the Ninth International Workshop on Dynamic Analysis* (Vol. 1, pp. 24–29).

89. Wróblewska, K. B., Plewa, S., Długaszewska, J., Froelich, A., & Muszalska-Kolos, I., (2021). Design and evaluation of pharmaceutical availability, stability and quality of modified viscosity eye drops with choline salicylate. *European Journal of Pharmaceutical Sciences, 159*, 105725.

90. Xu, X., Wang, L., & Newman, S. T., (2011). Computer-aided process planning–A critical review of recent developments and future trends. *International Journal of Computer Integrated Manufacturing, 24*(1), 1–31.
91. Yin, S., Ding, S. X., Xie, X., & Luo, H., (2014). A review on basic data-driven approaches for industrial process monitoring. *IEEE Transactions on Industrial Electronics, 61*(11), 6418–6428.
92. Yourdon, E., & Constantine, L. L., (1979). Structured design. *Fundamentals of a Discipline of Computer Program and Systems Design* (Vol. 1, pp. 3–9). Englewood Cliffs: Yourdon Press.
93. Zeng, Y., (2020). Evaluation of physical education teaching quality in colleges based on the hybrid technology of data mining and hidden Markov model. *International Journal of Emerging Technologies in Learning (iJET), 15*(1), 4–15.

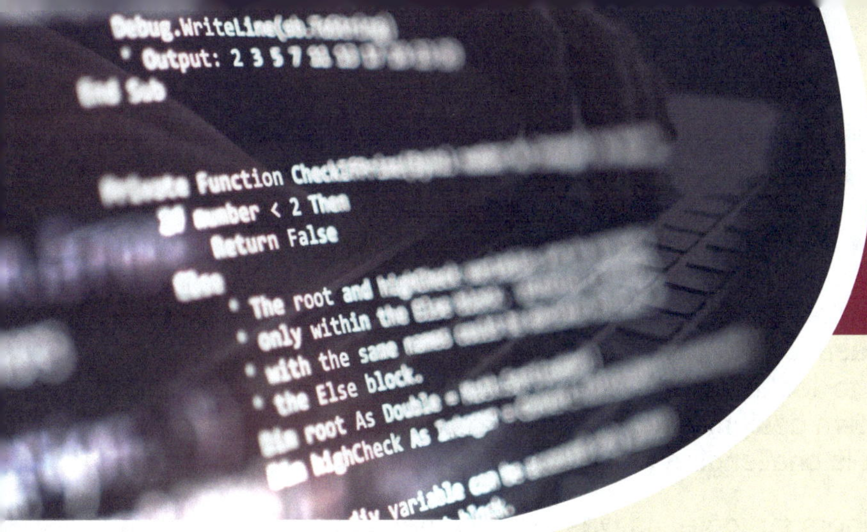

CHAPTER 4

DESIGN PRINCIPLES

UNIT INTRODUCTION

Activities of software design are governed at the most fundamental level by rules. Design strategies, which connect design activity to create well-organized design processes, are in the middle level. Software design methodology, or design methodologies study, is the level of abstraction that is highest (Kara, 2010).

Learning Objective

At the end of this chapter students will be able to learn:

- To comprehend the reasons behind the challenges in software development and the methods to difficulties;
- Recognize numerous methods for resolving issues with software design;
- To comprehend the fundamental layout of software design approaches.

Key Terms

- Design principles
- Design processes
- Dartmouth
- Prescriptive model
- Software design

BASIC RULES OF SOFTWARE DESIGN

Causes of Difficulties

Software development is challenging and complex. One of the most challenging aspects of software development is design (Fu et al., 2016). Prior to looking for techniques which helps us create good software system designs, it is important to comprehend why software development is challenging (Jalil et al., 2007).

All designers struggle, as was already mentioned. The question is if there are any particular factors, in addition to the basic ones, that make software creation even more challenging. Fred Brooks outlined some of the main reasons for the challenges of software development in his paper "No Silver Bullet: Essence and Accidents of Software Engineering." The accidents and the causes are divided into two categories. The challenges that come with software's nature are its essence. They cannot be resolved via technological means because they are intractable, persistent, and irreducible. Accidents are challenging that today's production faces, but they are not inherent. The following are Brooks' four main types of software development challenges (Ishikawa & Yoshioka, 2019).

Did you Know?

Software design principles are concerned with providing means to handle the complexity of the design process effectively. Effectively managing the complexity will not only reduce the effort needed for design but can also reduce the scope of introducing errors during design.

Complexity

Complexity is key characteristic of software. The extent of their state spaces and how these states are connected to one another make software entities complicated. Software conception, description, and testing become difficult as a result. Computer systems are more complicated than the majority of human-made objects. There are many states there. In comparison to computers, software systems have orders of magnitude more states. The quantity and nature of the parts that make up software entities makes them complex as well. A software entity's components are distinct from one another because if two of them are similar, we turn them into subroutines or procedures. As a result, each component of a software entity is fundamentally unique. Therefore, scaling up a software entity involves more than just raising the number of times the same pieces appear or increasing their sizes. It is inevitable that there will be more diverse elements. Most of the time, the interactions between these components in a software entity are nonlinear. For example, the state space of the entire system is frequently a non-linear function of the state spaces of the components (Galster et al., 2017).

The primary source of many challenges in software development is the intricacy of software and its nonlinear growth with size. The intricacy of the issue that has to be resolved by software makes it challenging for users and developers to communicate, which causes mistakes in requirements elicitation and specification, ultimately leading to the creation of incorrect software. Additionally, it hinders communication among members of the development team, which results in faults in the final product, cost overruns, timetable delays, etc. The intricacy of the state space makes it challenging to comprehend the program's behavior and even to list the states, which contributes to its unreliability. Software is challenging to use because the intricacy of the functions it offers leads to the complexity of how those functions are invoked. Program is difficult to extend with new functionalities, transport to other environments, rectify errors in the code or design, and even to identify the errors in the software due to the intricate nature of the structure of software systems. These technological issues are brought on by complexity, as are management issues. For instance, it hinders conceptual integrity by making it harder to get a broad overview of the product. The enormous learning and comprehension burden it generates makes staff turnover disastrous (Fiadeiro, 2012).

Conformity

Software must adhere to the standards set by current software, external organizations, or other components like hardware. Other scientists and engineers likewise deal with complexity, as Brooks noted. Due to the origin of complexity, the challenges that software engineers encounter are distinct from those that other people face. Scientists in the natural sciences, like Albert Einstein, were adamant that nature can be explained simply using a set of unified principles. For instance, some people think God is neither arbitrary nor capricious, whereas others think evolution is true. The software engineer, however, is not comforted by such a faith. A large portion of the intricacy that a software engineer must learn is arbitrary; it is imposed without rhyme or reason by the numerous human organizations and systems that the software system's interface must adhere to. Any software overhaul on its own cannot simplify this complexity (Oktafiani & Hendradjaya, 2018).

Changeability

There is a perpetual need for modification in software. Of course, practically all artifacts created by humans are subject to modification. For instance, there are times when specific automobile models are brought back, computers have their fields changed, buildings have room additions and rearrangements, and so on. Additionally, following models that modified versions of the original designs replace them. The frequency of these changes, however, pales in contrast to the updates made to publicly available software (Chaumun et al., 2000).

The rationale is partially due to the fact that a system's software is the component of the system under the most demand to change. It's partly because software is thought to be adaptable. Software is "pure thought-stuff," infinitely flexible, which is true to some extent.

In truth, a programmable general- purpose digital computer's only function is to provide the flexibility that special-purpose computers are unable to provide. The primary factor driving ongoing change in software is the enormous impact that computers and software have on our society as we move into the information era. These adjustments call for further adjustments to the software. According to Brooks, the software application is integrated within a cultural matrix of uses, people, rules, and mechanical vehicles. All of these undergo constant change, in part as a result of how computers and their software are used; hence, the software product must also undergo modification (Kabaili & Lustman, 2001).

Invisibility

Software is invisible, in contrast to practically all other human-made objects. The majority of currently used methods for visualizing and representing the structure and dynamics of other man-made objects rely on models, such as sketches, cardboard models, etc. Such models readily connect geometric structures to the nonlinear behavior as well as other characteristics of the system, capturing geometric actuality in a geometric abstraction. For instance, a building's floor plan aids in the evaluation of areas, traffic patterns, and views by the architect and the client. There are apparent inconsistencies and omissions. The same function is served by stick figure models of molecules and scale representations of mechanical components. However, due to software's invisibility, models based on geometric abstraction are seldom ever appropriate. The types of visual links that can offer a clearly understood connection between the representation and the system are essentially absent from the representations that are used to describe software. This deficiency not only makes it difficult for one mind to design, but also makes it difficult for minds to communicate with one another (Elerding, 2016).

These software fundamentals not only impede the development of software designs but also frequently result in flawed designs. Such errors can be divided into four categories, according to Parnas and Weiss: inconsistency, ambiguity, inefficiency, and rigidity. Of course, inflexibility and inefficiency are bad traits in software design. The inability to create software with the necessary quality, which can include any of the quality traits covered in the preceding chapter, is a typical mistake in software development. We can categorize design faults into the following four categories by include incorrectness as an obvious design error, which is by no means less common than other forms of design errors (van der Velden, 2008):

- **Incorrectness:** The functionality and features of the design do fulfill the needs of the users. Such a mistake could take the form of an incorrect interpretation of user requirements or even just a simple absence of user needs.
- **Inconsistency:** A design fails when there is inconsistency. The design

will not function, for instance, if two design statements make contradictory assumptions about a component's operation or the significance of a data item (Yang et al., 2012).

- **Ambiguity:** It happens when the design specification is either too vague or can be read in multiple distinct ways. Due to varying interpretations made during the implementation phase, ambiguity leads to problems in the design's implementation.
- **Inferiority:** The design somehow doesn't adequately handle quality needs. As a result, the created software falls short of the standards set by the users. Inefficiency, rigidity, and other issues are typical of inferior quality. The designed program becomes harder to modify due to rigidity. When a design creates a barrier to its efficient implementation, it is considered inefficient (Crutzen, 2006).

We went into great length in the previous section on how a design influences different software quality attribute. Design defects are frequently a cause of difficulties with the quality of software. Think about software efficiency, for instance. Assume that element A of a software system only requires information about a location's latitude from component B, and that element A can only request both the location's latitude and longitude from component B at once. Due to the needless computation of longitude in component B and the needless transmission of longitude data from component B to component A, the architecture of element B and the interface between elements A and B results in inefficiency (Carvalho et al., 2018).

Vehicles to Overcome Difficulties

Computer scientists studied why some rules can result in successful designs in the research on software design methodology. They also created a set of design principles as rules to direct design operations. Witt, Baker, and Merritt provided four simple statements as the foundation for the reasons why a principle can result in successful designs in the book Software Architecture and Design (Frasch et al., 2013).

These assertions were given the name axioms because they were thought to be true by default:

- **The Axiom of Separation of Concerns:** The ideal way to approach a difficult problem is to first come up with a workable intermediate solution that is defined in terms of smaller, independent problems.

The statement implies three important ideas (Kang & Jung, 2003):

- The combination of the identified simpler problems must resolve the original issue;

- The easier issues need to be independent. In fact, it's possible that dividing an issue into portions with a lot of interdependencies will make it more difficult rather than easier to solve; and
- The creation of the intermediate solution and the recognition of the constituent elements lead to simplification. While still important, the solutions to the simpler problems need to be handled separately from the simplification process (Angheluta & Costea, 2010).

- **The Axiom of Comprehension:** It states that the mind can only readily control around seven things at once. The Rule of Seven Minus or Plus Two is the common name for this principle. It was created when it was discovered in the 1950s that people have a short-term memory limit of seven (plus or minus two) random digits. The broad claim that we humans become overwhelmed when presented with a lot of different independent units of information seems self-evident, even though it is unclear to what extent the discovery relates to software design.
- **The Axiom of Translation:** Moving between equivalent contexts has no impact on design validity. As long as the new environment offers comparable services, a correct design that satisfies its interface and behavior standards in one environment will continue to do so in another. For instance, if a new operating system upgrade promises to start our application program and deliver the same services when we need them, our application program will continue to produce the same outcomes. Similar to this, a program can be run in a testbed during system development to gage its efficiency and storage efficiency. If the testbed accurately simulates the real environment, we can anticipate that the program will behave in a manner that is similar to the results obtained by test cases when it is run in its actual operating environment (Oubbati et al., 2016).
- **The Axiom of Transformation:** The substitution of equivalent components has no impact on the soundness of the design. Let's say we have a design with a number of components that adhere to the requirements for their interface and behavior. The axiom states that, as long as the replacement component satisfies the interface and behavior requirements of the original component, the overall design will continue to meet its specifications even if one of its components is replaced with a new design. The axiom implies that although a high-level design unit may refer to low-level unit specifications, the manner in which those criteria are met is irrelevant (or "transparent" to the high- level design). Referential transparency is the name given to this quality. These axioms provide the clear and unambiguous message that abstraction and separation of concerns are two crucial tools for managing complexity in software architecture (Husain & Yadav, 2022).

Basic Rules of Software Design

How to use these tools wisely is now the question. To match the design goals, we covered in section 2.3, Witt, Baker, and Merritt offered five design principles. Every guiding concept seeks to realize a specific design goal (Wan-Kadir & Loucopoulos, 2004).

The fundamental concepts of software design are based on these ideas:

- **The Modular Design Principle:** Large aggregates of components can be broken down into units with low inter-unit coupling and high internal cohesion, the behavior of each unit can be abstracted so that its overall goal can be understood, each unit's interface can be recorded and used, and each unit's design can be hidden so that it can be modified.
- **The Idea Behind Portable Designs:** Abstract context interfaces can be used to create designs that are portable.
- **The Concept of Malleable Designs:** Designs that mimic the end-perception users of the surrounding environment can be made malleable.
- **Conceptual Integrity** it is a principle that can be attained by applying a small number of design forms consistently (Rajesh & Sekar, 2021).
- **The Idea of Intellectual Control:** After creating a design strategy, designs can be recorded as hierarchies of progressively more specific abstractions. In addition to these guidelines, we offer one additional to address the challenges posed by invisibility in software design. The language is used in the Witt, Baker, and these serve as Merritt's guiding principles.
- **The Visualization Principle:** Visual representations of designs, such as diagrams, drawings, and figures, among others, can be used to describe the features of the behavior of parts of the system and the interactions among the components, so achieving (or partially achieving) visibility (Cai et al., 2013).

In reality, diagrams are used to illustrate software designs in practically all widely accepted software design methodologies. Data flow diagrams, entity-relationship diagrams, state transition diagrams, the Jackson structure diagram (also known as an entity life-history diagram), state charts, Petri nets, structure charts, structure graphs, and other visual notations are examples of existing visual notations. A wide range of diagrams, including as class diagrams, object diagrams, sequence diagrams, interaction diagrams, component diagrams, deployment diagrams, etc., are used in object-oriented analysis and design methodologies. Software architecture diagrams will be used in this book to analyze and describe software architecture designs (Lane, 1990).

DESIGN PROCESSES

Software design involves a broad range of tasks. Each activity has at least four components: the activity's action, the participants, the information provided as input, and the output, or the outcome of the action. There are further features of operations, such as the restrictions and conditions under which they must be completed. A process model explains the steps taken during the design process as well as how they relate to one another. We'll start by taking a look at a general process model that may be used for product design of any kind. After that, we'll examine software development process models and concentrate on software system design (Figure 4.1) (Mehalik & Schunn, 2007).

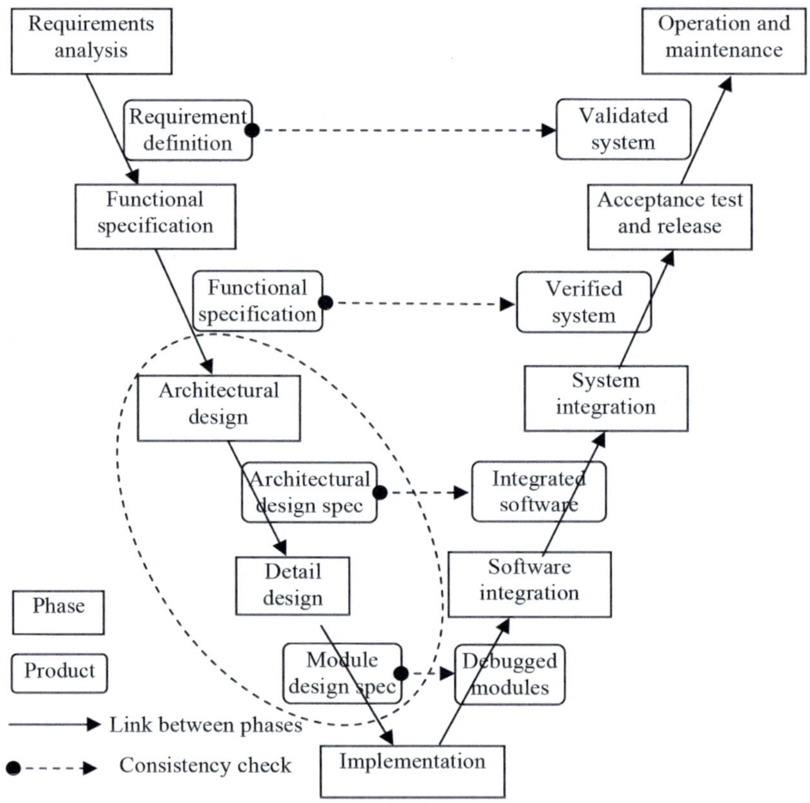

Figure 4.1. The software development lifecycle's "V" model.

Source: Image by geeksforgeeks.org.

Generic Design Process: Descriptive Models

Figure 4.3 illustrates a general design process model that extends Budgen's approach from his textbook on software design by creating many solutions and allowing for solution comparison. It holds true for software design as well (Howard & Dekoninck, 2008).

This model demonstrates that the essential actions in the design phase consist of:

- Creating models of each remedy;
- Comparing the models to the original specifications;
- Comparing the tested solutions to decide which should be developed further;
- Developing the model to create a "blueprint"-style definition of the solution in detail (Cross, 1997).

This process model has three crucial components that are important to remember. It emphasizes design activities' iterative nature first. This process model has two basic cycles. The first step in developing a solution is iteration. New limitations may be found whilst solutions are being developed, and as a result, new solutions may be suggested. Second iteration, or the postulation, assessment, and revision phase, may also be a part of this process. A crucial aspect of the design process is evaluation. It determines if a design is appropriate in light of the specifications. The iteration phase can end if the assessment demonstrates that the design satisfies all of the requirements; otherwise, the designer must complete another round of the design process. Take note that separate designers or design teams can postulate, validate, and revise several design solutions simultaneously. Various designers or design teams may collaborate or interfere with one another (Figure 4.2) (Eckert, 2006).

Remember

The generic process model is an abstraction of the software development process. It is used in most software since it provides a base for them.

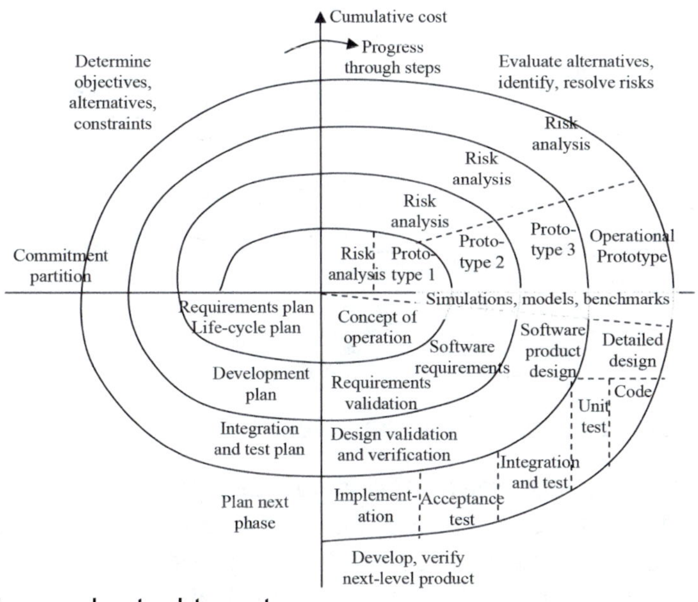

Source: Image by techtarget.com.

Figure 4.2. The software life cycle spiral model.

Second, it emphasizes the significance of model construction in the design process. A model like that can take many different forms. It could be structural or functional, dynamic, or static, abstract or concrete. Utilizing the model serves the objective of assessing the design. As a result, it is an illustration of the design. Last but not least, this process also emphasizes the creation of numerous solutions to the design problem, the evaluation of various answers, and the choice of a suitable solution for further development and execution. We may discover designs with the same or very similar functions but in various looks in practically every application field, including automobiles, structures, clothing, etc. It is crucial for a designer to comprehend the distinctions and benefits of several styles before developing his or her own. You should be aware that not every design challenge calls for the creation of multiple designs. A designer could occasionally have a favorite product style. In this situation, the comparison and choice are implied. The procedure of comparison and selection can be skipped if only one design is created. Therefore, the portion shown in Figure 4.3's dashed lines is optional (Macmillan et al., 2001).

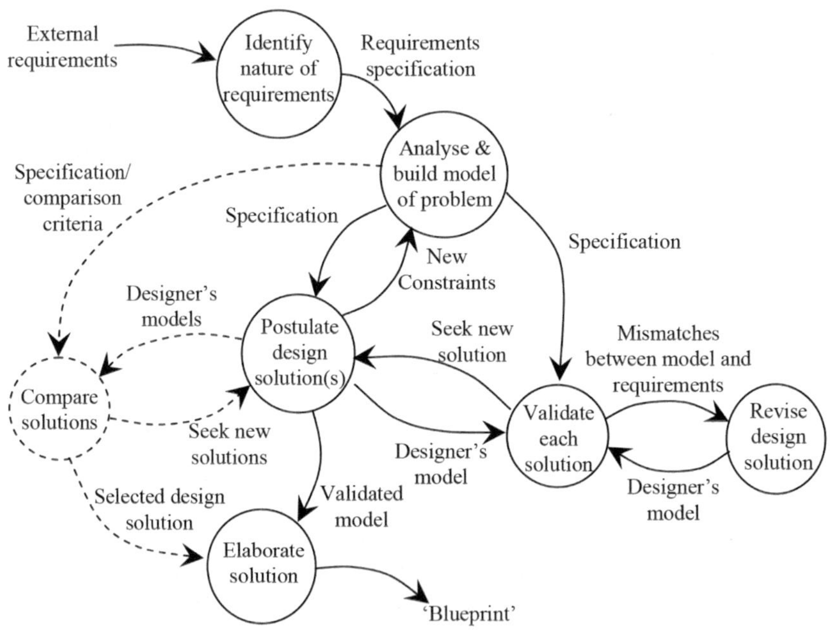

Figure 4.3. A representation of the overall design process.

Source: Image by David Laurence Dunne.

The initial recommendations of design concepts may be subjected to comparison and selection prior to validation and revision, and the chosen ones are then further evolved into a more comprehensive model of solution. It can also be done following the development of design concepts into established and verified solution models. There may be multiple iterations of comparisons and selections paired with assessments and adjustments in the majority of complex design processes (Lacour et al., 2005).

The design process we just covered is a part of what Cross called descriptive process models, which highlight the value of different design processes and exhibit design thinking (Brandt et al., 2008).

DESIGN STRATEGIES: PRESCRIPTIVE MODELS

Building models is one of the essential design activities, as was previously described. Several design strategies have been put forth in the literature and employed in a variety of design methodologies to direct the construction of design models. Decompositional, compositional, template-based, and evolutionary design methodologies are a few of the well-known ones (Visser et al., 1990).

Decompositional Methods

Decompositional approaches approach the design process from the top-down. It begins with an actual description of the issue or a model of the original problem, as seen in Figure 4.4. Then, this main problem is divided up into several smaller difficulties. Then, these related issues are resolved independently. A sub-problem is further broken down until it is straightforward enough to be solved directly if it is still too complex to do so. The answer to the main problem is formed by combining the answers to the subproblems (Fortin & Firpo, 2011).

Stepwise refinement, a decompositional process used in structured programming, is a classic example. The top-down component of the process model in the SSADM is also quite crucial (Abbaoui & Cherruault, 1995).

TIPS

A design method usually consists of three elements:

• The notations for representing the design problems and models of the solutions;

• The process model that consists of a sequence of design activities and the conditions for the application of the activities;

Compositional Methods

Compositional technique, as shown in Figure 4.5, initiates the construction of a model by identifying a group of specific things or objects implicated in the issue. These things and things are labeled, categorized, and grouped. The connections between the entities are determined for each category in order to create interconnections between them. These kinds of groups make up the model's elements. These elements are further divided and categorized.

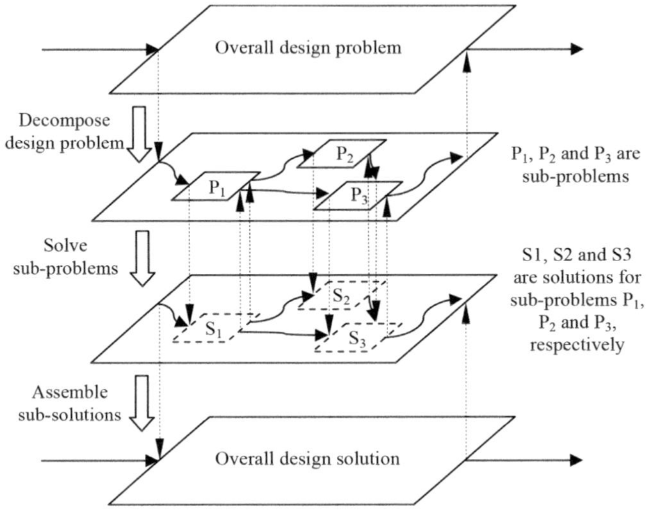

Figure 4.4. An example of a decompositional design approach.

Source: Image by Shaoying Liu.

To create larger components, the connections between the components are determined. Until a complete model is constructed, this composition process is continued. JSP and object-oriented design techniques are common compositional strategy implementations (Sluiter et al., 2010).

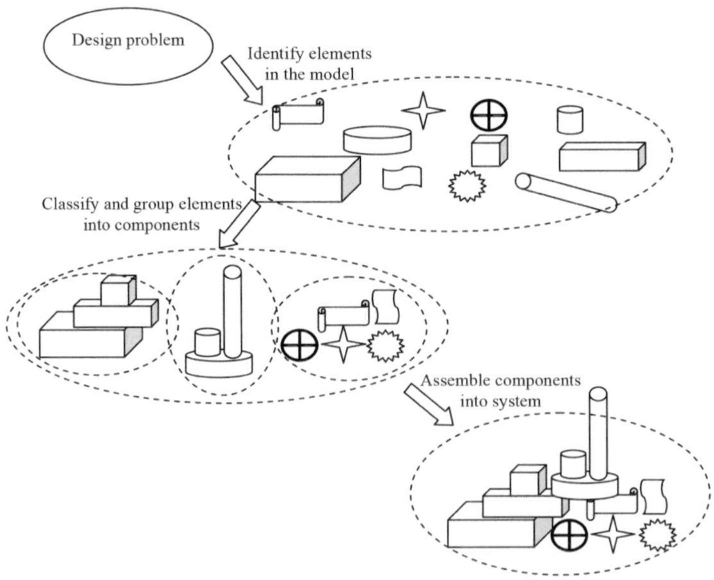

Figure 4.5. An example of a compositional design technique.

Source: Image by geekforgeek.org.

Design Template and Design Reuse

Over several years of research and practice in software development, people have discovered that there may be many commonalities in the designs that have been proven to be successful for a particular type of problem in a particular application domain. Once a problem is recognized as an instance of such a class of problems, the design template can be instantiated, making it relatively simple to produce a decent design. If such commonalities can be abstracted into a design template. Reusing designs means using a design template to address fresh design challenges (Jacome & Peixoto, 2001).

A sizable amount of design templates has been identified and documented in the literature in recent years. Design templates can be characterized and applied in a variety of ways, one of which is the software architectural style. The fundamentals of software architecture and how architectural style is used in software design are covered in this book. Design patterns are another successful attempt to investigate software designs in the object-oriented paradigm. In the broader framework of design methodology, research into the relationships between design challenges and design solutions in any given domain has given rise to a theory of design space based on topological mathematical concepts. Tools for computer-aided design have been created using this notion. We will provide a loose

introduction to theory in this book, which we will subsequently relate to software design and architecture (Ong, 2008).

Incremental and Evolutionary Design Strategies

Perhaps the simplest way to all designs is trial and error. It entails developing a design and assessing it in light of the limits and needs. If some limitations or needs are not met, the design is changed, and sometimes new designs are generated. Until an acceptable design is achieved, the cycle of development and evaluation is stopped. There is no assurance that a good design can always be produced, though. A prominent illustration of such a design process is the development of electric lighting by Thomas Edison (Juillé, 1995).

Starting with developing a design solution that only fulfills a carefully chosen subset of the most crucial and fundamental requirements is the first step in a methodical trial-and-error approach to design. In comparison to other requirements, this solution is assessed. When a need is not met, changes are made to the design to make it fulfill the requirement while maintaining the required properties that it has already met. Program transformation is a classic illustration of software evolutionary design techniques. It begins with the requirements being formally specified, perhaps in a functional programming language. The validity of this specification may be fairly easily ascertained because it is stated in a very high-level language. The formal specification is then subjected to a number of transformations to produce programs that are semantically equal to the specification but more effective, and so on, until a workable solution is attained. When a predetermined set of transformation rules are formally demonstrated to preserve the program's correctness, such transformations can be guaranteed to be right. The power of such a formal system is constrained, however, because the efficiency benefit from such a collection of rules can be confined (Hoffmann, 1998).

One particular approach to this type of evolutionary design and development is based on a comprehensive study of the needs to group functional criteria in a manner that some can be satisfied without affecting the others. To fulfill these needs, a design solution is therefore initially tried. With minimum adjustments to the earlier partial solutions, additional designs attempt to add a greater number of constituents to the earlier designs to satisfy more needs. This strategy is known as incremental design, as seen in Figure 4.6 (Stanton & Channon, 2013).

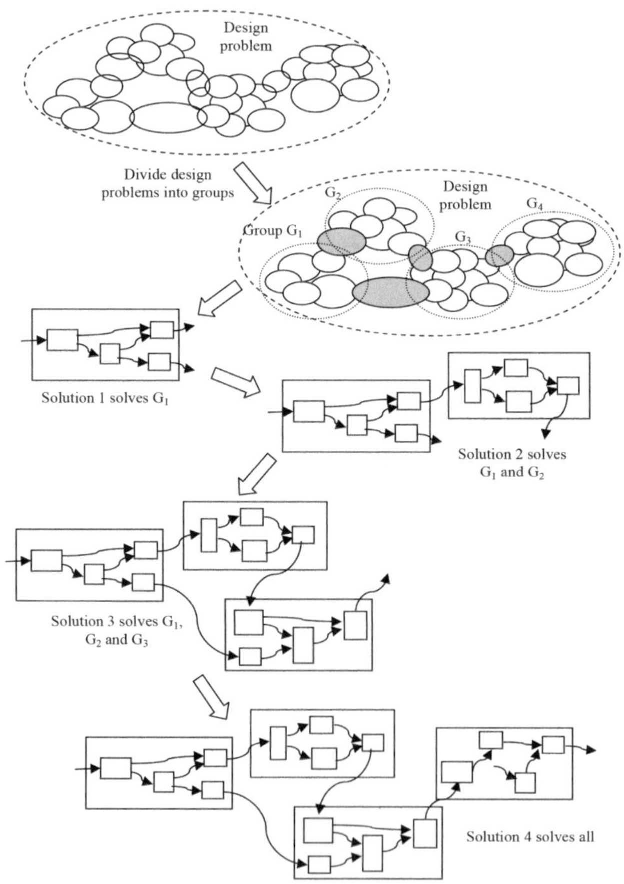

Figure 4.6. An example of the gradual design approach.

Source: Image by en.wikipedia.org.

The design techniques covered above offer more specific instructions for design procedures, particularly the creation of solutions. In Cross's terms, they might be thought of as models for prescriptive design processes. Compared to descriptive models, a prescriptive process model generally provides a more systematic design and algorithmic approach. They typically place a strong focus on the necessity for additional analysis before developing potential solutions. They frequently fall under a particular design methodology (Liu & Song, 2022).

STRUCTURE OF SOFTWARE DESIGN METHODS

Computer scientists have suggested a variety of software development methodologies in the literature and applied them in software design practices over the course of many years of study and practices in software design. Among them most popular design techniques are (Yau & Tsai, 1986). SSA/SD, SADT, and SSADM are examples of structured methods.

Object oriented and object based procedures include HOOD and more recent advancements in the UML and united process are examples of object-oriented and object-based methods. Model- oriented, axiomatic, and algebraic, refinement calculus, formal proof methods, program transformation methods, etc., are some examples of formal methods. Design techniques based on architecture. Software design at the level of software architecture has been the subject of immense research in recent years. There is a growing design methodology for software architectural design (Gomaa, 1984).

These approaches have a similar structure and characteristics. Generally speaking, a design technique must be built on an understanding of the issues that computer systems must answer as well as the structures and attributes of software systems to represent the developed software. Additionally, it must specify the broad approach the designer will use and offer some instructions for doing so. So, a well-known design process should have three fundamental parts, as shown in Figure 4.7 (Deumens et al., 2011).

The representation part comprises of one or more notations that can be used to model and/or explain the structure of the desired solution as well as the structure of the original design challenge from one or more points of view. Additionally, it ought to make the model analysis easier. A meta-model of the software's

ACTIVITY 4.1.

Make a presentation and discuss in what sense software is complex, and why software is inherently complex.

diagram and properties also the issues the software is intended to address serves as the foundation for such a representation (Sullivan et al., 2001).

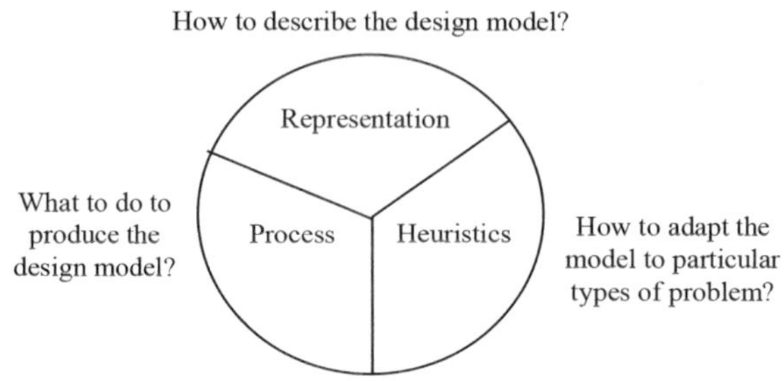

Figure 4.7. A software design method's components.

Source: Image by en.wikipedia.org.

The method section outlines the steps to take in creating the solution and the tactics to use when making decisions. Typically, the designer must perform a number of changes on the various shapes that make up the representation part. For particular classes of problems, a collection of heuristics offers recommendations on how to organize the actions indicated in the process section. These are typically based on experiences from previous applications of the method for a specific issue domain or type of structure. Software design approach is becoming more powerful and complex as computer systems are required to handle increasingly complex issues. The tools that support a design technique have a considerable impact on the actual applications of software design methodologies in addition to these fundamental elements. Such technologies are increasingly being used in software design techniques (Song & Osterweil, 1994).

SUMMARY

As per Fred Brooks, the intricacy of the issue to be solved, the constant changes in user needs, and the requirement for conformance to external standards are the key causes of the difficulties in software development, components, as well as the software system's invisibility. The fundamental Vehicles for overcoming the challenges include concern separation, abstraction, visualization, transformation, etc. Among the design strategies are decompositional, designs that are compositional, reuse design templates, and evolve. Typically, a design technique consists of three components: First, the notes for representing models of the design issues and solutions;

- the method that includes a series of design tasks and the requirements for the set of guidelines for using the method
- the application of the activities.

REVIEW QUESTIONS

1. Describe briefly the design principles.
2. What are the basic rules of Software design?
3. Explain design processes in detail.

MULTIPLE CHOICE QUESTIONS

1. The importance of software design can be summarized in a single word

a. Accuracy

b. Complexity

c. Efficiency

d. Quality

2. Which of these are characteristics of a good design?

a. Exhibits strong coupling between its modules

b. Implements all requirement in the analysis model

c. Includes test cases for all components

d. Provides a complete picture of the software

e. Both (b) and (d)

3. Which of the following is not a characteristic common to all design methods?

a. configuration management

b. functional component representation

c. quality assessment guidelines

d. refinement heuristics

4. Which of the following can be used to represent the architectural design of a piece of software?

a. Dynamic models

b. Functional models

c. Structural models

d. All of the above

5. Since modularity is an important design goal it is not possible to have too many modules in a proposed design.

a. True

b. False

Answers to Multiple Choice Questions

1. (d) 2. (e) 3. (a) 4. (d) 5. (b)

REFERENCES

1. Abbaoui, K., & Cherruault, Y., (1995). New ideas for proving convergence of decomposition methods.
2. *Computers & Mathematics with Applications, 29*(7), 103–108.
3. Angheluta, A., & Costea, C., (2010). Utilization of e-logistics in multinational companies to overcome difficulties of today's economic environment. *Management & Marketing, 5*(1). Archer, K. Rules and Software Architecture.
4. Atman, C. J., Chimka, J. R., Bursic, K. M., & Nachtmann, H. L., (1999). A comparison of freshman and senior engineering design processes. *Design Studies, 20*(2), 131–152.
5. Austin, S., Baldwin, A., Li, B., & Waskett, P., (1999). Analytical design planning technique: A model of the detailed building design process. *Design Studies, 20*(3), 279–296.
6. Brandt, S. C., Morbach, J., Miatidis, M., Theißen, M., Jarke, M., & Marquardt, W., (2008). An ontology-based approach to knowledge management in design processes. *Computers & Chemical Engineering, 32*(1, 2), 320–342.
7. Brazier, F. M., Jonker, C. M., Treur, J., & Wijngaards, N. J., (2001). Compositional design of a generic design agent. *Design Studies, 22*(5), 439–471.
8. Cai, Y., Wang, H., Wong, S., & Wang, L., (2013). Leveraging design rules to improve

software architecture recovery. In: *Proceedings of the 9th International ACM Sigsoft Conference on Quality of Software Architectures* (pp. 133–142).

9. Card, D. N., & Agresti, W. W., (1988). Measuring software design complexity. *Journal of Systems and Software, 8*(3), 185–197.
10. Carvalho, R. M., Andrade, R. M., Oliveira, K. M., & Kolski, C., (2018). Catalog of invisibility requirements for ubicomp and IoT applications. In: *2018 IEEE 26th International Requirements Engineering Conference (RE)* (pp. 88–99). IEEE.
11. Chaumun, M. A., Kabaili, H., Keller, R. K., Lustman, F., & Saint-Denis, G., (2000). Design properties and object-oriented software changeability. In: *Proceedings of the Fourth European Conference on Software Maintenance and Reengineering* (pp. 45–54). IEEE.
12. Cho, J., & Garcia-Molina, H., (1999). *The Evolution of the Web and Implications for an Incremental Crawler*. Stanford.
13. Cross, N., (1997). Descriptive models of creative design: Application to an example. *Design Studies, 18*(4), 427–440.
14. Crutzen, C. K., (2006). Invisibility and the meaning of ambient intelligence. *The International Review of Information Ethics, 6*, 52–62.
15. De Roever, W. P., De Boer, F., Hanneman, U., Hooman, J., Lakhnech, Y., Poel, M., & Zwiers, J., (2001). *Concurrency Verification: Introduction to Compositional and Non-Compositional Methods* (Vol. 54). Cambridge University Press.
16. Deumens, E., Lotrich, V. F., Perera, A., Ponton, M. J., Sanders, B. A., & Bartlett, R. J., (2011). Software design of ACES III with the super instruction architecture. *Wiley Interdisciplinary Reviews: Computational Molecular Science, 1*(6), 895–901.
17. Eckert, C. M., (2006). Generic and specific process models: Lessons from modelling the knitwear design process. In: *Proceedings of TMCE* (Vol. 6).
18. Elerding, C., (2016). The materiality of the digital: Petro-enlightenment and the aesthetics of invisibility. *Postmodern Culture, 26*(2).
19. Fiadeiro, J. L., (2012). The many faces of complexity in software design. In: *Conquering Complexity* (pp. 3–47). Springer, London.
20. Fortin, N., Lemieux, T., & Firpo, S., (2011). Decomposition methods in economics. In: *Handbook of Labor Economics* (Vol. 4, pp. 1–102). Elsevier.
21. Frasch, J. V., Gray, A., Zanon, M., Ferreau, H. J., Sager, S., Borrelli, F., & Diehl, M., (2013). An auto- generated nonlinear MPC algorithm for real-time obstacle avoidance of ground vehicles. In: *2013 European Control Conference (ECC)* (pp. 4136–4141). IEEE.
22. Fu, K. K., Yang, M. C., & Wood, K. L., (2016). Design principles: Literature review, analysis, and future directions. *Journal of Mechanical Design, 138*(10), 101103.
23. Galster, M., Zdun, U., Weyns, D., Rabiser, R., Zhang, B., Goedicke, M., & Perrouin, G., (2017). Variability and complexity in software design: Towards a research agenda. *ACM SIGSOFT Software Engineering Notes, 41*(6), 27–30.

24. Gero, J. S., (2000). Computational models of innovative and creative design processes. *Technological Forecasting and Social Change, 64*(2, 3), 183–196.
25. Gomaa, H., (1984). A software design method for real-time systems. *Communications of the ACM, 27*(9), 938–949.
26. Gomez, F., & Miikkulainen, R., (1997). Incremental evolution of complex general behavior. *Adaptive Behavior, 5*(3, 4), 317–342.
27. Gu, B., Gu, P., & Liu, G., (2017). Pattern generation rules for basic women's suits. *International Journal of Clothing Science and Technology.*
28. Ham, M., (1987). Software design rules. *Dr. Dobb's Journal, 7*, 112–116.
29. Hester, S. D., Parnas, D. L., & Utter, D. F., (1981). Using documentation as a software design medium. *The Bell System Technical Journal, 60*(8), 1941–1977.
30. Hoffmann, F., (1998). Incremental tuning of fuzzy controllers by means of evolution strategy. In:*Proceedings of the GP-98 Conference, Madison, Wisconsin* (pp. 550–556).
31. Howard, T. J., Culley, S. J., & Dekoninck, E., (2008). Describing the creative design process by the integration of engineering design and cognitive psychology literature. *Design Studies, 29*(2), 160–180.
32. Husain, A. A., Maity, T., Rai, M., & Yadav, R. K., (2022). *Detecting and Classifying Vehicles Under Uncontrolled Environmental Conditions: A Transfer Learning Based Approach. Available at SSRN 4174047.*
33. Ishikawa, F., & Yoshioka, N., (2019). How do engineers perceive difficulties in engineering of machine-learning systems?-questionnaire survey. In: *2019 IEEE/ACM Joint 7th International Workshop on Conducting Empirical Studies in Industry (CESI) and 6th International Workshop on Software Engineering Research and Industrial Practice (SER&IP)* (pp. 2–9). IEEE.
34. Jacome, M. F., & Peixoto, H. P., (2001). A survey of digital design reuse. *IEEE Design & Test of Computers, 18*(3), 98–107.
35. Jalil, M. A., & Noah, S. A. M., (2007). The difficulties of using design patterns among novices: An exploratory study. In: *2007 International Conference on Computational Science and its Applications (ICCSA 2007)* (pp. 97–103). IEEE.
36. Juillé, H., (1995). Incremental co-evolution of organisms: A new approach for optimization and discovery of strategies. In: *European Conference on Artificial Life* (pp. 246–260). Springer, Berlin, Heidelberg.
37. Kabaili, H., Keller, R. K., & Lustman, F., (2001). Cohesion as changeability indicator in object-oriented systems. In: *Proceedings Fifth European Conference on Software Maintenance and Reengineering* (pp. 39–46). IEEE.
38. Kang, D. J., & Jung, M. H., (2003). Road lane segmentation using dynamic programming for active safety vehicles. *Pattern Recognition Letters, 24*(16), 3177–3185.
39. Kara, L., (2010). *Design Principles.* (Vol. 1, pp, 1-25)
40. Kessler, J., Balc, N., Gebhardt, A., & Abbas, K., (2017). Basic design rules of unit cells for additive manufactured lattice structures. In: *MATEC Web of Conferences*

(Vol. 137, p. 02005). EDP Sciences.

41. Lacour, S., Pérez, C., & Priol, T., (2005). Generic application description model: Toward automatic deployment of applications on computational grids. In: *The 6th IEEE/ACM International Workshop on Grid Computing, 2005* (p. 4). IEEE.
42. Lane, T. G., (1990). *Studying Software Architecture Through Design Spaces and Rules*. (Vol. 1, pp, 1- 20)
43. Liu, T., Tan, L., Li, X., & Song, S., (2022). Incremental learning-inspired mating restriction strategy for evolutionary multiobjective optimization. *Applied Soft Computing, 127*, 109430.
44. Macmillan, S., Steele, J., Austin, S., Kirby, P., & Spence, R., (2001). Development and verification of a generic framework for conceptual design. *Design Studies, 22*(2), 169–191.
45. Mehalik, M., & Schunn, C., (2007). What constitutes good design? A review of empirical studies of design processes. *International Journal of Engineering Education, 22*(3), 519.
46. Melin, J., & Quake, S. R., (2007). Microfluidic large-scale integration: The evolution of design rules for biological automation. *Annual Review of Biophysics and Biomolecular Structure, 36*(1), 213–231.
47. Merrill, M. D., Barclay, M., & Van, S. A., (2008). Prescriptive principles for instructional design. *Handbook of Research on Educational Communications and Technology,* 173–184.
48. Morse, J. M., (2016). *Mixed Method Design: Principles and Procedures*. Routledge.
49. Oktafiani, I., & Hendradjaya, B., (2018). Software metrics proposal for conformity checking of class diagram to SOLID design principles. In: *2018 5th International Conference on Data and Software Engineering (ICoDSE)* (pp. 1–6). IEEE.
50. Ong, S. K., (2008). *Design Reuse in Product Development Modeling, Analysis and Optimization* (Vol. 4). World Scientific.
51. Oubbati, O. S., Lakas, A., Lagraa, N., & Yagoubi, M. B., (2016). UVAR: An intersection UAV-assisted VANET routing protocol. In: *2016 IEEE Wireless Communications and Networking Conference* (pp. 1–6). IEEE.
52. Rajesh, S., & Sekar, A. C., (2021). Evaluation of quality attributes of software design patterns using association rules. *International Journal of Advanced Intelligence Paradigms, 19*(3, 4), 314– 327.
53. Saad, G. H., (2001). Strategic performance evaluation: Descriptive and prescriptive analysis. *Industrial Management & Data Systems*.
54. Schuh, G., Lenders, M., Nussbaum, C., & Kupke, D., (2009). Design for changeability. In: *Changeable and Reconfigurable Manufacturing Systems* (pp. 251–266). Springer, London.
55. Sluiter, J. B., Ruiz, R. O., Scarlata, C. J., Sluiter, A. D., & Templeton, D. W., (2010). Compositional analysis of lignocellulosic feedstocks. 1. Review and description of

methods. *Journal of Agricultural and Food Chemistry, 58*(16), 9043–9053.

56. Song, X., & Osterweil, L. J., (1994). Experience with an approach to comparing software design methodologies. *IEEE Transactions on Software Engineering, 20*(5), 364–384.
57. Stanton, A., & Channon, A., (2013). Heterogeneous complexification strategies robustly outperform homogeneous strategies for incremental evolution. In: *ECAL* (pp. 973–980).
58. Sullivan, K. J., Griswold, W. G., Cai, Y., & Hallen, B., (2001). The structure and value of modularity in software design. *ACM SIGSOFT Software Engineering Notes, 26*(5), 99–108.
59. Van, D. V. M., (2008). Invisibility and the ethics of digitalization: Designing so as not to hurt others. In: *Information Security and Ethics: Concepts, Methodologies, Tools, and Applications* (pp. 859–871). IGI Global.
60. Visser, W., & Hoc, J. M., (1990). Expert software design strategies. In: *Psychology of Programming* (pp. 235–249). Academic Press.
61. Wakerly, J. F., (2008). *Digital Design: Principles and Practices, 4/E.* Pearson Education India.
62. Wan-Kadir, W. M., & Loucopoulos, P., (2004). Relating evolving business rules to software design. *Journal of Systems Architecture, 50*(7), 367–382.
63. Wasserman, A. I., Pircher, P. A., & Muller, R. J., (1990). The object-oriented structured design notation for software design representation. *Computer, 23*(3), 50–63.
64. Yang, F., Mei, Z. L., Jin, T. Y., & Cui, T. J., (2012). DC electric invisibility cloak. *Physical Review Letters, 109*(5), 053902.
65. Yau, S. S., & Tsai, J. J. P., (1986). A survey of software design techniques. *IEEE Transactions on Software Engineering*, (6), 713–721.
66. Yu, J., Cha, J., & Lu, Y., (2012). Design synthesis approach based on process decomposition to design reuse. *Journal of Engineering Design, 23*(7), 526–543.
67. Zamora, F., & Aceña, V (2019). *Regulatory Instructions and Guidance Published by the CSN to Overcome Some Difficulties to apply the Regulatory Requirements.* (Vol. 1, pp, 1-20)

CHAPTER 5

SOFTWARE ARCHITECTURE

UNIT INTRODUCTION

This chapter presents the concept of software architecture as well as several traditional architectural and analyzes the function that software architecture plays in the development of software (Hofmeister & Soni, 2000).

The following is the structure of this chapter: The very first part of the chapter investigates the application of the overarching concept of architecture to a variety of other fields, including the design of buildings as well as computer technology (Garlan, 2001). The second part of both chapters explores the responsibilities of software architecture within software design as well as offers the most prominent models of software architecture that have been found in the research literature. The concept of many software architecture styles is presented in Section 5.1 (Bosch, 2004).

Learning Objective

At the end of this chapter students will be able to learn:

- To get a grasp on the overarching concept of design;
- To have an understanding of the various perspectives on the topic of software architecture;
- To have a grasp on the concept of different software architecture styles;
- To have a solid understanding of the roles that software architecture as well as building features play in the creation of software.

Key Terms

- Software architecture
- Prescriptive models
- Descriptive models
- Multiple view models
- Software design

THE NOTION OF ARCHITECTURE

The Oxford English Dictionary's definition of an architect's original concept states that it is the "craft or technology of building, particularly the art or process of creating monumental structures to human use while taking into account equally esthetic and functional considerations." Additionally, it refers to a structure, mode, way, or manner of building, organization, or construction. So, let's begin the analysis of the idea with buildings (Galster & Avgeriou, 2011).

Architecture in the Discipline of Buildings

Buildings could be categorized based on their primary use or function. Dovecotes are used to house doves, and lighthouses include coastal towers having lights that alert approaching boats of risks, etc. For instance, houses are used for domestic accommodation. The most significant and fundamental lesson that could take away first from the architecture of structures is that a system's primary function defines its structure and serves as its determining factor. Whereas a building's primary purpose heavily influences its structure, other limitations also have an impact just on the building's structure as well as other elements. For instance, the structure and intended use of every type of building might be used as additional classification criteria. Homes known as pastel houses have living space atop stores and shelters for livestock. One-story homes are known as bungalows. Two houses are attached to create a single structure in a semi-detached home. A row of attached homes is referred to as a terraced home (Gruber, 2011).

Did you Know?

The history of software development began in England in 1948. The Manchester small-scale experimental machine, with a moniker of "baby," led the launch of all software in the world's history. Computer scientist Tom Kilburn is the genius that developed this early groundbreaking.

While structural in the sense described above plays a significant part in construction, the so- called style of architecture is the core of both the scientific and the artistry of architecture. Our family's home is not a Georgian or Victorian home, not only as it is not old enough, but also—and more pertinently it is not designed in a Georgian or Victorian manner. Symmetry, and simplicity, with classic elements like columns in Doric, Ionic, and Corinthian orders are characteristics of Georgian architecture. Large, paneled entrance doors have columns or other decorations on either side as well as a fanlight-style window above. Window frames are high and well-proportioned; they were first utilized in the 18th century. The glass panes have the same size and have exquisite wooden glazing bars. The Royal Crescent in Bath, which was constructed in the 18th century, is a perfect example of such a Georgian home. Victorian homes were constructed from 1837 to 1901, under the reign of Victoria. Terraced or semi-detached homes made up a large portion of residential Victorian architecture (Figure 5.1) (Hillier & Leaman, 1976).

Figure 5.1. The bath crescent with terraced Georgian homes from the 18th century.

Source: Image by wikiwind.com.

The evolution of building methodologies is seen in the historical shifts in architectural styles. The Romanesque architectural style was introduced to Britain by the Norman invasion and conquest of that country in 1066. Their enormous, solidly built churches as well as cathedrals served as examples of their craftsmanship as masons as well as engineers. They had advanced the Romans' ceiling vaulting technique, which had been around for 1,000 years. To create a barrel vault, semicircular stone bridges along the height of the ceiling area were used. The Norman style is characterized by sturdy walls, huge, rectangle-dressed stones having smooth faces, and the compaction of smaller stones. The walls are supported by wide buttresses. Windows have a slender, semicircular shape. Semicircular arches that frequently include colorful zigzag as well as dog-tooth patterns surrounding doors. Massive circular constructions called columns often have bases that are shaped like spirals or diamonds that rest on squared footings (Lukken & Searle, 1993).

Capitals either are round or rectangular with decorative cushions. When designing crossings among aisles of various lengths, Norman architects experienced difficulty. Since a pointing arch's height is independent of its breadth, their initial English predecessors either built arched to overcome these issues or raised the level of springers (the bottom stones) just on a shorter semicircular arch. Just after the 12th century, churches developed lighter, thinner architecture with aisles as well as naves that varied in breadth. The flying buttresses, which diverted the downwards thrusts to supports distant from the major interior wall, were invented to sustain the walls that were getting higher and thinner. As a result, windows could be bigger in buildings since less weight was being supported by the walls. The wideness of doors was no longer dependent upon the length of an arch due to the usage of pointed arches. Entrances started to seem more elegant. The following are the fundamental elements of Gothic church design. In the 14th century, architects were free to decorate every surface of their structures. A higher level of sculptural excellence matched advanced engineering abilities. Stained glass art reached new heights when tracery inside windows acquired intricate curves and incredible delicacy. Interior decoration also included the addition of pulpits, eagle lecterns, choir stalls, gargoyles, and fountains. Even by the 16th century, the interior had the appearance of more space thanks to repeated vertical crown molding and fluting, which gave origin to the phrase "perpendicular architecture." British Gothic reached its pinnacle in this fashion (Unwin, 2009).

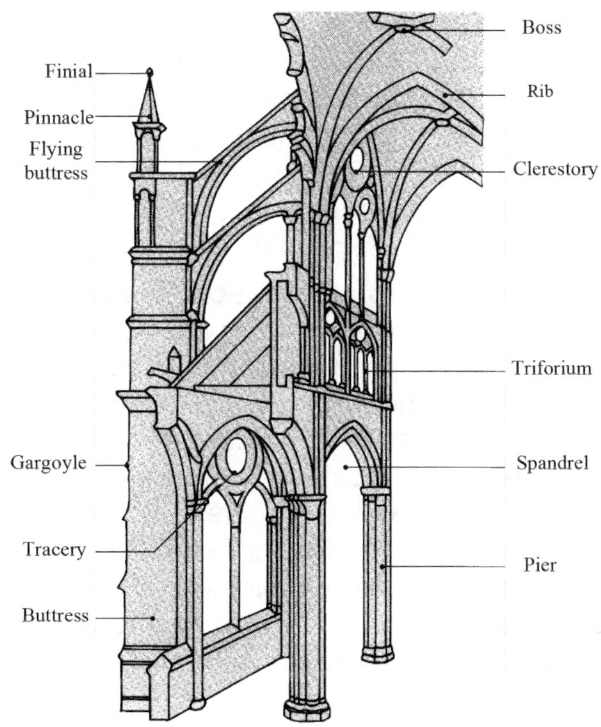

Figure 5.2. Characteristics of Gothic churches' structures.

Source: Image by simple.wikipedia.org.

It is important to note that such design is the process connected with a particular architectural style and is frequently formalized in the shape of a vocabulary which specifies the multiple kinds of architectures, as well as their functions and interactions.

Figure 5.2, for instance, illustrates the terminology used to describe the elements of Gothic churches. Even though the topics of building with the software are quite dissimilar, as Perry as well as Wolf (Unwin, 2009) noted, there are a lot of intriguing elements in building design that is equally relevant to the research of software architecture (Vives-Rego et al., 2015).

- **Multiple Views:** A building architect collaborates with the client using a variety of viewpoints that emphasize various aspects of the project. For instance, elevations with floor plans, provide views of the inside and outside, respectively. To give the consumer a sense of a building's appearance in its surroundings, contextual sketches and maybe even physical models could be added to the elevation viewpoints (Bachman, 2004).
- **Architectural Styles:** As we see from the debate above, architecture is crucial to both the science and art of construction. From such a prescriptive and descriptive standpoint, style is very helpful. Architectural style may be described as a specific coding of design components and formalized arrangements. Style restricts the types of design components and related formal groupings. In those other terms, a design's formal interactions with other design components are constrained by the style architecture (McGinley, 2015).
- **The Impact of Implementation Technique on Design:** The evolution of architectural styles served as a compelling example of how implementation methods affect architectural style. Romanesque engineering techniques, for instance, could not be used to construct the King's College, Cambridge, perpendicular design, which has an airy sense. The instruments, as well as the material, are also the two main components of the construction process. Without current construction technologies, a skyscraper could be constructed nowadays only using metal or timber pillars and beams (Rice, 2019).

Remember

The comparison between software design and (civil) architecture was first drawn in the late 1960s, but the term "software architecture" did not see widespread usage until the 1990s.

Architecture in the Discipline of Computer Hardware

Software engineers have created a variety of system architectures for effective designs for computer networks within the field of computer hardware. For instance, the vast majority of computers used every day now have von Neumann designs. The general layout of a von Neumann computer architecture is shown in Figure 5.3. The central processing unit (CPU), as well as the primary memory, are its two major components. The design's fundamental principles are (Esmaeilzadeh et al., 2012):

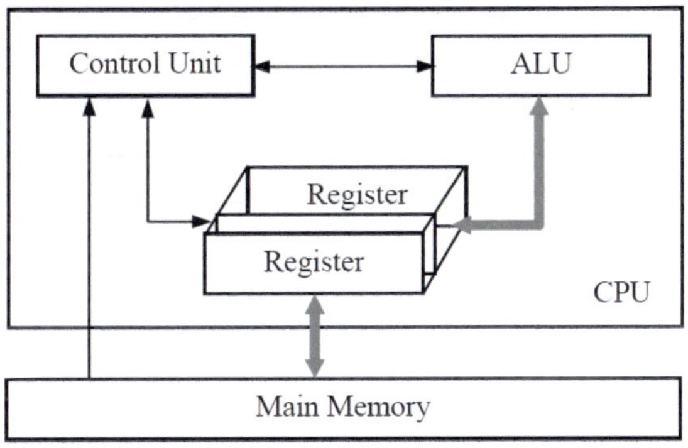

Figure 5.3. Von Neumann's architectural design.

Source: en.wikipedia.org.

- **Stored Program:** The strongest memory houses both the information as well as the instructions. Location can be used to access memory data without consideration of the contents of the location (Calazans & Moraes, 2001).
- **Sequential Execution:** Unless the sequence is expressly changed, tasks are performed consecutively from the first to the next in the order they are found in memory.

Executing the commands acquired first from system memory is the CPU's principal duty. The instruction directs the CPU to carry out one of its fundamental tasks, such as a logical or arithmetic operation, a data transmission to or from system memory, etc. Usually, there are three parts to it (Wolf, 2003). The control unit (CU) decodes as well as interprets the command that has to be carried out before directing some other components. The short storage capacity used to keep frequently needed data and interim outcomes is a series of registers. Logical and arithmetic tasks are carried out by the arithmetic/logic unit (ALU) (Wolf, 2003).

Withvon Neumann's design, a small number of circuits may be programmed to carry out a wide range of activities, based on the program that is performed during run time from storage. Inside the limits of logical and physical capacity, the multi-purpose computer programming aim is effectively met. Rapid integrated circuit innovation and novel architectural elements like big caches, many fast busses, pipelines, etc., have considerably improved the efficiency of von Neumann systems during the past 50 years. There are, however, a few significant flaws inside the architecture (Henzinger & Sifakis, 2007). For instance, von Neumann systems carry out instructions in a particular order. In several application fields, like flow field analysis including aerodynamics, systems with just a single CPU frequently fall short of the performance standards. Applications in these fields are characterized by extremely high mathematical calculations or data input volumes. The demand for high efficiency can be met by designs that have many processing elements running simultaneously. Parallel processing architectures have also been created as a result. A single instruction flowing multiple data (SIMD) flows architecture having memory space is seen in Figure 5.4 (Wolf, 2002).

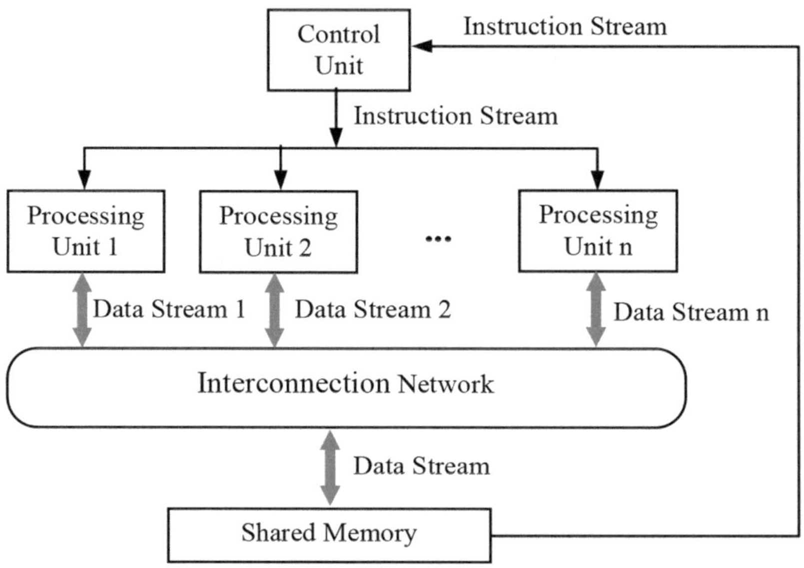

Figure 5.4. A SIMD architecture with shared memory.

Source: Image by Borko Furht.

The SIMD design consists of one control module with n (n>1) processor units coupled to such a memory space by a network interface. The control module instructs the processing elements to carry out logical and arithmetic operations just on data additionally obtained first from memory space after successively decoding and interpreting the commands fetched first from memory space. The data that the computer processors work with may vary even if they always follow the same set of instructions. The design features a single instructions flow and much information flows inside this sense (Harris et al., 2010).

The process within an organization experiences a sharp rise in traffic even as the number of processing units rises. Local memory could be added to prevent congestion on the communication link. The number of accesses to secondary storage made through linkages could be decreased since every processor unit has its local memory. By removing the memory space, the architecture's complexities may be decreased. An interconnecting network allows for information transfers among processing units. Figure 5.5 shows the SIMD architecture lacking shared memory (Kiran et al., 2010).

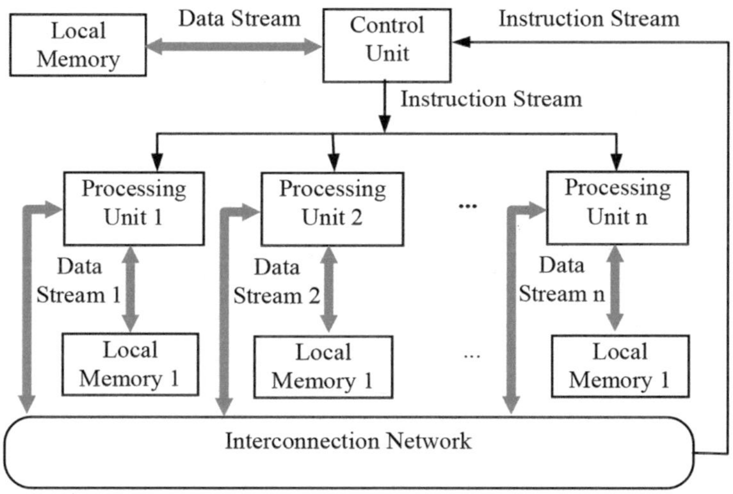

Figure 5.5. A SIMD architecture without shared memory.

Source: Image by geeksforgeeks.org.

SIMD computers have such a basic constraint, despite their exceptionally high efficiency. Consequently, only a select few programs may make use of the parallel which has been provided either by hardware or specifically coded either by software. MIMD designs may utilize a greater variety of parallelism seen in programs to obtain excellent performance. The design of MIMD is shown in Figures 5.7 without and with shared memory, respectively. We can observe how software engineers in the hardware field are using the concept of computer architectures to build and realize computer networks from the comments given above (Perry & Wolf, 1992).

- **The Concepts of Components:** It is acknowledged that only several fundamental components appear regularly in different structural architectures for computers at the top level. Their fundamental characteristics and functioning are known and clearly stated. These parts constitute the system's building blocks and the fundamental elements that create the architectural, or general design, of a system.

- **The Inference of System Property:** The assortment of components present inside a design and architecture and their connections may be used to deduce the characteristics of such a computer network at the network level. These conclusions rely less upon the specifics of how the component was implemented. However, they rely just on the components' abstract qualities. Construction architectures also incorporate analogous reasoning (Esmaeilzadeh et al., 2012).

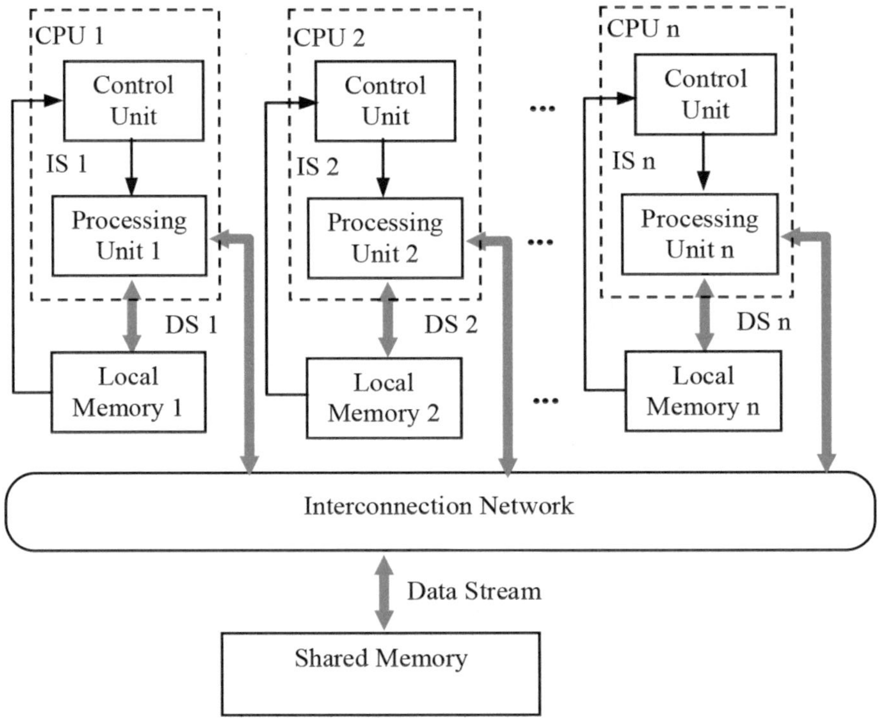

Figure 5.6. The shared memory architecture of MIMD. Source: Image by geeksforgeeks.org.

- **The Design Space:** Computer system categorization is based on that architecture. The highest-level architecture of several distinct computer networks may be used to categorize them. As was discussed above, there are three different categories of system architectures: von Neumann architectures (SISD), SIMD architectures, and MIMD architectures. The architecture's components could also be further categorized in a similar architectural manner. Depending on how it is implemented, the control system, for instance, might be categorized as either hardwired as well as microprogrammed. Linkage networks may also be categorized based on their design or implementation, such as employing busses or switching (Kain, 1988).

When a particular set of design restrictions and needs becomes apparent, these classifications offer suggestions again for the design of computer architecture. The development space is defined explicitly, but each potential design choice is linked to its effects and effects on system characteristics like cost and efficiency. The logic of the design choice, which is often supported by a substantial body of scientific study and experimental data, represents this relationship of design choices with the outcomes. The ability to standardize the parts is among the most significant benefits of having such a thorough grasp of computer architecture and its many classes. They may therefore be created and produced without the aid of other parts, and they can be employed in a wide range of various computer networks.

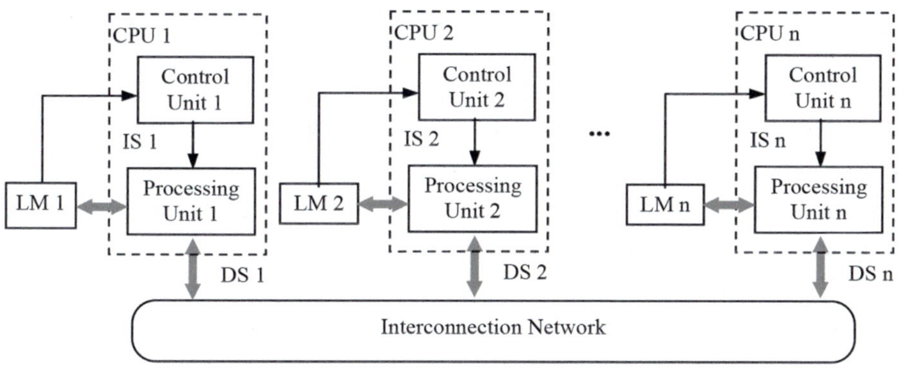

Figure 5.7. MIMD's architecture is devoid of shared memory.

Source: Image by Borko Furht.

The General Notion of Architecture

We note the following shared characteristics of the concept of architecture when comparing the architecture of buildings and computer hardware:

- **Architecture is an Abstract Model:** An intricate system is represented abstractly in architecture. Under a particular threshold, information is concealed. The application of the parts, which is not a problem just at the architectural level, is disregarded, for instance, in the discussion of hardware designs (Gruner, 2014).
- **Architecture is a Structural Model:** In terms of such a grouping of elements and the connections between both

elements, architecture is a representation of a complex system. In actuality, a key component of the definition of the term "architecture" designs. The representation of the elements and the connections between them reflects the abstractions from such a complicated system to that of an architectural pattern. Perhaps an abstract object with a set of attributes is used to describe an element, or even a composite of these elements is used instead. Selecting a subset of a program's parts as components and/or bundling specific subsets of components within one component are two further ways to abstract such a system out of its architectural pattern. The abstracted model could simply disregard some components (Simon, 1991).

- **Architecture is a Model with a Certain Engineering Purpose:** A design of architecture serves a single technical function or a collection of related ones. A descriptive objective often involves analyzing or demonstrating the system's important features. Along with the study and presentation of the relevant qualities, a prescriptive objective could be to offer suggestions for future system planning and implementation. An architecture framework must make it possible for its users—such as the engineer or client—to fulfill their objectives. What specifics of a system must be communicated and how specifics are expressed, such as the qualities of components and/or their interconnections, depends on the objective or the feature of interest.

Multiple perspectives in constructing architecture demonstrate how various aims and qualities of importance may lead to various sorts of models or various models of architecture. We provide the following discipline-neutral meaning of the term "architecture" in light of the aforementioned finding. Architecture is just an abstract concept, or modeling, of a complex system in terms of its organization. It is made up of several parts connected by relationships, which serve as a means of achieving certain technical goals and exhibiting a particular set of desirable features just on the system. The elements and their connections' specifics are concealed, and abstraction objects and relations are used in their stead. These abstract objects are composed of lesser tier different levels of abstraction or are defined by a variety of distinct attributes that have an impact upon that system's desired properties (Bax & Trum, 2004).

THE NOTION OF SOFTWARE ARCHITECTURE

People frequently use diagrams to represent the elements of a software system's make the best possible as well as connections between them. For instance, the software architecture of a WWW customer pair is shown in Figure 5.8 (Bosch, 2004).

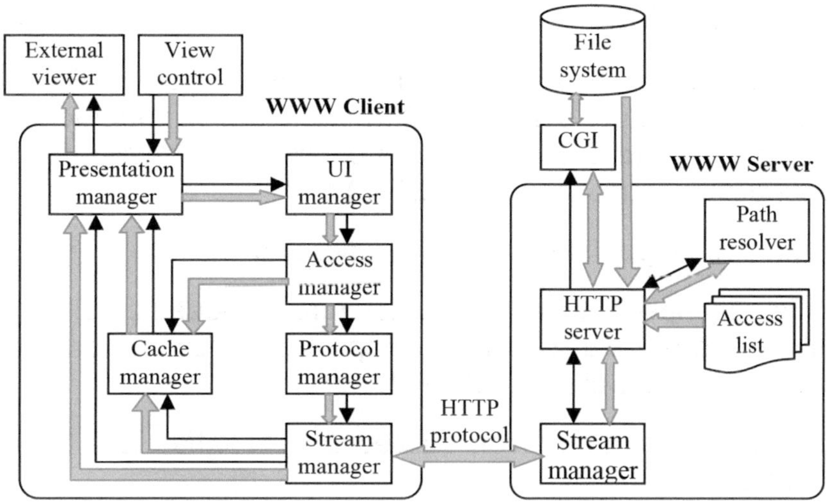

Figure 5.8. The WWW client-server pair's structure.

Source: en.wikipedia.org.

A diagram simplifies a complex system and offers an understandable depiction of the network to aid in thinking about the network, including demonstrating how it functions to complete the necessary tasks and also to evaluate its effectiveness. The concept of software architecture is intuitively understood as the overall organization of a software program as just a collection of interdependent components.

It is comparable to the concepts of computer architecture for hardware for computers, network architecture within networks for computers, and construction architecture in structures for buildings. The field of software architecture studies has expanded quickly during the last 10 years. The methodological and technological foundation for approaching design and architecture as such a field of engineering has come a long way (Perry & Wolf, 1992).

Knowing how well the highest possible level of software architecture influences a software system's properties as well as its ongoing development is among the key objectives of the research of software architecture. It has developed as a result of research on design concepts and behaviors that designers employ while working on actual systems. There isn't a single, widely acknowledged meaning of the word because it is a relatively new subject. On the other side, definitions are many as well. The majority of definitions that are frequently used have similar themes—structure, elements, and linkages between them—but they differ greatly in specifics and cannot be used interchangeably (Gruner, 2014).

PRESCRIPTIVE MODELS

In 1992, Perry & Wolf published one of the important definitions. Perry and Wolf created software architecture using the following equations after looking at concepts of architecture in various fields, such as computer hardware, computer networks, and construction (Eliasson et al., 2015).

Software Architecture = {*Elements*, *Form*, *Rationale*}

According to this description, software architecture is indeed a collection of architectural (or style) pieces with a certain shape. Architectural components were divided into three distinct classes. As follows:

- **Data Elements:** The information utilized and modified is included in the data items.
- **Processing Elements:** These are the components that offer the conversion for data pieces.
- **The Ties that Bind:** They serve as the "glue" that binds the various components of the building together. Instances of linking components that 'glue' architectural parts together include method calls, and access to common data, including messaging. The qualities and connections that make up the architectural form are weighted (Heldal et al., 2016; Clements et al., 2003).
- **Properties:** These are utilized to define limits on the components to the extent wanted either by architecture, which means they are used to limit the selection of architectural features.
- **Weight:** The minimal desirable limitations of this software architecture are defined by characteristics and connections taken together. Weight could be assigned to a feature or relation to convey a choice between many options or to emphasize the significance of a characteristic or connection (Pospieszny, 2017).

According to Perry and Wolf's description, software architecture includes the justification for all of the decisions that were taken while developing the architecture. The reasoning encapsulates the driving force behind the decision to choose a certain architectural style, set of materials, and shape. It explains how system restrictions set by customers' non-functional and functional criteria are satisfied (Neill et al., 2015).

In their concept, Perry & Wolf take a prescriptive approach to software architecture. According to this perspective, software architecture is just a design specification that details the system's construction. "Architecture is focused on the choice of architectural components, their relationships, and the limitations on such components and associated interrelations essential to provide a structure that can meet the criteria and serve as a foundation for the (detail) design," according to Perry and Wolf. As a result, the reasoning is considered a first-class resident as well as an essential component of software design.

DESCRIPTIVE MODELS

A declaration of a system's needs for stakeholders is another criterion put out by Barry Boehm as well as his students just at USC Center for Software Development. According to this viewpoint, not each complexity of diagrams and signs constitutes an architecture when there is insufficient justification to guarantee that the elements, interconnections, and restrictions will build a system that fulfills the criteria of both the group of stakeholders. A significant turning point within the software development process is the emergence of software architecture. Similar to this, Hofmeister, Soni, & Nord define system architectures also as the "purposeful proposed design of a mechanism," because although they concur with both the philosophical tenet that every software program that has been implemented does have an architecture, notwithstanding whether it has good or undesirable or has clear and specific precedent it:

- **Components:** System software is a piece of code that executes a specific task at run- time. Programs, objects, activities, customers, servers, networks, etc., are some instances of components.
- **Connectors:** A connector is a device that enables components to communicate, coordinate, or work together. Connectors explain how these elements interact with one another. Connector representations are frequently spread throughout a large variety of system elements and may not always match particular elements of active systems. Shared variables accessibility, process calls, remote method calls, message-passing mechanisms, data streams, and transactional streams are a few instances of connectors (Shaw, 2001).

Shaw and Garlan place a strong focus on the software architect's abstraction character, which defines the program's topology as well as structure. The architectural level conceals the specifics of how the connections and elements are implemented. Articulation, however, may be combined to describe more complex systems. An architecture of a sub-system could be used to specify an element (Medvidovic & Taylor, 2000).

MULTIPLE VIEW MODELS

Bass, Clement, as well as Kazman examine software architecture from a variety of perspectives, in contradiction to Shaw and Garlan who see elements as entities that perform some function at run-time. Consequently, a software system's architecture is not special. It may be seen from many angles, which leads to a range of structural models of a single system. For instance, the modules and how they interact may be used to analyze a software system. It may also be examined in light of the processes that are running at the moment and how they interact (Kruchten, 1995).

Typically, these two architectures are dissimilar. While each of these offers some architectural details about the system, according to Bass, Clements, and Kazman, neither of them provides a comprehensive description of the architecture. Therefore, they give the following definition of software architecture.

TIPS

IEEE 1471-2000, "Recommended practice for architecture description of software-

'A program's or computer system's system design refers to the structure(s) of the systems, which also are made up of software applications, those elements' externally observable characteristics, and the connections between them (Choi & Yeom, 2002).

The major ideas in the description are as follows:

- **Components:** There are several types of components and interactions between them since architecture can include various types of structures. By design, the definition omits a description of the linkages and architectural elements. "An architecture is firstly an abstraction of a network that suppresses aspects of elements which do not impact how they can use, are utilized by, link to, or communicate with one another," emphasize Bass, Clement, and Kazman (Liao, 2002).
- **Externally Visible Properties:** The term "externally visible qualities" refers to the conclusions that other elements could make about an element, including the services it offers, its efficiency traits, how it handles faults, how it uses common resources, and so forth. According to this concept, software architecture should abstract away certain network data while yet providing enough data to serve as a foundation for analysis, judgment, and risk mitigation (Robal & Kruus, 2002).
- **Structures:** Software systems have a variety of structures. Every architecture is an abstraction in terms of several standards. Every abstraction "boils away" components of the software which are unrelated to the issue it attempts to represent. Because of this, each building may define separately whatever is meant by such an element, an interrelationship, a reason, a principle, as well as a set of standards. It could also represent its selection of style architecture. What constitutes an architectural structure

is just not limited by the word itself. Nevertheless, they provided a list of some of the most typical and practical software architectures (Sztipanovits & Karsai, 1997).

- The following succinct summaries of software architectures are taken from the book by Bass, Clements, and Kazman. Every description gives the structure a personality based just on elements, referred to as units, as well as the connections between both units, referred to as links. Every structure has an application in application development that goes along with it (Robal & Kruus, 2002).
- **Module Structure:** The modules are work assigned for developing software systems, and they each have deliverables like an interface definition, code, testing phase, etc., attached to them. They have always been relation ties them together. For the creation and upkeep of the systems, the modular structure helps allocate labor as well as another resource.
- **Conceptual, or Logical, Structure:** The components are abstracts of the functional specifications of a system. The shares-data-with connection connects these abstractions. Analyzing the connections and changes of the elements in the issue space is made easier with the help of this viewpoint (Tu & Godfrey, 2001).
- **Process Structure, or Coordination Structure:** Processes, as well as threading, are also the units. The linkages comprise any relations relating to process synchronization and concurrently, such as synchronizes-with, cannot-run-without, couldn't, pre-empts, etc. This viewpoint addresses a system's dynamic features. Analyzing the program's run-time characteristics is helpful.
- **Physical Structure:** The connections are also the communication methods, whereas the units are physical hardware elements like CPUs. Connections are also the communicates-with relationships between the components. The mappings of hardware to the software are displayed in just this view. In dispersed or parallel applications, it is very relevant. It enables an engineer to make judgments regarding security, accessibility, and efficiency (Qin & Xing, 2008).
- **Uses Structure:** The units are either modules or processes. The supposed connection connects them. It is advantageous to design systems which can be quickly expanded or subset, for example, by integrating components incrementally.
- **Calls Structure:** Typically, the units include (sub) procedures. The calls or invites connection ties them together. The calls construct is employed to track the course of execution of a program (North & Saini, 2002).
- **Data Flow Structure:** The units are either modules or programs. The connections may communicate data to one another. The names of the

transferred data are shown next to the links. The best application of the information flow model is for needs traceability.

- **Control Flow Structure:** Programs, modules, or network states are making up the units. The relationship is after-becomes-active. This approach helps confirm the system's temporal characteristics along with its functional behavior. This is the same as the calls architecture if indeed the program call is the sole method of command transfer (Carpendale & Ghanam, 2008).
- **Class Structure:** Objects and classes seem to be the units. The relationship is either an example of or derives from. This viewpoint allows inference regarding sub-classing, which is utilized to capture groups of comparable behavior and parameterized deviations from the core.

Hofmeister, Nord, and Soni developed four loosely linked viewpoints of software architecture which are found in every system and give a somewhat full picture of such software architecture derived from observations and analyzes of industry practices. These perspectives include conceptual model, performance view, modules view, as well as code view (May, 2005):

- **Code View:** The code of a software program is often divided into several files of various types, such as files again for interface definition, the body of the module, and so on. The object code as well as binary code produced from the code base are granted their rights and are placed into libraries and/or directories to allow the complex construction of software systems. Because there are several variants of such software artifacts, configuration management is an essential responsibility. The organization of the code base into object files, binary code, library, and later into editions, files, as well as directories, etc., is the focus of a code view. The build speed of the systems and the reuse of the code are both significantly impacted by such an organization. The underlying engineering issues are crucial for this viewpoint (Tu & Godfrey, 2001).
  - How may product changes take less effort and time?
  - How ought product releases or versions to be handled?
  - How may build times be shortened?
  - How can the development environment be supported? What equipment is required?
  - How are testing and integration supported? (Hofmeister & Soni, 2000).
- **Module View:** Programming languages are applied to construct software systems, and different components or categories are used. The following inquiries are of importance to the module view:
  - How did the product fit into the software environment?

- What network services and support would it employ?
- How is assistance for testing possible? (Van Deursen et al., 2004).
- How may inter-module dependencies be reduced?

- How could we maximize the reusing of modules as well as subsystems? etc. (Javed & Zdun, 2014).
- **Execution View:** Systems have been dynamic from the beginning. The allocation of functional elements to operate objects, their handling of communications, coordination, and synchronization, and their mapping to hardware all are issues that fall under the purview of the executing view. Software developers should be able to respond to queries such as the following using this viewpoint (Bittencourt & Guerrero, 2009).
  - How can the system fulfill its demands for efficiency, restoration, and configurations?
  - How much resource utilization, including such load balancing, be balanced?
  - Could the required parallelism, duplication, and distribution be accomplished without overly complicating the control systems? (Hofmeister & Soni, 2000).
  - What steps may be taken to lessen the effects of modifications to a run- time framework? etc.
- **Conceptual View:** The major architectural components and their connections are described from the viewpoint of an application system's architectural style. The majority of authors who write about system design refer to it in terms similar to this. It is essential to the four views. The product creation addresses the following engineering problems (Hofmeister & Soni, 1999).
  - Which aspects of the system adhere to the specifications?
  - How might the effects of modifications to the domains or the objectives be minimized?
  - How are commercially off-the-shelf (COTS) parts combined, and how do they connect with the remainder of the system functionally? (Clements & Northrop, 1996).
  - How are product launches divided up into capabilities? etc.

We would primarily employ the basic software model systems as the architectural pattern for the duration of such a book. Our current working definition of the term "software architecture" is as follows.

An architectural pattern is just an abstraction, or design, of such a programming system in the sense of the framework that is made up of several pieces and the interactions between them to fulfill software design goals and to exhibit a particular set of architectural attributes of a system. The specifics of elements or connections are concealed and changed with more abstract computing entities known as connections and constituents, appropriately. These abstract objects either are represented by a series of distinguishing characteristics that have an impact on the system's characteristics or by a relatively low architecture design (Medina et al., 2020).

The Roles of Architecture in Software Design

Any architectural model of such a network is dictated either by the model's goal, as was covered in Section 4.1. Architectural models are mostly used in this book towards software development. There seem to be three primary reasons why system design is crucial, as Kazman emphasized in particular (Jaiswal, 2019).

Communication Among Stakeholders

As Mayall noted in the Rule of Relations, it is crucial for the design phase that the stakeholders develop a working connection. Several, if not all, of the program's stakeholders, may utilize the shared high- level abstractions of system design to build understanding, reach agreements, and communicate with one another (Woods & Palincsar, 2018).

Manifestation of Early Design Decisions

The design phase is a judgment method, as was previously mentioned. The initial design decisions taken regarding a system reveal themselves in the program's software architecture, and all these initial bindings have an impact just on the system's future growth, deployment, and management that is considerably greater than its gravitas. Architecture governs organizational structure, establishes implementing restrictions, and controls or promotes a program's quality characteristics. It's also the first time the system to also be constructed may be examined. Analyzing a system's design can help one forecast how good it will be. It facilitates decision-making and change management. In great concept, it is helpful (Kreye & Newnes, 2011).

Representation of Transferable Abstraction of a System

An architectural pattern is a condensed, cognitively understandable picture of the way a system is organized and how its parts interact. This model's representation of design knowledge is system transferable. It is particularly applicable to certain other systems with comparable needs and can encourage extensive reuse (Gomez & Giraldo, 2022).

From the point of view of a software design method, the thorough examination of software architecture style allows us to develop a fairly accurate representation of a design process for software products, to link the characteristics of software products to architecture and design choices as well as styles, and also to enabling design-stage disruptions. It represents an important turning point in the evolution of software system design 9 (Luo et al., 2017).

SOFTWARE ARCHITECTURAL STYLE

The employment of idioms forms of system organization is among the distinguishing characteristics of software architecture design, as Shaw and Garlan have noted. Numerous of these designs have now been created through time as architects have come to appreciate the benefits of particular organization structures as well as concepts for particular types of software platforms. Similarly, to the idea of architectural features in other fields like built forms and computer engineering, these forms of organizational principles as well as frameworks have a place in software design. The concept of program-style architecture is examined in this section (Santos et al., 2020).

Example 1: Audio Transcription System

Think about the voice transcription program (Santos et al., 2020) shown in Figure 5.9. The technology uses audio datasets of English speech during radio broadcasts to dynamically produce text transcribed (Lidy & Quereda, 2007).

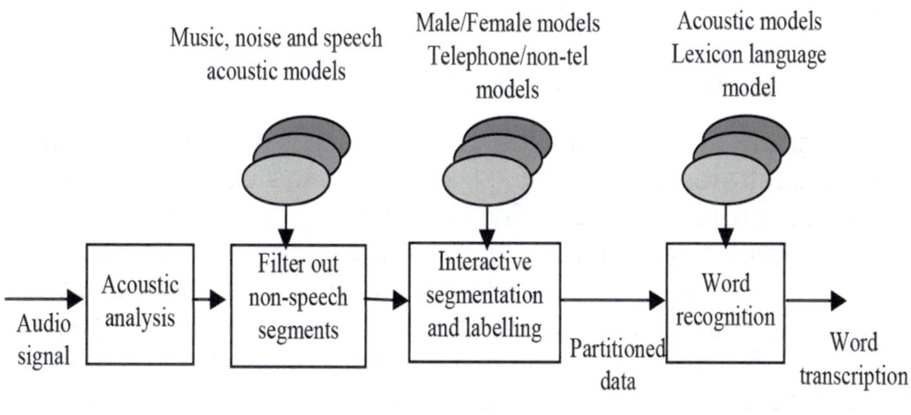

Figure 5.9. Overview of the audio stream transcription system.

Source: Image by T. Yoshioka.

It has four sections, as indicated by the figure. An ongoing flow of audio signals is indeed the program's input. The flow of speech data is divided into a series of homogenous acoustical sections by the acoustic features. The filter detects and eliminates non-speech parts. The segmented and labeling element groups and labels the voice segments based on gender as well as bandwidth. A series of voice segments including labels for the speakers, sexual identity, and phone line are the final result of such a partitioning process. Lastly, a transcribed is produced as a series of words by the word recognition element, which recognizes the words that used a language model. Figure 5.10 depicts the program's input, outputs, and intermediary data streams that move through its parts (Brugnara & Giuliani, 2000).

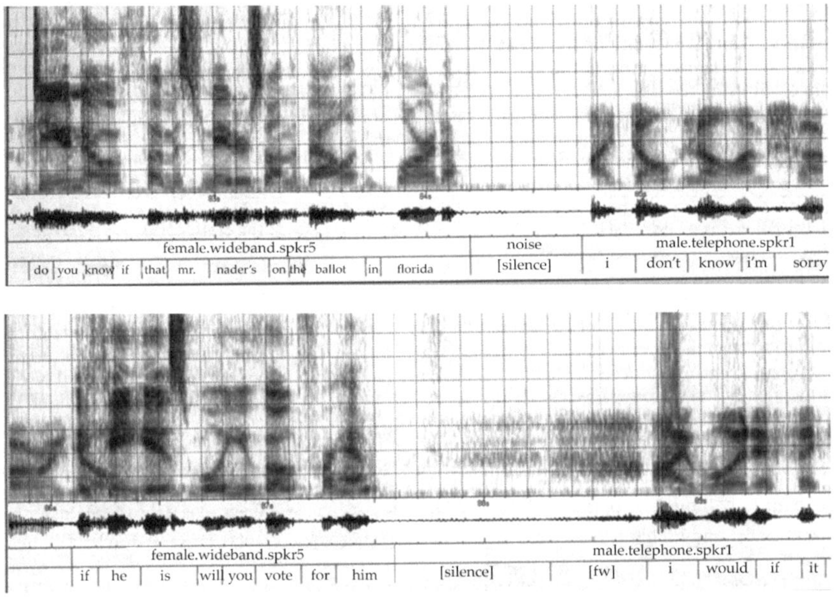

Figure 5.10. The input, output, and intermediate data streams that travel through the components are shown in spectrograms.

Source: Image by home.cc.umanitoba.ca.

Example 2: Projection Keyboard

The program that creates the projecting keyboards for portable devices illustrated in Figure 5.11 serves as the second illustration. A full-size prototype projecting keyboards, as shown in Figure 5.11, is completely formed of light that is projected upon surfaces like kitchen worktops, tablet trays for airplanes, and desktops. It behaves, feels, and makes the same sounds as its physical equivalent. A single small sensor just on the keyboard tracks the user's fingertips as they move and converts those movements into keystrokes. Using a full-sized keyboard, they can type as quickly as their fingers will allow. A physical keyboard is not required to be carried with you or folded up; it may simply be turned off. The projected keyboard created at Canesta Inc., San Jose, CA, would quickly be accessible to be incorporated into consumers' preferred devices such as mobile phones as well as PDAs using a few additional grams as well as a few fewer cubic millimeters, according to Tomasi, Rafii, and Torunoglu (2003).

Figure 5.11. A projection keyboard for portable electronics.

Source: Image by scorni.com.

According to Figure 5.11, the projected keyboard is made up of three basic physical components. The keyboard is projected over onto the writing surface by the imaging lens, shown by element An in Figure

5.12. An invisibility ray with the shape of a fan that is grazing that surface is produced by the infrared source of light (component B). The sensor (element C) is just a camera that has a wide lens delicate only to reflect light and takes pity at the keyboard at a shallow angle. The role of a finger here in trying to type surface would then be determined by triangulation after a finger trying to strike the keyboard breaks the infrared signal and becomes viewable to a camera (Sun, 2013).

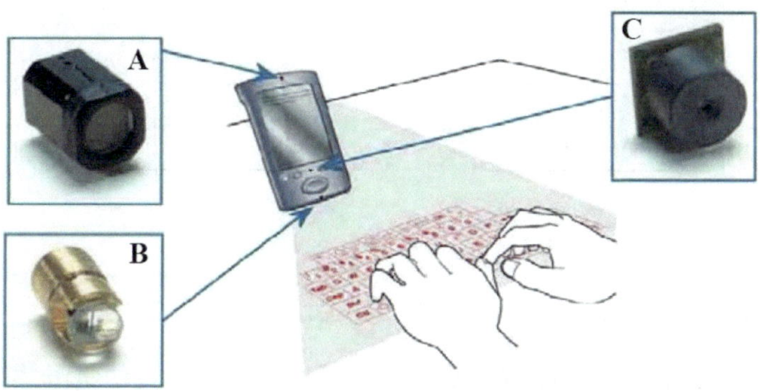

Figure 5.12. The projection keyboard's components.

Source: Image by robopeak.com.

The program that converts the pictures that the camera captures into keystrokes is seen in Figure 5.13. The classification component separates the candidate's fingers from those other potential background items from the constant stream of photos which the camera captures. It produces a stream of potential finger sections that have been discovered and outputs them to the localization component. The Localization component establishes the position and timing of such a keystroke for every picture segment using the camera's stream of pictures and the initial stream of sections as input. It creates a series of finger motions using the dimensions of a sensor. The Events Classification module takes this sequence of data to categorize the activity as landing, pause, motion, or takeoff. Additionally, the Triangulation element, which converts picture points to keyboard locations, receives a stream of finger positions. Every sensing coordinate point is mapped to the name of a key linked with it using a table. The outcome of the triangulation element is a flow of key identification, that, along with streaming of event kinds, lets the events generating portion choose the right streaming of keystrokes events. Even though the voice transcribing software and the projected keyboards interpreting software come from distinct application sectors, their general architectures share a few characteristics (Wang & Hedge, 2008).

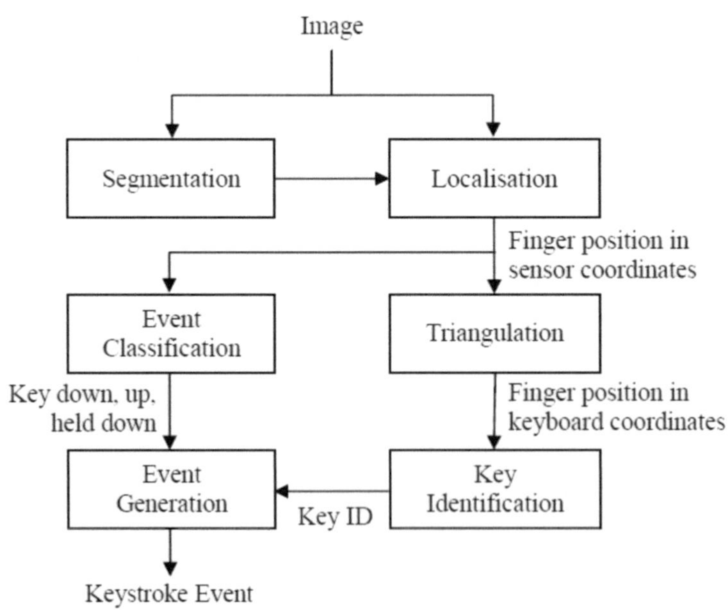

Figure 5.13. The keystroke interpretation algorithm's structure.

Source: Image by Stefan Ciprian Arseni.

Firstly, even if the formats, as well as semantics of input information again for two software products, may differ greatly, each component accepts continual streams of information as input. These pipes by which these data travels from one element to another are, secondly, the links here between parts. Lastly, each component processes data a little at a time. That would not depend on the overall knowledge of the entire input sequence. There are no globally interconnected state variables across the elements that are system wide. They don't rely on one another (Rashid & Smith, 2008).

These shared characteristics lead to a variety of shared characteristics between the systems' run-time behaviors in addition to their developmental and construction characteristics. For instance, both systems are capable of processing endless streams of continual data input while producing a stream of equivalent data output with the same ordering also as the input dataset. We recognize that the system's specific functions may be readily altered by only swapping out relevant components as an illustration of developmental and servicing qualities. The voice transcribing system may be readily updated to recognize utterances in French, German, as well as other languages simply altering the sight word element. The table that links sensor locations to key IDs within the Key Recognition element of the projected keyboard interpreting software is simply interchangeable with alternative tables for various keyboard designs. The software makes it possible to modify the keyboard layout dynamically thanks to customizable tables. On a standard keyboard, it would be challenging to provide this functionality. These similar run-time behaviors and developmental and servicing qualities are natural outcomes of their shared architecture traits. Furthermore, it follows that every system with the aforementioned architectural characteristics will likewise have the corresponding run-time and developmental characteristics. We may argue that such architectural constructions of the aforementioned systems have the same style of architecture since they share certain characteristics. In reality, they follow one of the extensively researched software architecture styles, the piping system architectural style; see Chapter 6 for additional information. In other terms, software architecture is an assortment of software products that fulfill a set of regular architectural criteria (Shah, 2017).

Example 3: DVD Rental Management System

Let's look at one further instance of a software program that is not designed in a similar style also as the two examples before to further clarify the idea of style architecture. A system for managing information for just a DVD rental store serves as the third instance software application which we are looking at. The technology is necessary to assist in managing the shop's inventory of DVDs available for rent by consumers. Numerous clients of the store are listed as members and are eligible to rent DVDs. The management of client data, including identities, locations, telephone numbers, including payment methods (including such credit card numbers), is another need for the program. The system must do the following activities in particular (Doherty, 2017):

- **A User Interface:** Customers (i.e., the employees of a DVD rental store) should be able to access the system by entering a password and username as well as receiving and executing orders through a graphical interface as well as showing data on the screen.
- **DVD Management:** It ought to oversee the DVD library. It should perform specific responsibilities in specific (Jung & Sriskandarajah, 2015).
    - Include a new DVD title in the inventory and give every DVD copy a bookshelf number;
    - Eliminate a DVD or video from the collections that are already there;
    - Use the DVD's title, bookshelf number, or even other details to find it;
    - View and print a DVD title that is actually or disc's comprehensive information;
    - Whenever consumer rents a DVD, verify it;
    - Whenever a consumer returns a DVD, make sure you check it in;
    - The background of DVD or disc rentals will be shown and printed;
    - List each DVD which is available for rent;
    - Listing every DVD which is currently available (Jung & Sriskandarajah, 2015).
- **Customer Management:** It should perform the following responsibilities and maintain the client list.
    - Add a new participant;
    - Delete a current participant;
    - Find out as much as you can about just a participant;
    - Verify that even a member meets the requirements for leasing a disc, such as that there are no past-due discs and that the quantity of discs leased is not exceeded (Verhoef, 2010);
    - Renting history for a member may be seen and printed.
- **User Management:** It ought to maintain a list of customers and associated passwords for logging in. It performs the following duties in specific (Lin et al., 2010).
    - New user added;
    - Changing the password for a current user;
    - Altering a user's category, such as changing a store assistant's category to manager;
    - Remove a current user (Doll, 1987);

- Display and publish the participant's transactions that were issued during a particular date and time.

Every one of the program's primary functions is implemented by an element inside the format of such a module that contains a set of instructions or operations. A database table is used to build the element, as well as the specifics of the data types it manages are contained within the modules and kept secret from those other elements. During the process and functional calls, components communicate with one another. For instance, while renting a DVD to a client, the DVD Manager element contacts the Consumer Manager to confirm that the customer is authorized to lease the DVD. Just administrators can remove a DVD from the collections, thus the DVD Manager additionally contacts the Users Manager to confirm that the users have the necessary access rights. In Figure 5.14, the system architecture is shown as follows (Yuan et al., 2018).

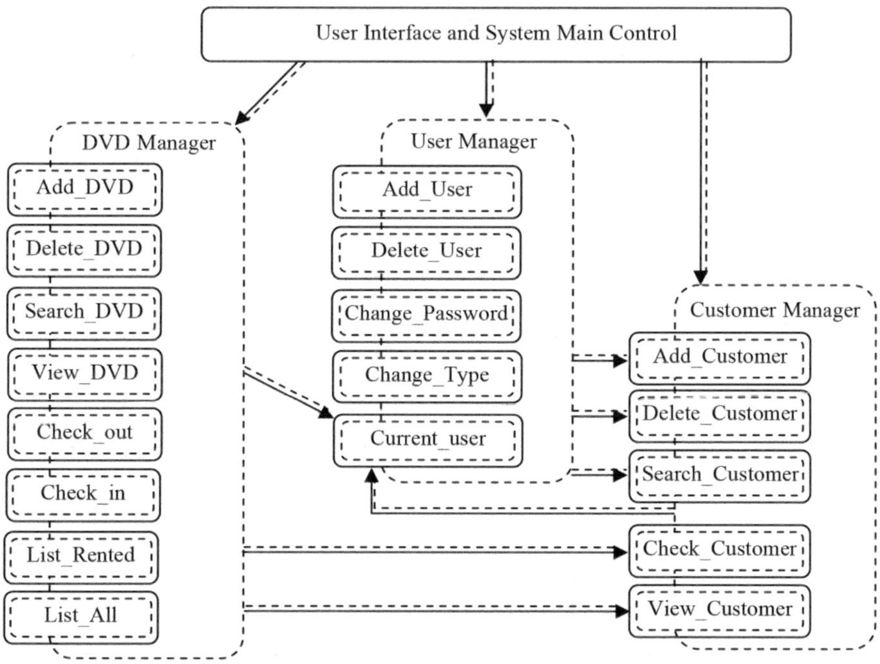

Figure 5.14. The design of the DVD store management system.

Source: Image by freeprojectz.com.

The characteristics of the projected keyboard interpreting and voice transcribing systems are not present in this general arrangement. It is different from the comparable system in the following architectural ways (Bianchessi et al., 2007).

First off, the DVD booking and reservation system's elements aren't filters. They don't change incoming data and don't accept streams of information as input. Rather, every element has a variety of distinct functions that other elements can call. Sometimes processes even fail to provide an output in response to a phone call. To maintain the confidentiality of the information and keep details of the implementation concealed from the elements that utilize the information, parts of the system typically combine data with their function into a single unit. These parts are frequently referred to as managers (Jøsang & Pope, 2005).

Second, they are still not data pipes—they are just links between the parts. Conversely, these are calls to procedures and functions that transfer both information and control. The program's computer simulation is also distinct from pipe-and-filter designs. There is no concurrent execution of elements. An element is only put into action when one of its processes or functions is used. Additionally, whenever one element calls the method or operation of some other element, control is transferred to the second component, which then picks up where it left off after the called process is finished and returned control.

As a result, the management solution for the DVD store is indeed not pipe-and-filter in design. Therefore, we cannot assume that now the DVD system will have the same operating behavior traits or maintenance and development characteristics associated with the piping system design. In actuality, it belongs to a different, well-known architectural approach called data abstractions, which will also be covered in further depth in Chapter 6 (Regan & Jensen, 2001).

THE NOTION OF SOFTWARE ARCHITECTURAL STYLE

We can conclude from the aforementioned examples that software architecture is somewhat comparable to either a building style architecture like Gothic or Greek revival. It comprises a few essential architectural aspects as well as guidelines for mixing features while maintaining architectural consistency. The above sorts of characteristics establish a software design esthetic (Zhu, 2005):

- **A Set of Component Types:** Not that all element kinds are allowed to be used in system design. However, the sorts of elements that may be used in the systems are frequently restricted by the architecture. Such a pipe-and-filter arrangement, for instance, consists of many filters. That system cannot accommodate further element kinds. Many examples of abstract data and/or entities make up a data abstraction architecture. These particular sorts of elements frequently have particular names, including managers within information abstraction style architecture and filters in the piping system's traditional architecture (Medvidovic, 1995).
- **A Set of Connectors:** Connections are the devices that allow devices to communicate, coordinate, or work together. The system connections' possible usage is restricted by the system design. For instance, only

pipes may be used to link filters in a piping system arrangement. Pipes, for instance, are one of the particular titles given to a connection type that might be employed in the piping system style architecture (Fielding et al., 2017).

- **A Topological Structure:** The topology architecture which elements can be joined to via connections is also constrained by a system design.
- **A Set of Semantic Constraints:** The architectural pattern could apply semantic restrictions just at the systems level as well as restrictions placed on elements, connections, and topological structures. For instance, calls to that an object's functions are the sole way to alter its state under a data annotation architecture. Inside a pipe- and-filter design, the filters need not exchange states. Consequently, a design is not the system's architecture. However, it serves as that an abstract for a group of architectural designs that share several characteristics. Software architecture identifies a set of structures that adhere to the limits of the style, just like the word Gothic identifies the appearance of a building. Styles are therefore frequently purposefully unclear on some specific topics. A style specifically avoids information regarding the following facets of systems (Fielding, 2000).
- **The Function of the System and Components:** The type of database files, for instance, may differ depending just on style architecture.
- **The Number of Components Involved:** A pipe-and-filter design might, for instance, contain 20 filters linked by 19 pipes and 2 filters linked by 1 pipe. Architecture is also not concerned with the number of filters or pipelines within the system.
- **The Mechanism of Interaction:** For instance, a call to a bottom division in component layers may be made via a localized procedure call, the remote method call, or another process communication service. Each of these techniques is suitable again for multilayered systems design and architecture (Fielding, 1999).

ACTIVITY 5.1.

Recall all the models discussed in this chapter and describe their benefits, drawbacks, and history, then state which model you believe is better.

The architectonic design for software products that have evolved throughout the years is abstracted in software architectural features. Several of the elements and concepts that make up a design are typically applied to a wide range of application areas and frequently recur within the same application domain. We will use Shaw and Garlan's description of the term "software style architecture" to summarize the subject. The family with a system is defined by such an architectural style as a result of a style for the structural organization. A certain lexicon of parts and connecting kinds, as well as limitations on how they might be joined, are defined by a style of architecture. One or even more semantics models which describe how to infer a system's total attributes from its component properties could also exist for many different styles (Fielding, 2000).

SUMMARY

Construction and computer hardware constitute two engineering fields where the concept of architecture has been created. In the words of the structure which is made up of a collection of elements with these relationships between themselves, the architect is often a model or abstracted description of a complex system. An architecture model may be used to accomplish certain technical goals and exhibit a specific set of desirable system attributes. Various architectural designs could be constructed for a single system to suit various engineering requirements. The architectural pattern conceals the specifics of the parts and how they relate to one another. In their substitute, abstraction concepts and relationships are used. Such abstract objects are composed of lower-tier different levels of abstraction or are characterized by a variety of distinct attributes that have an impact on the system's desired properties. We could gain the following insights from research on complex system designs in those other engineering areas. First, relevant architectural models may be used to infer specific system attributes. A constant collection of design choices that have been demonstrated to be established and that may be used to address a specific type of related challenge is what is meant by a style architecture, according to the second point.

Many different software architectural designs have indeed been put out in the research. A predictive model utilizes the software architecture also as a blueprint with rules again for the system's future design and execution. Whether systems are still to be created already or existing, a description model represents it as existing. The necessity to display a complex system to use a variety of distinct representations for various reasons is highlighted by multiple perspective models. The following models of system design rank some of the most significant:

- According to Perry as well as Wolf, software architecture consists of three things: components, styles, and logic;
- Software architecture is described by Shaw and Garlan as having structures built up of connections and elements;
- According to Bass, Clements, and Kazman, a collection of structures built up of software applications is defined as a set of those components' interactions with one another and their externally observable attributes.;
- Boehm et al.'s software architecture serves as a software design milestone for the thorough documenting of architecture, defined as a triad of architecture, criteria, and justification;
- Definitions by Hofmeister, Nord, and Soni using four perspectives: coding view, modules view, execution view, and concept view.

Three main functions of software architecture are present in software development. This is a program that makes communication between stakeholders easier. It is a simulation of a system to show the impact of early design options. This is a notation that, on such an abstract, conveys transferrable knowledge about a system. The accompanying definition of system design is used in the remaining chapters of this book while discussing software development.

An architectural pattern is just an abstraction, or model, of a programming system in the sense of a framework that is made up of several pieces and the interactions between them to fulfill software design goals and also to exhibit a particular set of design attributes of a system. The specifics of the elements as well as connections, which are dubbed components as well as connectors correspondingly, are disguised and changed. Such abstract objects are either composed of these lesser tier different levels of abstraction within the shape of such an architectural pattern or are expressed by a variety of distinct attributes that influence the system's features.

A family of structures is defined by an architecture and design style as a result of a sequence of structural organization. A certain lexicon of parts and connection types, as well as limitations upon how they might be joined, are defined by a style of architecture. There might also be one or even more semantic designs for several styles that explain how to infer a system's overall characteristics from its component properties.

REVIEW QUESTIONS

1. Describe the notion of architecture.
2. Differentiate between prescriptive and descriptive models.

MULTIPLE CHOICE QUESTIONS

1. Which of the following factors are influenced on the architect?

a. Background and experience of the architects
b. Developing an organization
c. Customers and end users
d. All of the above

2. Seeheim model later evolve to_model.

a. Slinky model
b. Arch model
c. None of the these
d. All of the above

3. Software design defines__.

a. Software design is an activity subjected to constraints
b. Software design satisfies client needs and desires
c. Software design specifies the nature and composition of software product
d. All of the above

4. How do architects influence on developing organization?

a. Long term business

b. Immediate business

c. Organization structure

d. All of the above

5. Which are the layers introduce in Arch Model?

a. Virtual application

b. Virtual toolkit

c. All of the above

d. None of these

Answers to Multiple Choice Questions

1. (d) 2. (d) 3. (d) 4. (d) 5. (c)

REFERENCES

1. Alden, D., (1997). Recreational user management of parks: An ecological economic framework. *Ecological Economics, 23*(3), 225–236.
2. Arias, T. B. C., America, P., & Avgeriou, P., (2009). Defining execution viewpoints for a large and complex software-intensive system. In: *2009 Joint Working IEEE/IFIP Conference on Software Architecture & European Conference on Software Architecture* (pp. 1–10). IEEE.
3. Bachman, L. R., (2004). *Integrated Buildings: The Systems Basis of Architecture* (Vol. 9). John Wiley & Sons.
4. Bagheri, H., Song, Y., & Sullivan, K., (2010). Architectural style as an independent variable. In: *Proceedings of the IEEE/ACM International Conference on Automated Software Engineering* (pp. 159–162).
5. Bass, L., Clements, P., & Kazman, R., (2003). *Software Architecture in Practice*. Addison-Wesley Professional.
6. Bax, M. F., & Trum, H. M. G. J., (2004). On the notion of level in architecture. In: *Recent Advances in Design and Decision Support Systems in Architecture and Urban Planning* (pp. 279–292). Springer, Dordrecht.
7. Bianchessi, N., Cordeau, J. F., Desrosiers, J., Laporte, G., & Raymond, V., (2007). A heuristic for the multi-satellite, multi-orbit and multi-user management of earth observation satellites. *European Journal of Operational Research, 177*(2), 750–762.
8. Bittencourt, R. A., & Guerrero, D. D. S., (2009). Comparison of graph clustering algorithms for recovering software architecture module views. In: *2009 13th European Conference on Software Maintenance and Reengineering* (pp. 251–254). IEEE.

9. Bosch, J., (2004). Software architecture: The next step. In: *European Workshop on Software Architecture* (pp. 194–199). Springer, Berlin, Heidelberg.
10. Brugnara, F., Cettolo, M., Federico, M., & Giuliani, D., (2000). A system for the segmentation and transcription of Italian audio news. In: *RIAO* (pp. 364–371).
11. Budgen, D., Brereton, P., & Turner, M., (2004). Codifying a service architectural style. In: *Proceedings of the 28th Annual International Computer Software and Applications Conference, 2004; COMPSAC 2004* (pp. 16–22). IEEE.
12. Calazans, N. L. V., & Moraes, F. G., (2001). Integrating the teaching of computer organization and architecture with digital hardware design early in undergraduate courses. *IEEE Transactions on Education, 44*(2), 109–119.
13. Carpendale, S., & Ghanam, Y., (2008). *A Survey Paper on Software Architecture Visualization*. University of Calgary.
14. Chaloupka, J., (2019). A prototype of audio-visual broadcast transcription system. In: *2019 42nd International Conference on Telecommunications and Signal Processing (TSP)* (pp. 543–547). IEEE.
15. Choi, H., & Yeom, K., (2002). An approach to software architecture evaluation with the 4+ 1 view model of architecture. In: *Ninth Asia-Pacific Software Engineering Conference, 2002* (pp. 286– 293). IEEE.
16. Clements, P. C., & Northrop, L. M., (1996). *Software Architecture: An Executive Overview*. Carnegie- Mellon Univ Pittsburgh PA Software Engineering Inst.
17. Clements, P., Garlan, D., Little, R., Nord, R., & Stafford, J., (2003). Documenting software architectures: Views and beyond. In: *25th International Conference on Software Engineering, 2003. Proceedings.* (pp. 740–741). IEEE.
18. Doherty, J., (2017). *Edge of Tomorrow DVD Rentals* (Vol. 1, pp, 1-20).
19. Doll, W. J., (1987). Encouraging user management participation in systems design. *Information & Management, 13*(1), 25–32.
20. Ducasse, S., & Pollet, D., (2009). Software architecture reconstruction: A process-oriented taxonomy. *IEEE Transactions on Software Engineering, 35*(4), 573–591.
21. Eliasson, U., Heldal, R., Pelliccione, P., & Lantz, J., (2015). Architecting in the automotive domain: Descriptive vs prescriptive architecture. In: *2015 12th Working IEEE/IFIP Conference on Software Architecture* (pp. 115–118). IEEE.
22. Esmaeilzadeh, H., Sampson, A., Ceze, L., & Burger, D., (2012). Architecture support for disciplined approximate programming. In: *Proceedings of the Seventeenth International Conference on Architectural Support for Programming Languages and Operating Systems* (pp. 301–312).
23. Esmaeilzadeh, H., Sampson, A., Ringenburg, M., Ceze, L., Grossman, D., & Burger, D., (2012). Addressing dark silicon challenges with disciplined approximate computing. In: *Proc. 4th Workshop on Energy-Efficient Design* (pp. 1, 2).
24. Fielding, R. T., (1999). *Software Architectural Styles for Network-Based Applications*. Unpublished manuscript.

25. Fielding, R. T., (2000). *Architectural Styles and the Design of Network-Based Software Architectures*. University of California, Irvine.
26. Fielding, R. T., (2000). *Software Architectural Styles for Network-Based Applications* (Vol. 1). Phase II Survey Paper, draft.
27. Fielding, R. T., Taylor, R. N., Erenkrantz, J. R., Gorlick, M. M., Whitehead, J., Khare, R., & Oreizy, P., (2017). Reflections on the REST architectural style and "principled design of the modern web architecture" (impact paper award). In: *Proceedings of the 2017 11th Joint Meeting on Foundations of Software Engineering* (pp. 4–14).
28. Galster, M., & Avgeriou, P., (2011). The notion of variability in software architecture: Results from a preliminary exploratory study. In: *Proceedings of the 5th Workshop on Variability Modeling of Software-Intensive Systems* (pp. 59–67).
29. Garlan, D., & Perry, D. E., (1995). Introduction to the special issue on software architecture. *IEEE Trans. Software Eng., 21*(4), 269–274.
30. Garlan, D., (2000). Software architecture: A roadmap. In: *Proceedings of the Conference on the Future of Software Engineering* (pp. 91–101).
31. Garlan, D., (2001). *Software Architecture.* (Vol. 1, pp, 1-22).
32. Gauvain, J. L., Lamel, L., & Adda, G., (2002). The LIMSI broadcast news transcription system. *Speech Communication, 37*(1, 2), 89–108.
33. Gomez, D., Quijano, N., & Giraldo, L. F., (2022). Information optimization and transferable state abstractions in deep reinforcement learning. *IEEE Transactions on Pattern Analysis and Machine Intelligence*.
34. Gruber, P., (2011). *Biomimetics in Architecture: Architecture of Life and Buildings* (pp. 418–426). New York: Springer.
35. Gruner, S., (2014). On the historical semantics of the notion of software architecture. *TD: The Journal for Transdisciplinary Research in Southern Africa, 10*(1), 37–66.
36. Guessi, M., Neto, V. V., Bianchi, T., Felizardo, K. R., Oquendo, F., & Nakagawa, E. Y., (2015). A systematic literature review on the description of software architectures for systems of systems. In: *Proceedings of the 30th Annual ACM Symposium on Applied Computing* (pp. 1433–1440).
37. Hamilton, D., & Pajari, R., (1997). Effective communication among stakeholders: A key component for successful internship programs. *Journal of Public Administration Education, 3*(2), 203–215.
38. Harris, D., & Harris, S. L., (2010). *Digital Design and Computer Architecture*. Morgan Kaufmann.
39. Heldal, R., Pelliccione, P., Eliasson, U., Lantz, J., Derehag, J., & Whittle, J., (2016). Descriptive vs prescriptive models in industry. In: *Proceedings of the ACM/IEEE 19th International Conference on Model Driven Engineering Languages and Systems* (pp. 216–226).
40. Henzinger, T. A., & Sifakis, J., (2007). The discipline of embedded systems design. *Computer, 40*(10), 32–40.

41. Hillier, B., & Leaman, A., (1976). Architecture as a discipline. *Journal of Architectural Research, 28*– 32.
42. Hofmeister, C., Kruchten, P., Nord, R. L., Obbink, H., Ran, A., & America, P., (2007). A general model of software architecture design derived from five industrial approaches. *Journal of Systems and Software, 80*(1), 106–126.
43. Hofmeister, C., Nord, R. L., & Soni, D., (1999). Describing software architecture with UML. In: *Working Conference on Software Architecture* (pp. 145–159). Springer, Boston, MA. Hofmeister, C., Nord, R., & Soni, D., (2000). *Applied Software Architecture*. Addison-Wesley Professional.
44. Jaiswal, M., (2019). Software architecture and software design. *International Research Journal of Engineering and Technology (IRJET)*. e-ISSN, 2395-0056.
45. Jansen, A., & Bosch, J., (2005). Software architecture as a set of architectural design decisions. In: *5th Working IEEE/IFIP Conference on Software Architecture (WICSA'05)* (pp. 109–120). IEEE.
46. Javed, M. A., & Zdun, U., (2014). A systematic literature review of traceability approaches between software architecture and source code. In: *Proceedings of the 18th International Conference on Evaluation and Assessment in Software Engineering* (pp. 1–10).
47. Jøsang, A., & Pope, S., (2005). User centric identity management. In: *AusCERT Asia Pacific Information Technology Security Conference* (Vol. 22, p. 2005).
48. Jozefowicz, J. J., Kelley, J. M., & Brewer, S. M., (2008). New release: An empirical analysis of VHS/DVD rental success. *Atlantic Economic Journal, 36*(2), 139–151.
49. Jung, K. S., Chung, C., Niu, S. C., & Sriskandarajah, C., (2015). Inventory and shipment policies for the online movie DVD rental industry. *Service Science, 7*(4), 249–271.
50. Kain, R. Y., (1988). *Computer Architecture: Software and Hardware* (Vol. 1). Prentice-Hall, Inc.
51. Kazman, R., Woods, S. G., & Carrière, S. J., (1998). Requirements for integrating software architecture and reengineering models: CORUM II. In: *Proceedings Fifth Working Conference on Reverse Engineering (Cat. No. 98TB100261)* (pp. 154–163). IEEE.
52. Khan, R., (2011). Secure software development: A prescriptive framework. *Computer Fraud & Security, 2011*(8), 12–20.
53. Kiran, M., Richmond, P., Holcombe, M., Chin, L. S., Worth, D., & Greenough, C., (2010). FLAME: Simulating large populations of agents on parallel hardware architectures. In: *Proceedings of the 9th International Conference on Autonomous Agents and Multiagent Systems* (Vol. 1, pp. 1633–1636).
54. Kracklauer, A. H., Mills, D. Q., & Seifert, D., (2004). Customer management as the origin of collaborative customer relationship management. In: *Collaborative Customer Relationship Management* (pp. 3–6). Springer, Berlin, Heidelberg.

55. Kreye, M. E., Goh, Y. M., & Newnes, L. B., (2011). Manifestation of uncertainty-a classification. In: *DS 68-6: Proceedings of the 18th International Conference on Engineering Design (ICED 11), Impacting Society Through Engineering Design: Design Information and Knowledge* (Vol. 6). Lyngby/Copenhagen, Denmark, 15.

56. Kruchten, P. B., (1995). The 4+ 1 view model of architecture. *IEEE Software, 12*(6), 42–50.

57. Liao, L., (2002). *From Requirements to Architecture: The State of the Art in Software Architecture Design* (pp. 1–13). Department of Computer Science and Engineering, University of Washington.

58. Lidy, T., Rauber, A., Pertusa, A., & Quereda, J. M. I., (2007). Improving genre classification by combination of audio and symbolic descriptors using a transcription systems. In: *ISMIR* (pp. 61–66).

59. Lin, J., Lu, X., Yu, L., Zou, Y., & Zha, L., (2010). VegaWarden: A uniform user management system for cloud applications. In: *2010 IEEE Fifth International Conference on Networking, Architecture, and Storage* (pp. 457–464). IEEE.

60. Lukken, G., Hirschfeld, Y., & Searle, M., (1993). *Semiotics and Church Architecture: Applying the Semiotics of AJ Greimas and the Paris School to the Analysis of Church Buildings* (No. 34). Peeters Publishers.

61. Luo, Z., Zou, Y., Hoffman, J., & Fei-Fei, L. F., (2017). Label efficient learning of transferable representations across domains and tasks. *Advances in Neural Information Processing Systems, 30.*

62. May, N., (2005). A survey of software architecture viewpoint models. In: *Proceedings of the Sixth Australasian Workshop on Software and System Architectures* (pp. 13–24). Australia: Melbourne.

63. McGinley, T., (2015). A morphogenetic architecture for intelligent buildings. *Intelligent Buildings International, 7*(1), 4–15.

64. Medina, O. C., Romero, M. S., Romero, R. A., Martin, S. M., & Marciszack, M. M., (2020). Using architecture patterns in the conceptual model of an eGov software. In: *International Conference on Information Technology & Systems* (pp. 54–63). Springer, Cham.

65. Medvidovic, N., & Taylor, R. N., (1997). Exploiting architectural style to develop a family of applications. *IEE Proceedings-Software, 144*(5), 237–248.

66. Medvidovic, N., & Taylor, R. N., (2000). A classification and comparison framework for software architecture description languages. *IEEE Transactions on Software Engineering, 26*(1), 70–93. Medvidovic, N., & Taylor, R. N., (2010). Software architecture: Foundations, theory, and practice. In: *2010 ACM/IEEE 32nd International Conference on Software Engineering* (Vol. 2, pp. 471– 472). IEEE.

67. Medvidovic, N., (1995). *Formal Definition of the Chiron-2 Software Architectural Style.* (Vol. 1, pp, 1-20).

68. Mesbah, A., & Van, D. A., (2007). An architectural style for Ajax. In: *2007 Working*

IEEE/IFIP Conference on Software Architecture (WICSA'07) (pp. 8–9). IEEE.

69. Mesbah, A., & Van, D. A., (2008). A component-and push-based architectural style for ajax applications. *Journal of Systems and Software, 81*(12), 2194–2209.
70. Muccini, H., Inverardi, P., & Bertolino, A., (2004). Using software architecture for code testing. *IEEE Transactions on Software Engineering, 30*(3), 160–171.
71. Neill, C. J., Sangwan, R. S., & Kilicay-Ergin, N. H., (2015). A prescriptive approach to quality-focused system architecture. *IEEE Systems Journal, 11*(4), 1994–2005.
72. Neslin, S. A., Grewal, D., Leghorn, R., Shankar, V., Teerling, M. L., Thomas, J. S., & Verhoef, P. C., (2006). Challenges and opportunities in multichannel customer management. *Journal of Service Research, 9*(2), 95–112.
73. North, C., Conklin, N., Indukuri, K., & Saini, V., (2002). Visualization schemas and a web-based architecture for custom multiple-view visualization of multiple-table databases. *Information Visualization, 1*(3, 4), 211–228.
74. Perry, D. E., & Wolf, A. L., (1992). Foundations for the study of software architecture. *ACM SIGSOFT Software Engineering Notes, 17*(4), 40–52.
75. Pospieszny, P., (2017). Software estimation: Towards prescriptive analytics. In: *Proceedings of the 27th International Workshop on Software Measurement and 12th International Conference on Software Process and Product Measurement* (pp. 221–226).
76. Qin, Z., Zheng, X., & Xing, J., (2008). *Introduction to Software Architecture* (pp. 1–33). Springer Berlin Heidelberg.
77. Ramachandran, R., Arya, P., & Jayanthy, P. G., (2017). A novel method for intrusion detection in relational databases. In: *2017 International Conference on Advances in Computing, Communications and Informatics (ICACCI)* (pp. 230–235). IEEE.
78. Rashid, D. R., & Smith, N. A., (2008). Relative keyboard input system. In: *Proceedings of the 13th International Conference on Intelligent User Interfaces* (pp. 397–400).
79. Recordon, D., & Reed, D., (2006). OpenID 2.0: A platform for user-centric identity management. In:
80. *Proceedings of the Second ACM Workshop on Digital Identity Management* (pp. 11–16).
81. Reddy, A. R. M., Govindarajulu, P., & Naidu, M., (2007). A process model for software architecture.
82. *International Journal of Computer Science and Network Security, 7*(4), 272–280.
83. Regan, J. T., & Jensen, C. D., (2001). Capability file names: Separating authorization from user management in an internet file system. In: *10th USENIX Security Symposium (USENIX Security 01)*.
84. Rice, L., (2019). A health map for architecture: The determinants of health and wellbeing in buildings.*Designing for Health & Wellbeing: Home, City, Society*, 155–184.
85. Robal, T., Viies, V., & Kruus, M., (2002). The rational unified process with the "4+

1" view model of software architecture-a way for modeling web applications. In: *BalticDB&IS* (pp. 119–132).

86. Rockart, J. F., & Flannery, L. S., (1983). The management of end user computing. *Communications of the ACM, 26*(10), 776–784.
87. Roeber, H., Bacus, J., & Tomasi, C., (2003). Typing in thin air: The canesta projection keyboard-a new method of interaction with electronic devices. In: *CHI'03 Extended Abstracts on Human Factors in Computing Systems* (pp. 712, 713).
88. Salmansha, P. N., Parveen, S., Yohannan, F., Vasavan, A., & Kurian, M., (2017). Mini keyboard: Portative human interactive device. In: *2017 International Conference on Communication and Signal Processing (ICCSP)* (pp. 1531–1535). IEEE.
89. Santos, L., Silva, E., Batista, T., Cavalcante, E., Leite, J., & Oquendo, F., (2020). An architectural style for internet of things systems. In: *Proceedings of the 35th Annual ACM Symposium on Applied Computing* (pp. 1488–1497).
90. Shah, S., Patel, D., Patel, J., & Patel, R., (2017). A survey of virtual keyboard with its senses.
91. *International Journal of Recent Trends in Engineering & Research, 3*, 184–190.
92. Shaw, M., & Garlan, D., (1996). *Software Architecture: Perspectives on an Emerging Discipline*. Prentice-Hall, Inc.
93. Shaw, M., (2001). The coming-of-age of software architecture research. In: *Proceedings of the 23rd International Conference on Software Engineering* (p. 656).
94. Simon, H. A., (1991). The architecture of complexity. In: *Facets of Systems Science* (pp. 457–476). Springer, Boston, MA.
95. Singh, H., & Mookerjee, V., (2011). *Inventory as a Driver of Demand: The Case of Blockbuster Online Rental System*. (Vol. 1, pp, 1-10).
96. Sun, B., Ding, J. F., Su, L. D., Zhong, Y. L., & Yin, Y. Y., (2013). The projection keyboard based on the image processing. In: *Applied Mechanics and Materials* (Vol. 373, pp. 634–637). Trans Tech Publications Ltd.
97. Sztipanovits, J., & Karsai, G., (1997). Model-integrated computing. *Computer, 30*(4), 110, 111. Tamzalit, D., & Mens, T., (2010). Guiding architectural restructuring through architectural styles. In:
98. *2010 17th IEEE International Conference and Workshops on Engineering of Computer Based Systems* (pp. 69–78). IEEE.
99. Tomasi, C., Rafii, A., & Torunoglu, I., (2003). Full-size projection keyboard for handheld devices. *Communications of the ACM, 46*(7), 70–75.
100. Tu, Q., & Godfrey, M. W., (2001). The build-time software architecture view. In: *Proceedings IEEE International Conference on Software Maintenance. ICSM 2001* (pp. 398–407). IEEE. Unwin, S., (2009). *Analyzing Architecture*. Routledge.
101. Van, D. A., Hofmeister, C., Koschke, R., Moonen, L., & Riva, C., (2004). Symphony: View-driven software architecture reconstruction. In: *Proceedings. Fourth Working IEEE/IFIP Conference on Software Architecture (WICSA 2004)* (pp. 122–132). IEEE.

102. Verhoef, P. C., Reinartz, W. J., & Krafft, M., (2010). Customer engagement as a new perspective in customer management. *Journal of Service Research, 13*(3), 247–252.

103. Vives-Rego, J., Uson, E., & Fumadó, J., (2015). Passive designed buildings for active citizens became schools of sustainability: A proposal for sustainable architecture. *Journal of Green Building, 10*(1), 85–96.

104. Wang, X., & Hedge, A., (2008). A usability evaluation of a laser projection virtual keyboard. In: *Proceedings of the Human Factors and Ergonomics Society Annual Meeting* (Vol. 52, No. 6, pp. 537–541). Sage CA: Los Angeles, CA: SAGE Publications.

105. Wolf, W., (2002). What is embedded computing? *Computer, 35*(1), 136–137.

106. Wolf, W., (2003). A decade of hardware/software codesign. *Computer, 36*(4), 38–43.

107. Woods, A. D., Morrison, F. J., & Palincsar, A. S., (2018). Perceptions of communication practices among stakeholders in special education. *Journal of Emotional and Behavioral Disorders, 26*(4), 209–224.

108. Yoshioka, T., Abramovski, I., Aksoylar, C., Chen, Z., David, M., Dimitriadis, D., & Zhou, T., (2019). Advances in online audio-visual meeting transcription. In: *2019 IEEE Automatic Speech Recognition and Understanding Workshop (ASRU)* (pp. 276–283). IEEE.

109. Yuan, H., Chen, X., Jiang, T., Zhang, X., Yan, Z., & Xiang, Y., (2018). DedupDUM: Secure and scalable data deduplication with dynamic user management. *Information Sciences, 456*, 159– 173.

110. Zhu, H., (2005). *Software Design Methodology: From Principles to Architectural Styles*. Elsevier.

CHAPTER 6

TYPICAL ARCHITECTURAL STYLES

UNIT INTRODUCTION

An architectural style is an approximation of the structural designs of a group of software systems, as was addressed in the previous knowledge. These idioms act as organizational patterns for systems. They have evolved as designers have come to appreciate the benefits of particular organizational principles and frameworks for particular types of software systems. Similar to the idea of architectural styles in other fields like building design and computer architecture, such patterns of organizational principles and structures have a role in software design. In this chapter, we go into great detail on a few well- known software architectural approaches (Liao et al., 2017).

Depending upon the definition of software architectural designs in the preceding chapter, Shaw & Garlan (1996) noted that a particular style can be identified by the responses to the questions below:

- **What terms are used in the design?** Clarification of the kinds of connectors and elements that may be utilized in systems of a particular style has been provided by the response to this question. The type of vocabulary that software developers use to identify these kinds of elements and connectors as well as the ways they are coupled, reflects a portion of the design knowledge linked with the architectural style. Moreover, design vocabulary can also refer to design processes, run-time events, and other concepts in addition to such names for connectors and elements of a certain architectural style (Shalunts & Sablatnig, 2012).
- **What structural patterns have been permitted?** In the type of restrictions on how parts and connectors may be joined and coupled in a system in the style,

the response to this question defines the features and characteristics of the topological system's structure.

- **What's the computational model that underlies this?** The typical response to this query explains the system's execution, or more specifically, the mechanics that make the system work. The characteristics of the run-time behaviors of the systems are made clear in this manner.
- **What are the style's fundamental constants?** The response to this query offers extra traits of the architectural style, like semantic limitations, which aren't handled by the questions above. Such traits have a significant role in defining architectural style. It frequently allows us to deduce additional characteristics about maintenance and development procedures as well as run-time behaviors (Zhu, 2005).
- **What crucial characteristics of software systems may be gleaned from the style? What are the style's benefits and drawbacks, in particular?** An answer to this query offers guidelines for the application of the style, forming an essential design knowledge that connects architectural aspects to design factors like quality.
- **What are some of the style's typical specializations?** The response to this query will reveal details about the flexible features of the architectural design. It defines the options available to designers and illustrates a design area inside the architectural design. A sub-type of the design is frequently formed by a specialization. These connections can help create a systematic understanding of software architectural design and offer extra guidance on how to employ architectural designs in software architecture (Wang & Xu, 2010).
- **What are some common instances of its applications?** Instances of actual software systems that adhere to the architectural style serve to clarify its applications, highlight its value, and point out any potential drawbacks. Learning from past experiences and best practices is beneficial for software designers. The application domains that frequently advantage of the architectural style are also shown in instances. It is important to remember, nevertheless, that an architectural style is typically not restricted to such application areas. As a result, we will group the explanations of every architectural style in the sections that follow by focusing on its design vocabulary, computational model, structural pattern, key invariants, and features deriving from the style, like the benefits and drawbacks, and sub-types of the styles. Additionally, we'll give examples to demonstrate each style and talk about how its typical applications are integrated and coupled to form a system (Sevcikova & Fabian, 2016).

Learning Objective

At the end of this chapter students will be able to learn:

- To learn various software architectural styles;
- To learn how different software architectural styles are interrelated.

Key Terms

- Architectural styles
- Data flow
- Batch sequential processing
- Independent components
- Call and return

DATA FLOW

Data processing plays a crucial part in many application domains, and the flow of data is a software architecture style that's also frequently employed in these environments. A particular instance of the data flow architectural style is the pipe-and-filter style that is discussed in the knowledge. To demonstrate how design knowledge might be connected to an architectural style, we begin with the information flow architectural design in this instance. In the chapter, further software architectural designs would be discussed (Khedker & Sathe, 2017).

Did you Know?

The three most prevalent styles of software architecture are data-centric style, layered style, and object-oriented style.

The General Data Flow Style

Computational Model

The entire mechanism through which a system in an architectural style operates is represented by its computational model. The system is viewed as a sequence of transformations applied to consecutive bits of input information in the data flow approach. Data flow into the system, moving through each element individually until they have been allocated to a specific destination (data store or output). The design's structure has been governed by the systematic transfer of data from element to element. Data accessibility determines calculation (Sussman, 1973).

Design Vocabulary

Particular elements and connector kinds may be utilized in the systems of every architectural design, special design concerns that frequently preoccupied the designers of this type of system, and other topics that are linked with every architectural style. For instance, a system designed in the data flow design includes several parts referred to as processing units or elements. When the inputs are accessible, the computation of a processing element begins. The outputs are then given as input into further processing elements after the data has been processed. Data flows, or simply flows, refer to the links and connections between such processing components (Khowaja & Salim, 2020).

Structural Pattern

Systems of a certain type frequently have a particular topologic structure where their constituent parts are related to one another. A directed graph can be used to visualize a data flow system, with nodes representing processing units and arcs representing the flow of data between the components. The information flow style is shown in Figure 6.1 (Pavlidis, 2013).

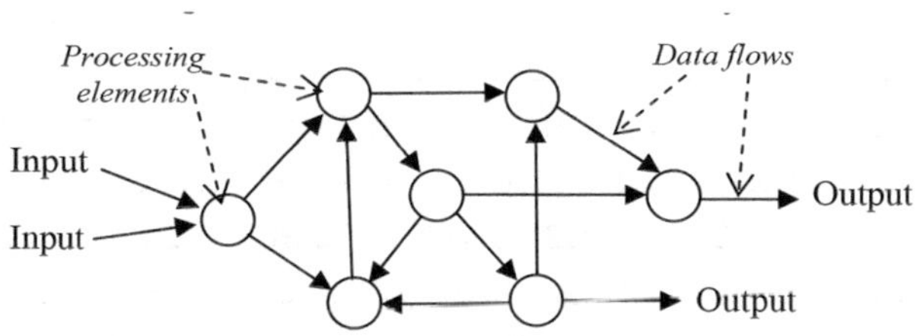

Figure 6.1. Illustration of data flow style.

Source: Image by brainkart.com.

The diagram in Figure 6.2 in the software architecture visual notation may be utilized to show the structure of an information flow system (Paulston, 1970).

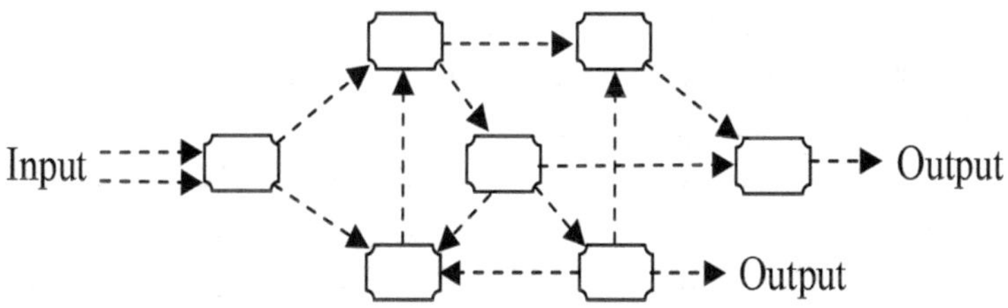

Figure 6.2. Information flow style depiction using a visual notation.

Source: Image by brainkart.com.

Essential Invariants

Systems of a particular style may differ from one another in several ways. For various systems to differ while still being viewed as belonging to a similar style, this is crucial to establish what components are flexible and what the fundamental characteristics of the style are. There is no contact between processing units other than data flows, which is one of the fundamental assumptions behind information flow systems. Every processing component also needs to be on a pathway from an input to an output (Taubes, 2001).

Sub-Types of the Style

Recognizing a style's sub-styles is a method to comprehend what might be distinctive for systems within that style. They are the most significant variations of the style, which explains the style's design decisions. The two primary subtypes of information flow style include pipe-and-filter and batch sequential processing. In the earlier section, we looked at 2 illustrations of pipe-and-filter systems (Fletcher et al., 2013).

Characteristics Resulting From the Architecture

Remember

The software system architecture is the term that refers to specific formats and patterns used by software programs.

Systems of a similar kind frequently share several characteristics, as we've seen earlier. These shared characteristics of every architectural design give transferrable design knowledge that may be utilized as standards for software design. Elements in the information flow architecture are quite independent of one another. The behavior of the elements is not under global control. Even on multiple computers, the processing pieces can run simultaneously. They are capable to process continuous data streams, the length of which theoretically has no upper bound, and offer continuous monitoring and controlling capabilities of actual process control systems. The parts can be reused and integrated very quickly into other systems with the same architectural design (Atzori et al., 2012).

At 2 levels, the system alteration is simple to carry out. If the formats and kinds of information flow in and out of the processing component at the component level seem to be identical to the original ones, the processing component may be changed without needing changes to another processing component. To increase the system's functionality, additional processing components and information flow can be reasonably readily incorporated into the system's structural level. The efficiency of an information flow architecture may be examined by using tried-and-true techniques like queue theory (Xu et al., 2011).

The synchronization of the calculations of several processing elements, if such synchronizations are required, could be a challenge in the design and execution of an information flow architecture.

Examples

We may better know how this type of system functions and the benefits and drawbacks of creating systems in the style by looking at typical instances of software systems in that style. When the approach applies to a design issue, we can draw lessons from such cases (Raney et al., 2010).

Information flow architectural style may be applied to numerous web-based applications. For instance, the following graphic (Figure 6.3) shows the four elements of an e-business system. The consumer's computer hosts the client side, which communicates with the web server over the internet. The web server handles consumers' request patterns in the format of messages and forwards the requests to a database server for database query processing.

The HTML page generator processes the outcomes of database queries to create an HTML file, which is then delivered back to the consumer's side for display on the consumer's computer screen (Kumar et al., 2022).

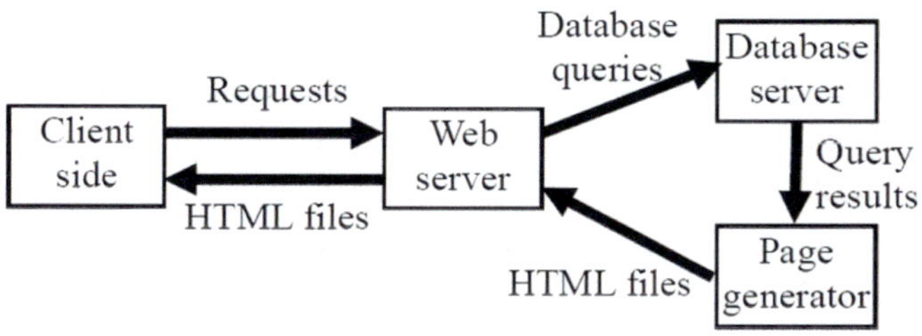

Figure 6.3. The general layout of a web application.

Source: Image by Ayman Hussein Odeh.

The Pipe-and-Filter Sub-Style

Computational Model

A subtype of the information flow architectural style has been the pipe-and-filter style. As a result, the pipes-and-filters design style has been represented by the computational model of information flow. Specifically, every element in a software system designed in the pipe-and-filter paradigm gradually reads in streams of information on its inputs and gradually generates streams of information on its outputs. In most cases, it is done by performing a local modification on every individual datum of the data input and calculating gradually, allowing output to start as soon as a new component of the input stream enters the system and before the entire input stream has been used. One element's outputs are used as the inputs for another component's outputs. These connectors carry streams from one filter's output to another filter's input by acting as conduits for the streams (Seo et al., 2009).

Design Vocabulary

Filters are the elements of pipes-and-filters architecture. In pipe-and-filter systems, the connectors have been referred to as pipes. There are three important restrictions on the parts and connectors of a pipe- and-filter architecture (Sussman, 1973).

- **Independence:** Filters need to be autonomous entities. They shouldn't, particularly, share states. Additionally, there shouldn't be any global main parameters (Cairns et al., 2019).

- **Anonymity:** The names of their downstream and upstream filters are unknown to filters. The elements at the endpoints of such pipes can't be identified, even though their requirements can limit what can show on the input pipes or ensure what can display on the output pipes (Allen, 1997).
- **Concurrency:** Even while fair scheduling may be expected, the output accuracy of a pipe-and-filter network shouldn't be dependent on the order in which the filters carry out their periodic processing. The best way to comprehend dynamic execution is to imagine all filters operating simultaneously or in parallel (Dashofy et al., 2001).

As a result, there are 2 methods that a filter varies from a processing component in the basic data flow architectural style. Firstly, although anonymity is a crucial component of filters, a processing component isn't necessary to be anonymous to its downstream or upstream processing components. Secondly, while it is possible in some systems, processing units are often not necessary to run concurrently in an information flow architecture. However, filters should operate simultaneously in a filter and pipe system (Coch, 1998).

Structural Pattern

There are no structure constraints in addition to the information flow architectural style constraints. Figure 6.4 depicts the architecture of a pipe and filter system in pictorial notation (Thoen & Catthoor, 2012).

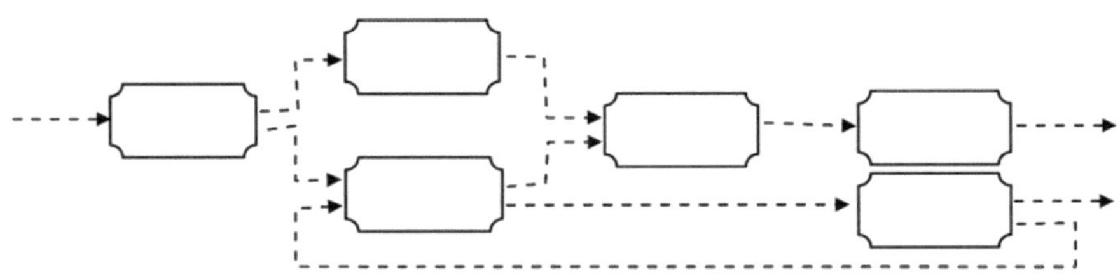

Figure 6.4. Visual representation of a pipe-and-filter architecture.

Source: Image by Hyun Jung Cho.

Characteristics Resulting From the Architecture

The advantages of pipe-and-filter systems are numerous. They initially enable the designer to comprehend the general input or output behavior of a particular system as a straightforward combination of the particular filter behaviors. They also encourage reuse. As long as the data being communicated among any 2 filters agrees, they may be connected. Third, systems are simple to improve and maintain (Atzori et al., 2012).

Systems already in place may be expanded with new filters, and outdated filters can be upgraded. For the transcription system shown in Figure 6.5, for instance, the word recognition element may be swapped out for elements that can recognize new transmissions in German and French with an appropriate error rate for data acquisition. Data processing is done in stages. This allows the system to interpret large input data streams. The audio transcription machine, for instance, is capable of processing hours' worth of unconstrained radio and television news broadcasts. Additionally, they allow for specific types of specialized analysis like performance and deadlock analysis. Furthermore, they enable concurrent execution by default. Every filter can be designed as a distinct task and may run concurrently with other filters (Locke, 1992). Such systems do, although, also have some drawbacks. Firstly, pipe-and-filter systems frequently result in batch-processing organization. Since filters are independent and may process data progressively, the designer should consider every filter as offering a full modification of input information to output data. Pipe-and-filter systems are often not capable of handling interactive applications due to their transformational nature. Maintaining correspondence among 2 distinct but connected streams may also pose a challenge. Depending upon how they are implemented, they might make data transmission adhere to a lowest common denominator, which would make it more difficult for every filter to interpret and unparsed its data. As a result, efficiency may suffer and writing the filters themselves may become more difficult (Qin et al., 2022).

TIPS

The main software architecture patterns and styles include data-centric, layered, and object-oriented styles.

Sub-Types of the Style

The pipeline is the primary sub-type of this fashion. There isn't a cycle of information flows in pipes- and-filters systems with a pipeline architecture. The architectural design of a pipeline is depicted in Figure 6.5. In actuality, pipelines are used as instances (Fletcher et al., 2013).

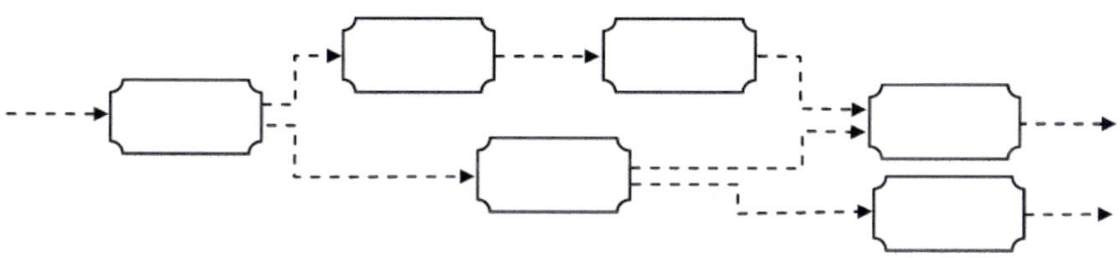

Figure 6.5. An example of a pipeline-architectural design.

Source: Image by geeksforgeeks.org.

Illustrations

We saw 2 illustrations of software systems using the pipe-and-filter architectural design, including voice projection transcription keyboards translation. UNIX shell programs are the most well-known instances of pipe-and-filter designs. By offering run-time techniques for implementing pipes, UNIX supports this fashion. For instance, entering the command 'ls-l more' onto the command prompt of a UNIX system creates a program utilizing the pipe-and-filter architecture. It utilizes the pipe connection to unite the programs "ls" and "more" (Mayer, 2019).

THE BATCH SEQUENTIAL PROCESSING SUB-STYLE

Computational Model

An architectural subtype of the flow of information is batch sequential processing. In addition to the computational model's shared characteristics with the information flow architectural style, elements in the batch sequential architectural style have been separate programs. They are carried out in order, so one runs through to completion before the next begins. Instead of being sent as a stream of individual data elements, the data has been sent among components as a single batch (Shaw et al., 1997).

Design Vocabulary

Processing phases or steps are common names for the computational elements in a batch sequential processing architecture.

Structural Pattern

Architectures for batch sequential processing often have a limited amount of linearly linked steps. But certain batch sequentially processing systems have loops that repeatedly perform particular processing operations a set amount of times (Arronte & Gómez, 2021).

Characteristics Resulting From the Architecture

Almost all of the benefits of the information flow architectural style, particularly the modifiability and reusability, are carried over into batch sequential processing structures. Additionally, running the components one after another eliminates complex problems with synchronization between them. However, since the elements don't operate simultaneously, the system's efficiency cannot be as good as that of other information flow systems. Particularly, it frequently is unable to handle continuous input streams having unbounded lengths (Huang et al., 2019).

Examples

The transaction processing system shown in Figure 6.6 is an illustration of batch sequential processing, wherein data is saved on tapes as it is passed from one stage to the next.

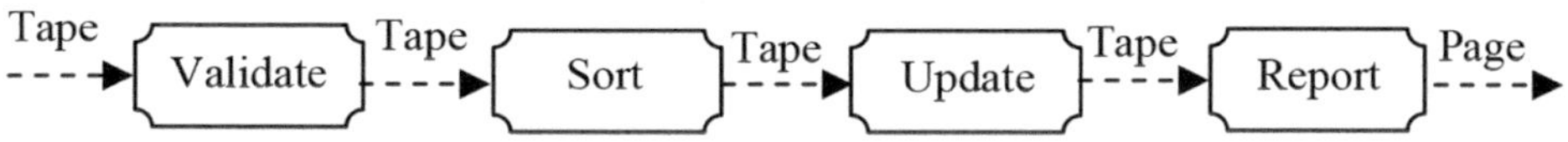

Source: Image by L. M. Honorio.

Figure 6.6. An illustration of the batch sequential processing paradigm.

There are four parts to the system. Every transaction saved on a tape is verified by the Validate element to ensure its legitimacy. All valid transactions are stored on another tape after the invalid transactions have been removed. Whenever validation has been finished, the Sort element is put to use. All of the transactions that were written to the tape in the previous phase are read in, and they are then sorted by the time that they were issued. The outcome is then recorded on a different tape. All transactions placed on the tape should be valid and presented in the order that prior transactions have been listed first because this phase comes after the validation process has been completed (Patro et al., 2017).

Upon categorizing the transactions, the Update element processes each one individually by the order they are placed on the tape created by the Sort element, updating the contents of a business database. The outcomes of the update are captured on a different tape that was fed into the Report element's last stage of processing to create a summary report. Compilers primarily employ batch sequential processing techniques. Figure 6.7 shows a condensed perspective of the compiler architecture (Locke, 1992).

The modules' source code, which takes the shape of a string of characters kept in a text file, is read into by the lexical analysis. Every token in the generated sequence indicates a lexical component in the source code, and a table of identifiers is also produced. The outputs are kept in various folders. The syntax analysis phase then parses the token series into a parsing tree and generates additional tables, such as those that link factors to their kinds, etc. Such files, along with files that were already created during the compilation of the imported modules, are passed to the syntax analysis phase. Additionally, files containing these outputs are kept for use by the code generation stage. Such files are read during the code creation phase, which also generates object codes and additional tables, like those containing details about the exported methods, variables, and kinds for the linker program. Additionally, files are kept for such outputs. The optional *optimization* phase increases the object code's effectiveness. Mistakes in the program's source code could be found during every stage. When this occurs, an error report can be produced and put into a file or displayed on the screen. When a mistake is found, the compilation would stop (Qin et al., 2022).

Figure 6.7. Compiler architecture simplification.

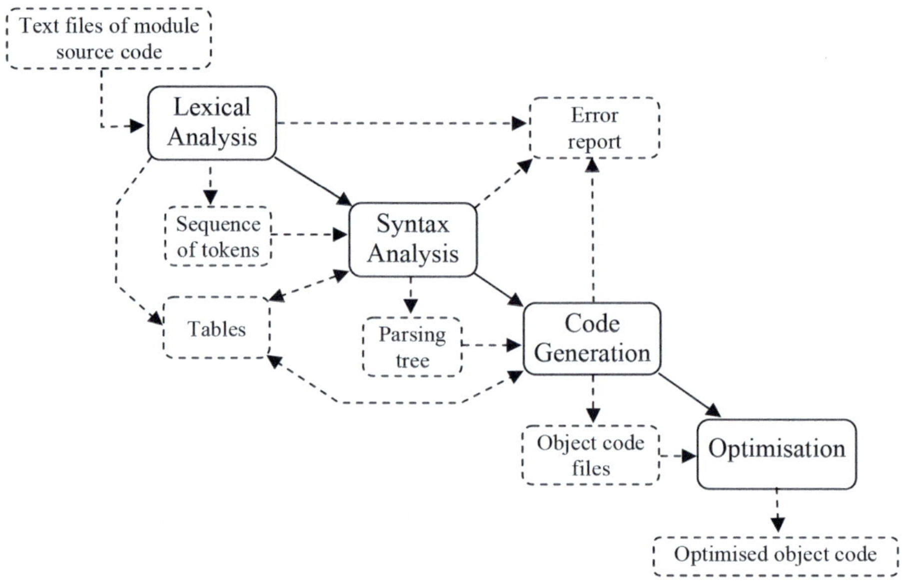

Source: Image by Rodrigo Rocha.

INDEPENDENT COMPONENTS

Because of the convenience of integrating independent elements into a system, the architectural style of independent elements has recently received growing interest because of its strong support for software reuse and evolution. It has a lot of subtypes of style, including multiagent systems, event-based implicit invocation, communicative processes, and subtypes of style (Beckmann, 2012).

The General Independent Components Style

Computational Model

A collection of elements that connect via messages make up an independent element architecture. They exchange data but normally do not have direct control over one another. When employing the publish or subscribe paradigm, the message can be sent to specifically identified participants or distributed to unidentified users (Xie et al., 2022).

Design Vocabulary

In a system with separate elements, each component should be able to be executed. If the element is active, they have been frequently referred to as processes. If not, they are frequently just referred to as modules. The vocabulary for each particular sub-type of the architectural style, which would be covered subsequently, is different (Bell & Sejnowski, 1997).

Structural Pattern

Regarding the topological structures of the systems, there isn't an overarching pattern of system structure that can be applied to the entire class of architectural styles that utilize independent element components (Shapiro & Faloutsos, 2006).

Essential Invariants

Message passing is the only method that may be used to communicate information between the different components, which is a fundamental invariant that is shared by all subtypes of the independent element style. There is not a single state variable or piece of data that is shared among the components. Elements are considered autonomous when it comes to the sense that they do not exert any form of control over one another. This means that a single element can't decide whether or not the recipient of a message would then take an action in response to it, nor can it decide which action, if any, should be taken. When more than one element receives a message, the sender is unable to choose among the receivers who would respond to the message initially because they all received the message simultaneously (Iadecola et al., 1994).

Characteristics Derived From the Architecture

Independent element architectures enable modification by disconnecting different compute components. It allows for the simultaneous or even parallel execution of the elements on several computers connected to a network. By distributing the workload between the servers, which are often powered by more powerful hardware, and the clients, the system may be scaled. To provide load balancing, different software functional element partitions that could be distributed among computers in a two-tier client-server system have been shown in Figure 6.8 (Tabassum et al., 2017).

Decoupling computing into separate components also makes it easier to integrate the components. At two levels, it greatly encourages system evolution. A component can be changed at the element level without impacting how other elements in the system interact with it. At the system level, adding new elements to the system is simple, for example, by just identifying it for the system's events. The fundamental drawback of independent element architectures results from the components' independence from one another. A component cannot expect that the recipients would respond when it sends a message or declares an event to another element. Designing and implementing interaction protocols that all elements can adhere to will help solve this issue. The system can have significant overhead as a result. Furthermore, because of elements' autonomous behavior, thinking about correctness might sometimes be challenging (Fu et al., 2011).

Sub-Types of the Style

The communicative process systems and event-based implicit invoke systems are two sub-types of independent element architectural styles that will be studied in depth. There have also been interrupt-driven procedure systems and multicast messages having dynamic binding systems in addition to such subtypes. A subtype of the independent element style is multi-agent systems. They evolved from artificial intelligence research and have recently received a lot of attention (Qian et al., 2015).

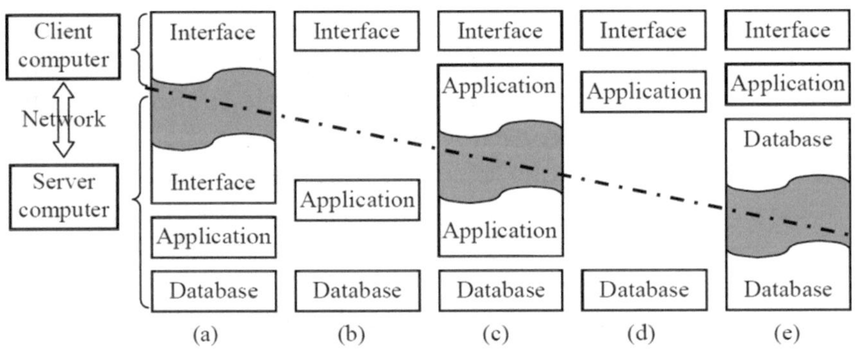

Figure 6.8. Distribution of software's functional components to server and client computers may be divided in this way.

Source: Image by spiceworks.com.

Examples

The client-server architecture is a perfect illustration of the principal components of architecture and may be regarded as a subtype of the architectural style. As depicted in Figure 6.9, a client-server system typically includes several consumers and one or many servers (Spector et al., 1980).

A consumer element sends messages to a server to request that the server execute a specific computing activity. The server determines whether to do the requested task after obtaining such a request and if it does, the conclusion or outcome of the operation is communicated to the client via a message. Web- based applications provide several real instances of such client-server systems (Cacioppo & Berntson, 1999).

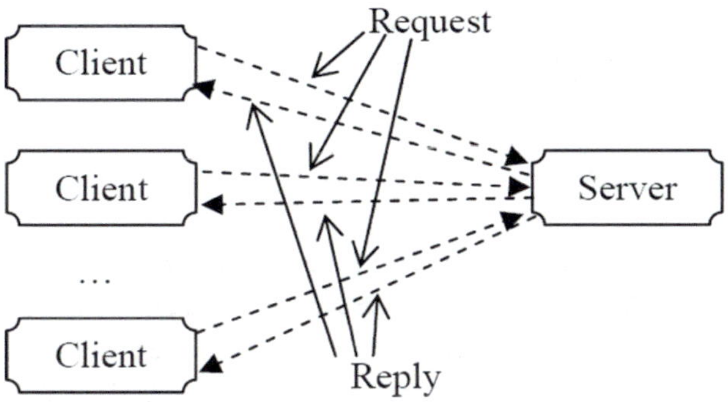

Source: Image by teachcomputerscience.com.

Figure 6.9. Client-server structure.

THE EVENT-BASED IMPLICIT INVOCATION SYSTEMS SUB-STYLE

Control is an element of the paradigm for event-based systems, which are a subtype of independent element architectures (Seo, 2008).

Computational Model

A ceremony-based implicit invocation system uses individual elements to declare data that they desire to convey with its environment, which consists of a group of nameless elements. These additional elements might signal an interest throughout this data class. If they do, they have been called upon and given the data when it appears. Message managers are frequently used in event systems to govern the communication between the elements by calling an element when a message is sent to it. Since it dissociates element execution from knowing each other's locations and names, this approach is significant. Element integration is made simpler by this decoupling (Mui et al., 2002).

Design Vocabulary

The act of publishing data by an element is commonly referred to as *publishing* the data. Such an announcement has been referred to as an *event*. *Subscription* is the act of a component registering its interests in a certain set of data. In an event-based implicit invocation system, a message manager is also frequently referred to as an *event handler*. It is in charge of keeping track of all parts that expressed an interest in particular events. The event handler delivers the information to such registered elements when an event occurs (Cairns & Haynes, 2019).

Structural Pattern

Figure 6.10 depicts the overall structural layout of event-based implicit invocation systems. In event- based implicit invocation systems, an element's interface typically includes several events that it may raise and several functions or processes that other elements may directly invoke. Thus, elements can directly communicate with one another through function/process calls in addition to messages passing through the event handler (Pavlidis, 2013).

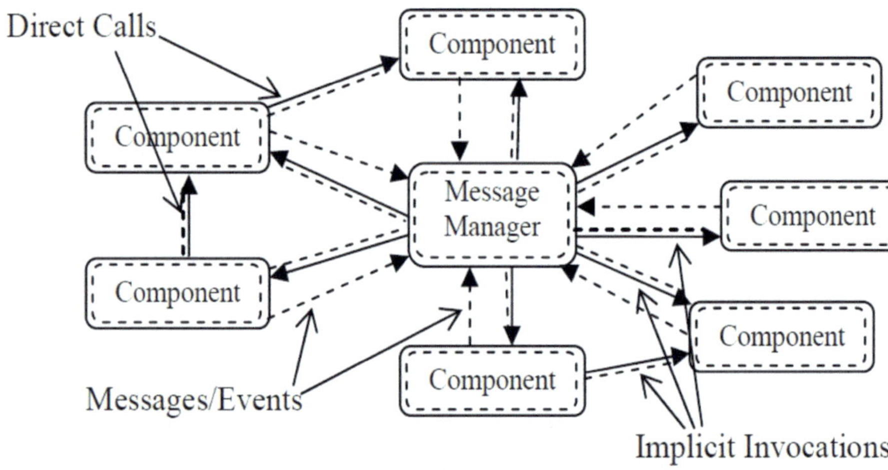

Figure 6.10. Structure of event-based implicit invocation systems.

Source: Image by Jeremy Bradbury.

Properties Derived From the Architecture

Event-based implicit invocation style, a sub-type of independent elements architectural designs, inherits all the benefits and drawbacks of independent elements architectures. Reuse and software evolution has been significantly supported by the implicit invocation architecture. Essentially by registering it for the functions of that system, a new element may be incorporated into the system as it is running. The connections of other system elements are unaffected when one element is switched out for another one or more elements. Such a replacement is possible without pausing the system's operation. For systems like continuous procedure control systems that must function flawlessly and constantly for an extended length of time, this quality is very crucial (Grabowski & Schneider, 2007).

Examples

Database management systems to guarantee different consistency limitations, visual user interface systems to segregate displays of information from applications that handle the data, and other typical instances of software systems in the event-based implicit invocation style may be found.

The comprehensive programming environment Domain, which blends a range of tools including an event-based implicit invocation architecture, is an instance of this. As seen in Figure 6.11, the system's structure is explained. The Field system is made up of several programming tools, some of which are listed below, as seen in Figure 6.11 (Newitt et al., 2002):

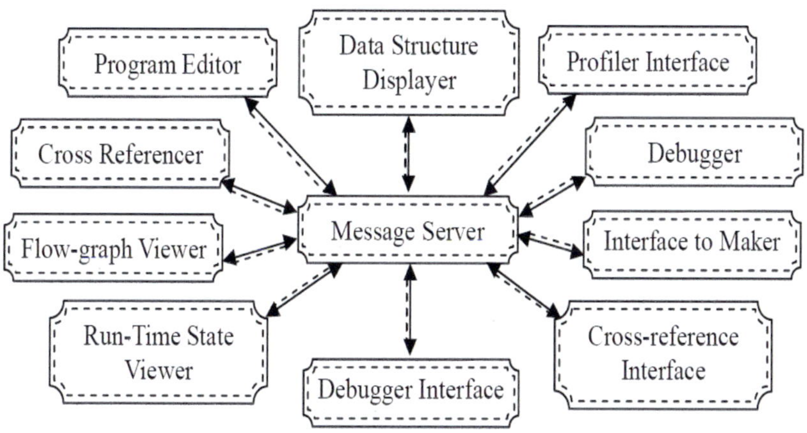

Figure 6.11. The design of the field programming environment architecture.

Source: Image by Laura K. Dillon.

- **Program Editor:** An extensible editor with complete functionality for C and Pascal code. Every line of code can have annotations associated with it. Annotations may be added, deleted, and searched for. The editor's window may have multiple active windows at once (Zadeck, 1984).
- **Cross References:** It gathers information on a software system in a relational database. Cross-referencing creates

the database for the first time. Only such source files which have been modified are then gradually rescanned.

- **Cross Reference Interface:** A menu-based user interface that lets users fill out dialog boxes to do simple database queries. It's utilized by other devices to execute instructions like "find and show the declaration of this process" and "create thresholds at all allocations to this parameter," etc. It is also utilized by the debugger to execute high-level commands (Lennox & Cooke, 2014).
- **Data Structure Displayer:** This is integrated as a combination of tools that graphically display a data structure and specify how the data structure must be displayed, correspondingly. It is an adaptation from another programming environment (Sammon, 1969).
- **Flow Graph Viewer:** It shows a hierarchical flow graph of a software section that the consumer has interactively chosen.
- **Run-Time State Viewer:** Whenever the program is executed for debugging, it shows different forms of run-time state, including the run-time stack, the values of expressions, parameters, and debugger occurrences like breakpoints. The system contains more tools as well. The readers are directed to (McKinley, 2004) for additional information. The component known as the Message Server is what connects these tools. Every tool register with the server a set of signal patterns. By transmitting letters to the server and getting those that fit their recorded patterns, devices can communicate. The Field system's message management is the message server. The messages are text messages of varying lengths. The message server retransmits them to other tools after the tools have transmitted them. A conventional event-based implicit invocation system is present in this system. By allowing independent instruments to collaborate using the basic convention of implicit invocation, the Field system was able to attain tremendous flexibility (Kasten & McKinley, 2004).

THE COMMUNICATING PROCESSES SUB-STYLE

The architectural design of communication processes is another kind of independent element of architecture. Such multi-process systems are the traditional ones (Janusheva & Jurukovska, 2017).

Computational Model

In a system with communicating processes, active procedures make up its constituent parts. They use established lines of communication to communicate with one another. To coordinate their actions and establish mutual exclusion when gaining access to shared resources, they relay messages to one another.

Design Vocabulary

The parts of a system having communicating processes have been referred to as processes, and they exchange messages among themselves through ports or channels of communication. The system may leverage a variety of various communication systems that are offered by distinct operating systems. Synchronous communication among procedures is when two processes engage in communication at a similar time to send a message between one of them. Alternately, the communication may be asynchronous, in which a single message is sent without the receiver's participation (Rafe & Hajvali, 2014).

Whenever a message has only been received by one particular process, communications between processes may also be point-to-point or one-to-one. Alternatively, it may be broadcast to a subset of the processes or all procedures in the system.

Structural Pattern

A system of processes linked by channels of communication makes up the basic framework of systems that communicate with one another. The key distinction between it and event-based implicit invocation is that no event handler is in charge of redistributing the messages across the processes. Although communicative process systems having constant channels of communication may be considered a sub-style of the information flow architectural style, they typically contain a more intricate information flow between procedures instead of just more or less simple patterns of information flow. Instead of only the information to be processed, the messages transferred between processes typically include requests to carry out specific activities (Wong et al., 2008).

Sub-Types of the Style

A famous sub-type of communicating processes is a client-server architecture. One or many clients, who are often spread out across a network, are served data by a server. The server receives a call from the consumer and response to it either asynchronously or synchronously.

CALL AND RETURN

For the past 30 years, call-and-return architecture has dominated the design of big systems. The traditional and contemporary programming paradigms directly facilitate this. A range of sub-types of the style has arisen, like object-oriented systems, layered systems, main programs and subroutines having shared data, and others. Each of such has unique and intriguing characteristics (Durand, 1987).

The General Call and Return Style

Computational Model

A call and return style software system is broken down into smaller sections to handle complications and aid in modifiability. Usually, there is just one control thread. When an element receives control from another element it begins to operate, and when it completes, it returns control to the original element. It may hand off control to other elements during execution. Every component typically has a specific entry where its implementation begins. Exits are permanent areas within a component when executions come to an end. Subroutines are the name for these parts. Invocations or subroutine calls are the control transfers between components; they frequently include the parameter-passing of data. Typically, the main program seems to be the part of the program that has the gateway. It manages how subroutines are executed. In a system of this type, there might also be a few passive data components that house shared data that the subroutines can access. Global parameters or the worldwide state of the system are terms used to describe shared data that all elements may access (Di Tella & Rotemberg, 2018).

The function or procedure feature in virtually all higher-level programming languages directly supports the call and return style's hierarchical organization and dynamic control of implementation. As a result, subroutines are also known as processes and function calls to subroutines are known as function/procedure calls.

Structural Pattern

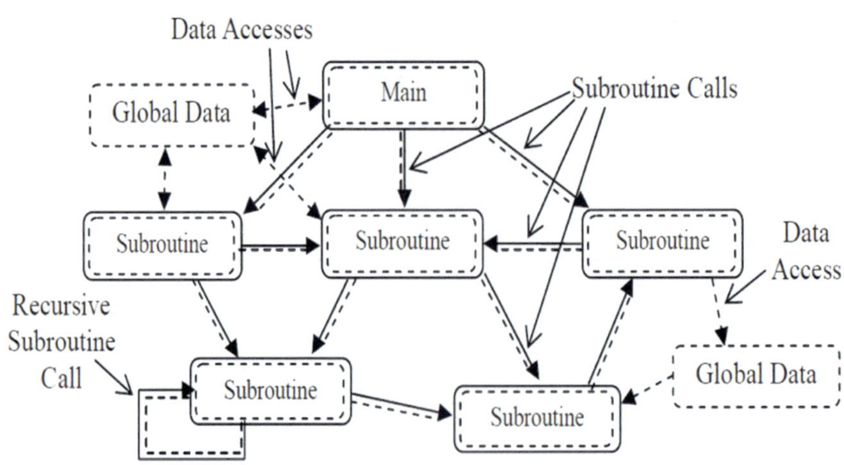

Figure 6.12. Call and return architectures' structure.

Source: Image by Vincent Pijpers.

As depicted in Figure 6.12, a call and return system may have any topological structure which connects subroutines through subroutine calls. Nonetheless, this is normal practice to organize the links amongst subroutines in specific patterns and to bundle multiple interconnected subroutines into program components. This produces several subtypes of the style (Asness, 2016).

Design Vocabulary

As depicted in Figure 6.13, it is typical practice in the design of call and returns systems to structure subroutines hierarchically. The main program and subroutine having shared data is a common name for a call-and-return architecture with a hierarchical structure. In actuality, it is a subtype of the call and return style. Figure 6.13 depicts the structure of these types of systems.

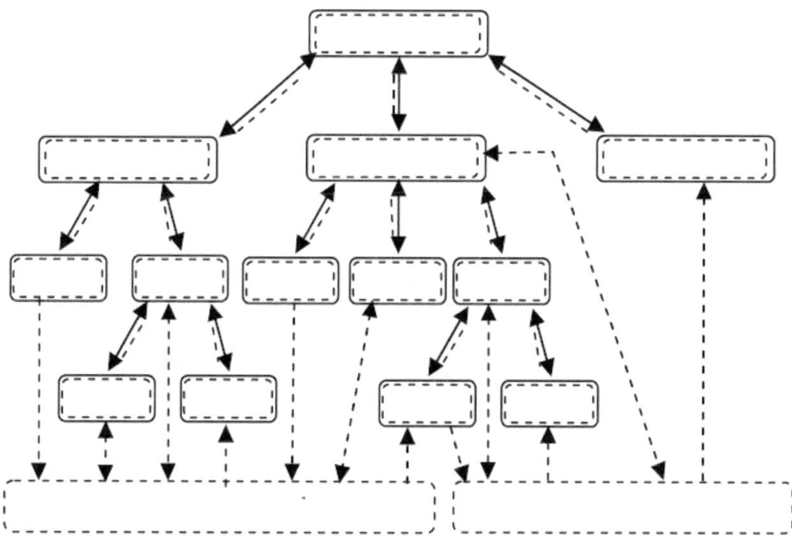

Figure 6.13. The shared data architecture of the main program and subroutine.

Source: Image by Vincent Pijpers.

A module is composed of a collection of subroutines which use the same data stored in a call-and-return system. The module feature in nearly all high-level programming languages allows for granular control over the accessibility of procedures, parameters, and functions specified in a module, allowing execution details to be concealed from module consumers. Figure 6.14 depicts the modular organization of call and return structures (Kelsey, 1995).

Loose coupling and strong cohesion serve as guiding principles for arranging subroutines into modules. High cohesiveness indicates that the subroutines inside a module must be well interconnected with the number of calls among them and, maybe more crucially, the frequency with which one subroutine calls the other during execution. Loose coupling indicates that there are minimal linkages across the boundary of modules, both statically in consideration of the connections among subroutines of various modules and interactively with the frequency of subroutine calls over the module boundary at runtime. The fundamental concept of this principle also holds for the division of software into subroutines. We prefer a subroutine to contain lots of internal interaction (strong cohesion) and minimal external interactions (weak binding) with other subroutines. Granularity is a different idea associated with the modular structure of a software application through the division of software into subroutines and the collection of subroutines into modules. A module's (or a subroutine's) size shouldn't be too tiny as this will lead to a lot of interactions between them. Additionally, it shouldn't be too big because it would negate the advantages of modularity (Boutier & Kerneis, 2012).

Properties Derived From the Architecture

As was previously mentioned, complexity is one of the fundamental reasons why software development is challenging. Separation of concerns is a fundamental tool for dealing with complexity.

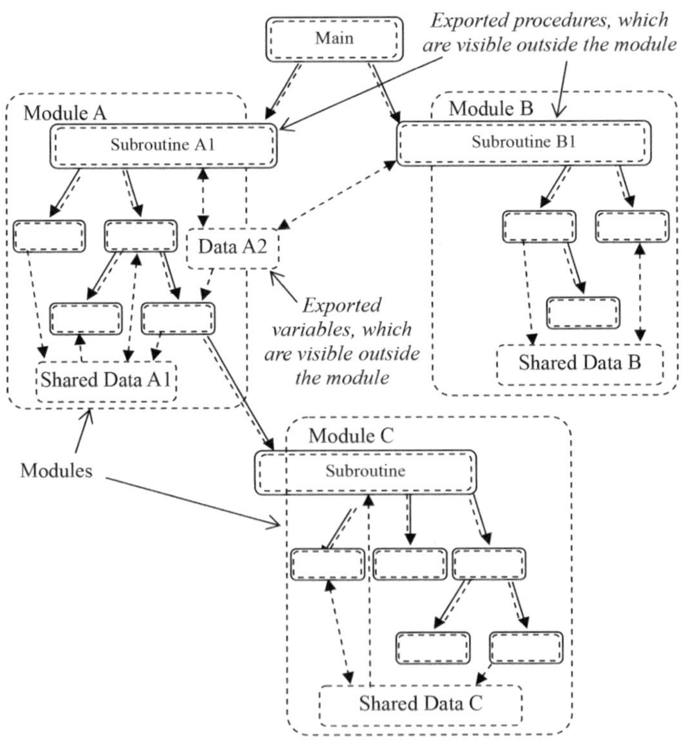

Figure 6.14. Architecture with a modular call and return design.

Source: Image by brainkart.com.

Programmers can divide the worries involved in creating a huge system into a variety of simpler programming difficulties by breaking a complex program down into subroutines. Thus, by working together as a team of software engineers, each of whom works with a smaller and simpler sub-problem, bigger-scale software systems may be created (Duta & Grust, 2020).

ACTIVITY 6.1.

Draw the different illustration of data flow.

Software engineers can further break down even larger-scale systems into controlled-sized parts thanks to the idea of hiding data and the modular programming capability, which also offers a more flexible way to integrate them into a system. Additionally, the system's modifiability was improved by this. A procedure's internal structure can be changed without impacting the interface, and this won't have an impact on the entire system. Similar to how changing a module's body without changing its interface won't change the entire system (Shackleton & Wojakowski, 2002).

SUMMARY

In this chapter, we examined a number of software architectural styles. The following summaries the interrelationships between the software architectural styles discussed in this chapter.

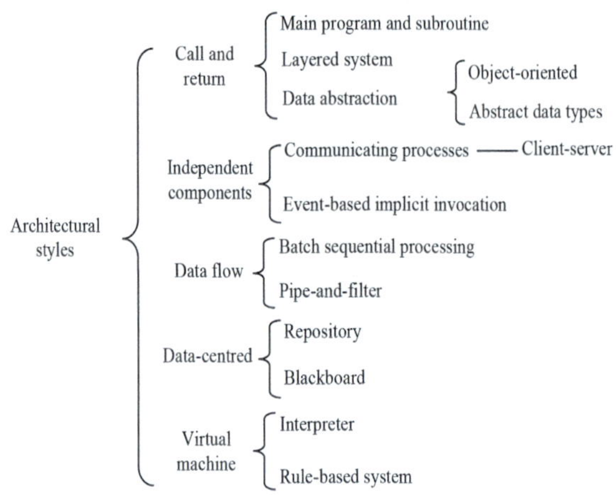

REVIEW QUESTIONS

1. Briefly explain the typical architectural styles.
2. What do you understand by the term "data flow"?
3. What do you understand by the term "independent components"?

MULTIPLE CHOICE QUESTIONS

1. Architectural styles are composed of which of the following?

a. A set of component types that perform some function at run-time
b. A topological layout of these components indicating their run-time inter relationships
c. A set of semantic constraints
d. All of the mentioned

2. Which architectural style goal is to achieve integrability?

a. Data flow architecture
b. Call and return architecture
c. Data centered architectures
d. None of the mentioned

3. Which architectural style goal is to achieve modifiability with scalability?

a. Data flow architecture

b. Call and return architecture
c. Virtual machine architecture
d. None of the mentioned

4. Type of system in which data is collected together as a single unit is considered as

a. batch processing
b. batch unit
c. batch system
d. batch functioning

5. Architectural styles is composed of which of the following?

a. A set of component types that perform some function at run-time
b. A topological layout of these components indicating their run-time inter relationships
c. A set of semantic constraints
d. All of the mentioned

Answers to Multiple Choice Questions

1. (c) 2. (c) 3. (b) 4. (a) 5. (d)

REFERENCES

1. Allen, R. J., (1997). *A Formal Approach to Software Architecture*. Carnegie Mellon university.
2. Amit, Y., & Geman, D., (1999). A computational model for visual selection. *Neural Computation, 11*(7), 1691–1715.
3. Arronte, A. A., & Gómez, F., (2021). *Motivic Pattern Classification of Music Audio Signals Combining Residual and LSTM Networks*. EEE.
4. Asness, C. S., (2016). Invited editorial comment: The siren song of factor timing aka "smart beta timing" aka "style timing." *The Journal of Portfolio Management, 42*(5), 1–6.
5. Atzori, L., Iera, A., Morabito, G., & Nitti, M., (2012). The social internet of things (SIoT)–when social networks meet the internet of things: Concept, architecture and network characterization. *Computer Networks, 56*(16), 3594–3608.
6. Beckmann, C. F., (2012). Modeling with independent components. *Neuroimage, 62*(2), 891–901. Bell, A. J., & Sejnowski, T. J., (1997). The "independent components" of natural scenes are edge filters. *Vision Research, 37*(23), 3327–3338.
7. Boutier, M., & Kerneis, G., (2012). *Generating Events with Style*. arXiv preprint arXiv:1210.4263.

8. Cacioppo, J. T., & Berntson, G. G., (1999). The affect system: Architecture and operating characteristics. *Current Directions in Psychological Science, 8*(5), 133–137.

9. Cairns, P., Power, C., Barlet, M., & Haynes, G., (2019). Future design of accessibility in games: A design vocabulary. *International Journal of Human-Computer Studies, 131*, 64–71.

10. Chithra, P., Chandrikha, C., Kannan, A. S., Sundararajan, S., Srinivasan, V., & Jayanthi, V., (2012). Clinical and life style variables in functional dyspepsia and its sub-types. *Tropical Gastroenterology, 33*(1), 33–38.

11. Choi, T. M., (2013). Optimal return service charging policy for a fashion mass customization program. *Service Science, 5*(1), 56–68.

12. Coch, H., (1998). Bioclimatism in vernacular architecture. *Renewable and Sustainable Energy Reviews, 2*(1,2), 67–87.

13. Dashofy, E. M., Van, D. H. A., & Taylor, R. N., (2001). A highly-extensible, XML-based architecture description language. In: *Proceedings Working IEEE/IFIP Conference on Software Architecture* (pp. 103–112). IEEE.

14. De Muga, B. J., (2010). *Implementation of a 2D Graph Viewer* (Vol, 1 pp, 13–19).

15. Di Tella, R., & Rotemberg, J. J., (2018). Populism and the return of the "paranoid style": Some evidence and a simple model of demand for incompetence as insurance against elite betrayal. *Journal of Comparative Economics, 46*(4), 988–1005.

16. Dimitrov, V., & Koptchev, V., (2010). PSIRP project--publish-subscribe internet routing paradigm: New ideas for future internet. In: *Proceedings of the 11th International Conference on Computer Systems and Technologies and Workshop for PhD Students in Computing on International Conference on Computer Systems and Technologies* (pp. 167–171).

17. Durand, V. M., (1987). "Look homeward angel": A call to return to our (functional) roots. *The Behavior Analyst, 10*(2), 299.

18. Duta, C., & Grust, T., (2020). Functional-Style SQL UDFs with a capital 'F.' In: *Proceedings of the 2020 ACM SIGMOD International Conference on Management of Data* (pp. 1273–1287).

19. Fletcher, K., Parker, G., & Manicavasagar, V., (2013). Cognitive style in bipolar disorder sub-types. *Psychiatry Research, 206*(2, 3), 232–239.

20. Fu, C., Zhang, G., Yang, J., & Liu, X., (2011). Study on the contract characteristics of internet architecture. *Enterprise Information Systems, 5*(4), 495–513.

21. Grabowski, K., & Schneider, G., (2007). Properties and architecture of drugs and natural products revisited. *Current Chemical Biology, 1*(1), 1-115.

22. Huang, J., Ren, Z., Zhao, W. X., He, G., Wen, J. R., & Dong, D., (2019). Taxonomy-aware multi-hop reasoning networks for sequential recommendation. In: *Proceedings of the Twelfth ACM International Conference on Web Search and Data Mining* (pp. 573–581).

23. Iadecola, C. O. S. T. A. N. T. I. N. O., & Zhang, F. A. N. G. Y. I., (1994). Nitric oxide-dependent and- independent components of cerebrovasodilation elicited by

hypercapnia. *American Journal of Physiology-Regulatory, Integrative and Comparative Physiology, 266*(2), R546–R552.

24. Janusheva, V., & Jurukovska, J., (2017). The orthography of the dash in the Macedonian standard language and the journalistic sub-style. *International Journal of Language Academy, 19*(5, 6), 331–342.
25. Kasten, E. P., & McKinley, P. K., (2004). Perimorph: Run-time composition and state management for adaptive systems. In: *24th International Conference on Distributed Computing Systems Workshops, 2004; Proceedings* (pp. 332–337). IEEE.
26. Kelsey, R. A., (1995). A correspondence between continuation passing style and static single assignment form. *ACM SIGPLAN Notices, 30*(3), 13–22.
27. Khedker, U., Sanyal, A., & Sathe, B., (2017). *Data Flow Analysis: Theory and Practice*. CRC Press.
28. Khowaja, K., & Salim, S. S., (2020). A framework to design vocabulary-based serious games for children with autism spectrum disorder (ASD). *Universal Access in the Information Society, 19*(4), 739–781.
29. Kumar, U., Hsieh, H. W., Liu, Y. C., Deng, Z. Y., Chen, K. L., Huang, W. M., & Wu, C. H., (2022).
30. Revealing a highly sensitive sub-ppb-level NO2 gas-sensing capability of novel architecture 2D/0D MoS2/SnS heterostructures with DFT interpretation. *ACS Applied Materials & Interfaces, 14*(28), 32279–32288.
31. Lee, E. A., & Messerschmitt, D. G., (1987). Synchronous data flow. *Proceedings of the IEEE, 75*(9), 1235–1245.
32. Lennox, R., & Cooke, S. J., (2014). State of the interface between conservation and physiology: A bibliometric analysis. *Conservation Physiology, 2*(1).
33. Liao, C. F., Bao, S. W., Cheng, C. J., & Chen, K., (2017). On design issues and architectural styles for blockchain-driven IoT services. In: *2017 IEEE International Conference on Consumer Electronics-Taiwan (ICCE-TW)* (pp. 351, 352). IEEE.
34. Lieberherr, K. J., & Holland, I. M., (1989). Assuring good style for object-oriented programs. *IEEE Software, 6*(5), 38–48.
35. Locke, C. D., (1992). Software architecture for hard real-time applications: Cyclic executives vs. fixed priority executives. *Real-Time Systems, 4*(1), 37–53.
36. Mayer, R. E., (2019). Illustrations that instruct. In: *Advances in Instructional Psychology* (pp. 253– 284). Routledge.
37. Mui, L., Mohtashemi, M., & Halberstadt, A., (2002). A computational model of trust and reputation. In: *Proceedings of the 35th Annual Hawaii International Conference on System Sciences* (pp. 2431–2439). IEEE.
38. Newitt, D. C., Majumdar, S., Van, R. B., Von, I. G., Harris, S. T., Genant, H. K., & MacDonald, B., (2002). *In vivo* assessment of architecture and micro-finite element analysis derived indices of mechanical properties of trabecular bone in the radius. *Osteoporosis International, 13*(1), 6– 17.

39. Nyman, T., Ekberg, J. E., Davi, L., & Asokan, N., (2017). CFI CaRE: Hardware-supported call and return enforcement for commercial microcontrollers. In: *International Symposium on Research in Attacks, Intrusions, and Defenses* (pp. 259–284). Springer, Cham.
40. Patro, S., Potey, M., & Golhani, A., (2017). Comparative study of middleware solutions for control and monitoring systems. In: *2017 Second International Conference on Electrical, Computer and Communication Technologies (ICECCT)* (pp. 1–10). IEEE.
41. Paulston, C. B., (1970). Structural pattern drills: A classification. *Foreign Language Annals, 4*(2), 187– 193.
42. Pavlidis, T., (2013). *Structural Pattern Recognition* (Vol. 1). Springer.
43. Qian, W., Zhu, J., Zhang, Y., Wu, X., & Yan, F., (2015). Condiment-derived 3D architecture porous carbon for electrochemical supercapacitors. *Small, 11*(37), 4959–4969.
44. Qin, H., Zhang, B., Wang, C., Wang, D., & Ou, X., (2022). Engineering the pin effect through selective doping and architecture design towards high-rate sodium storage performance. *Energy Storage Materials, 52*, 189–200.
45. Rafe, V., & Hajvali, M., (2014). A reliable architectural style for designing pervasive healthcare systems. *Journal of Medical Systems, 38*(9), 1–10.
46. Raney, R. K., Spudis, P. D., Bussey, B., Crusan, J., Jensen, J. R., Marinelli, W., & Winters, H., (2010). The lunar mini-RF radars: Hybrid polarimetric architecture and initial results. *Proceedings of the IEEE, 99*(5), 808–823.
47. Sackett, J. A., (1977). The meaning of style in archaeology: A general model. *American Antiquity, 42*(3), 369–380.
48. Sammon, J. W., (1969). A nonlinear mapping for data structure analysis. *IEEE Transactions on Computers, 100*(5), 401–409.
49. Sannier, N., Adedjouma, M., Sabetzadeh, M., & Briand, L., (2017). An automated framework for detection and resolution of cross references in legal texts. *Requirements Engineering, 22*(2), 215–237.
50. Seo, C., (2008). *Prediction of Energy Consumption Behavior in Component-Based Distributed Systems*. University of Southern California.
51. Seo, C., Edwards, G., Popescu, D., Malek, S., & Medvidovic, N., (2009). A framework for estimating the energy consumption induced by a distributed system's architectural style. In: *Proceedings of the 8th International Workshop on Specification and Verification of Component-Based Systems* (pp. 27–34).
52. Sevcikova, H., Machovcakova, E., & Fabian, R., (2016). Typical architectural elements of socialist realism in Czech Republic. In: *3rd International Multidisciplinary Scientific Conference on Social Sciences and Arts SGEM 2016* (pp. 853–860).
53. Shackleton, M., & Wojakowski, R., (2002). The expected return and exercise time of Merton-style real options. *Journal of Business Finance & Accounting, 29*(3, 4), 541–555.

54. Shalunts, G., Haxhimusa, Y., & Sablatnig, R., (2012). Architectural style classification of domes. In: *International Symposium on Visual Computing* (pp. 420–429). Springer, Berlin, Heidelberg.
55. Shapiro, A., Cao, Y., & Faloutsos, P., (2006). Style components. In: *Graphics Interface* (Vol. 2006, pp. 33–39).
56. Shaw, M., & Clements, P., (1997). A field guide to boxology: Preliminary classification of architectural styles for software systems. In: *Proceedings Twenty-First Annual International Computer Software and Applications Conference (COMPSAC'97)* (pp. 6–13).
57. Shaw, M., & Garlan, D., (1996). *Software Architecture: Perspectives on an Emerging Discipline*. Prentice-Hall, Inc.
58. Spector, S. A., Gardiner, P. F., Zernicke, R. F., Roy, R. R., & Edgerton, V. R., (1980). Muscle architecture and force-velocity characteristics of cat soleus and medial gastrocnemius: Implications for motor control. *Journal of Neurophysiology, 44*(5), 951–960.
59. Sussman, G. J., (1973). *A Computational Model of Skill Acquisition.* (Vol,1 pp. 6–13)
60. Tabassum, H., Guo, W., Meng, W., Mahmood, A., Zhao, R., Wang, Q., & Zou, R., (2017). Metal- organic frameworks derived cobalt phosphide architecture encapsulated into B/N Co-doped graphene nanotubes for all pH value electrochemical hydrogen evolution. *Adv. Energy Mater, 7*(9), 1601671.
61. Taubes, C. H., (2001). The Seiberg–Witten invariants and 4–manifolds with essential tori. *Geometry & Topology, 5*(2), 441–519.
62. Thoen, F., & Catthoor, F., (2012). *Modeling, Verification and Exploration of Task-Level Concurrency in Real-Time Embedded Systems*. Springer Science & Business Media.
63. Wang, Z. J., & Xu, X. F., (2010). Classifications and comparisons of service architectural styles. *International Journal of Services Sciences, 3*(4), 269–292.
64. Wong, S., Sun, J., Warren, I., & Sun, J., (2008). A scalable approach to multi-style architectural modeling and verification. In: *13th IEEE International Conference on Engineering of Complex Computer Systems (ICECCS 2008)* (pp. 25–34). IEEE.
65. Xie, X., Li, Y., Huang, H., Fu, H., Wang, W., & Guo, Y., (2022). Artistic style discovery with independent components. In: *Proceedings of the IEEE/CVF Conference on Computer Vision and Pattern Recognition* (pp. 19870–19879).
66. Xu, J., Huang, F., Yu, Y., Yang, A., & Wang, Y., (2011). SnO2/α-Fe2O3 nanoheterostructure with novel architecture: Structural characteristics and photocatalytic properties. *CrystEngComm, 13*(15), 4873–4877.
67. Youssef, M. I., (1968). Structural pattern of Egypt and its interpretation. *AAPG Bulletin, 52*(4), 601– 614.
68. Zadeck, F. K., (1984). Incremental data flow analysis in a structured program editor. In: *Proceedings of the 1984 SIGPLAN symposium on Compiler Construction* (pp. 14–132).
69. Zhu, H., (2005). *Software Design Methodology: From Principles to Architectural Styles*. Elsevier.

CHAPTER 7

USING STYLES IN DESIGN

UNIT INTRODUCTION

This chapter explores the application of architectural styles to design software. When a design-related problem is presented, we will initially provide a variety of guidelines for selecting an architectural style. The combination of architectural styles to address a design issue is then covered. Finally, we give an example of how to use multiple architectural features to solve a design issue and produce various designs with specific attributes (Zhu, 2005). Additionally, we will analyze the design casually to show how the architectural styles differ.

Learning Objective

At the end of this chapter, students will be able to learn:

- To learn how to design software systems in various architectural styles;
- To understand how architectural styles affect the quality of the software.

Key Terms

- Styles
- Hierarchy
- Heterogeneous styles
- Simultaneously heterogeneous styles
- Frequency vector

CHOICES OF STYLES

Which architectural style for software should you adopt for a given design issue? Numerous architectural designs are frequently appropriate for the calculation required to solve the problem (Shaw, 1995).

The most important quality characteristics in that situation often determine the architectural style. System structure offers the most substantial influence on quality for several quality criteria. As a result, a style that addresses the quality issue should be taken into account. The design expertise in the architectural styles covered in the earlier chapters is compiled in Table 7.1 as a general guideline for selecting an architectural style (Shaw & Clements, 1997).

Table 7.1. Rules for Using Appropriate Architectural Styles

Style	Computational Nature	Quality Concerns
Data flow	The problem that has to be solved has clearly defined and simple to identify input & output information. The purpose of the computation is to generate output directly from input by successively and independently manipulating the input.	Integrability from reasonably simple component interfaces. Reusability through component substitutions to alter functionality.
Batch sequential	Reading and analyzing a single collection of input results in a single output procedure. A collection of progressively interconnected intermediate transformations makes up the input computation (Le Métayer, 1998).	Reusability as well as flexibility, especially when performance isn't a top priority and the complexity associated with synchronization can be decreased.
Pipe-and filter	On-going data streams are transformed as part of the process. The modifications are executed incrementally or on the individual components of the data stream. Before the preceding stage is finished, one transformation may start.	Scalability, especially when processing data streams with infinite lengths as input. Performance, the ability to react to information even before the system has received the entirety of the input data stream.

Call and return	There is a set order to the computations. Waiting for the responses to requests made by other components prevents components from moving forward productively.	Reusability, modifiability, and integrability
Layered systems	There are two types of computational tasks: those that	Portability between computing platforms.
	are particular to the application and those that are generic to numerous applications yet distinctive to the supporting computing platform.	Reuse of a layer of the computer infrastructure that has already been established, such as a software system, network modules, etc.
Main program/subroutine with shared information	The higher-level issue can be resolved by dissecting it into several simpler problems at a reduced level of abstraction, which can then be solved individually, and their solutions combined to solve the higher-level issue (Shaw & Clements, 1997).	By sharing memory with other components, performance, particularly the memory used, holds intermediate results, and can be considerably improved without duplication. Complete direct access to the intermediate results can also speed up access times compared to alternative communication methods. Reusability, particularly when a subroutine resolves a dilemma that commonly arises in the application domain (Le Métayer, 1996).
Data abstraction	Each object has a set range of operations, and computation	Reusability, particularly the utilization of parts that

	depends on a relatively constant variety of these entities.	represent computational objects commonly encountered in the application area. Modifiability is especially important when it comes to modifying computational entities' representations (Galster et al., 2010)

It is important to note that while the rules mentioned above offer a set of guidelines for the use of architectural styles in architectural system designs, it is still a good idea to create multiple architectural solutions to the same problem and then compare and contrast these solutions to fully comprehend the quality attributes of each solution in the unique context of the design problem. Making so many designs and performing many evaluations and comparisons typically leads to a greater knowledge of the design issue and, as a result, better design adjustments. Before a final design decision can be reached to settle on a particular architectural design, this design, review, and modification process may continue for multiple cycles. In this situation, the design guidelines previously covered can be utilized as a rapid guide to exclude some style selections that are manifestly wrong for the issue at hand and to choose potential candidate designs as a first step quickly (Monroe et al., 1997).

Did you Know?

The use of architectural styles is to establish a structure for all the components of the system.

DIFFERENT STYLES USED FOR A COMBINATION

Many software systems don't follow a single design pattern. Instead, to tackle the design issue, it is frequently necessary to blend many design philosophies at the standard of a software system architecture. Heterogeneous styles refer to software systems that do not adhere to a single style. There are three distinct criteria by which architectural styles can be mixed (Fritz et al., 2014).

Hierarchy of Heterogeneous Styles

One architectural style is used at one level of abstraction. In contrast, another is used in designing a component at a higher level in a hierarchical mix of several styles in the architecture of a software system (Lee, 2010).

For instance, at the highest level of abstraction, Java virtual machine (JVM) can be designed using the virtual machine approach, as seen in Chapter 6. The executing engine is the most important part of the architecture. To design this component, we can employ the main program-and-subroutine design pattern. The component comprises a supervisor that chooses which instruction should be carried out while a procedure performs each instruction, as shown in Figure 7.1 (Faulkner, 2000).

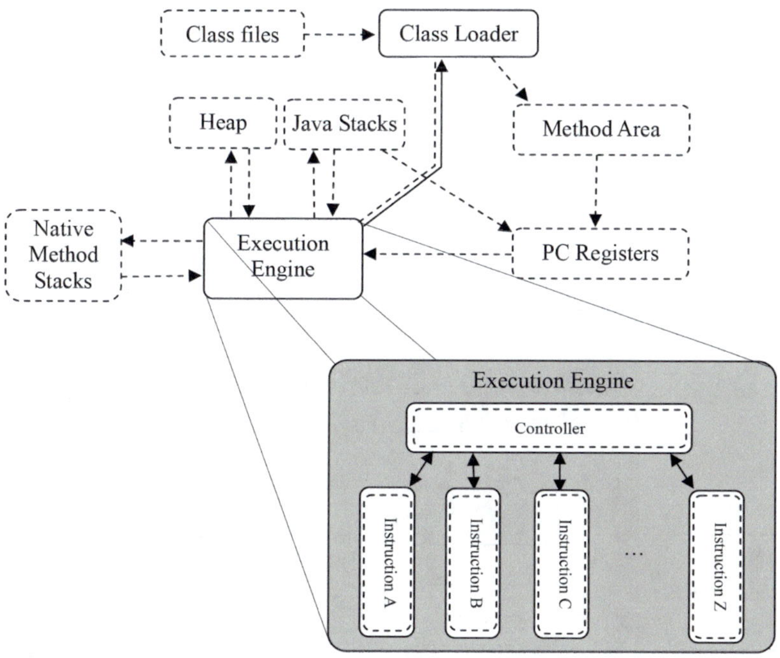

Figure 7.1. JVM (Java virtual machine) in the hierarchy of heterogeneous design.

Source: Image by dzone.com.

Simultaneously Heterogeneous Designs

The previous chapter's discussion of software architectural styles did not result in a confusing taxonomy of software architectures. A software system's architecture is frequently best defined as incorporating various architectural styles. As an illustration, the shared information component of a data-centered architecture is accessed and updated by a variety of clients (Nunez-Yanez et al., 2019). When the data integration is an active source, and every client has its own set of controls, the system can frequently be seen as having an independent component style.

The pipe-and-filter system is yet another illustration of how two architectural styles can overlap. A pipe-and-filter system can be built as a variety of independent operations that wait till input arrives at their ports before operating. A system like this can also be considered an independent component system. The MISOC 2000 system is a real-world illustration of a concurrently heterogeneous system (Pu & Bell, 2017).

Additionally, the system is developed using a mainly object-oriented programming language. The system can also be seen from an object-oriented perspective. When a system, such as MISOC 2000, can be effectively defined in several ways, we can analyze the system as it is represented differently to better understand its characteristics and issues. Each type may offer a unique perspective on the behavior and structural elements. Consequently, it is crucial to comprehend the system from all angles (Figure 7.2) (Verkest et al., 1996).

Figure 7.2. JVM example of heterogeneous locational design.

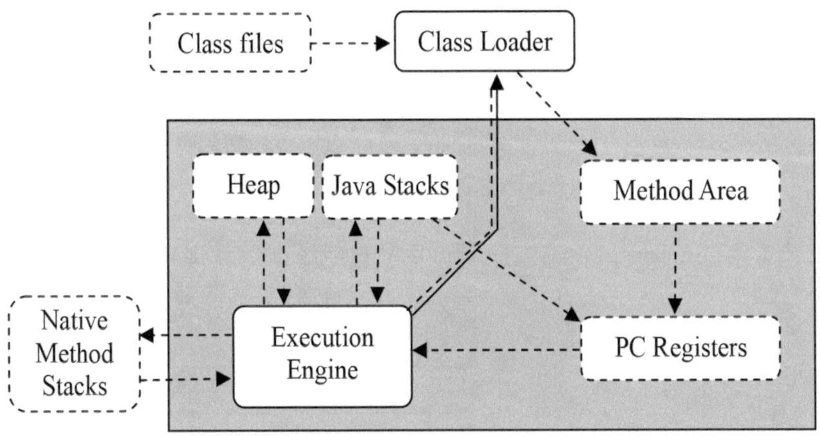

Source: Image by geeksforgeeks.org.

Due to the overlap between several architectural styles used in software system design, several designs in various styles can be combined into one design that shares all of the benefits of those styles while avoiding their drawbacks. Therefore, comprehending diverse contemporary styles is crucial while applying architectural styles. Naturally, there is a chance that integrating several architectural designs could result in a heterogeneous architecture that inherits all the drawbacks of the individual styles but none of their benefits (Mignolet et al., 2003).

KEYWORD FREQUENCY VECTOR (KFV) CASE STUDY

This chapter shows how to create designs in a specific architectural style. To demonstrate the variations in the qualitative characteristics of the designs of various styles, we implement four distinct architectural styles to a single design challenge (Hossny et al., 2018).

Remember

The term "architectural design styles" refer to the features of a building that make it historically distinguishable. Such as the clean lines of mid-century a modern house design, or the intricately sculpted facades of Gothic cathedrals. These features range from form to the materials from which a building is made.

Description of an Issue

A text file's keyword frequency vector (KFV) lists keyword pairs with information on how frequently they appear in the text. It is an accurate reflection of the text's contents. In information extraction, KFVs are frequently employed. As an illustration, the KFV for this passage is as follows (Hou & Chan, 2003).

The vector makes it clear that the chapter concerns a vector, a keyword, a periodicity, and a text. Because the requested words frequently occur in the text, when users make searches for information about the "keyword frequency vector," this chapter satisfies the search. The fact that the KFV is typically more compressed than the actual text is another benefit. Small terms like "a," "the," "is," and "it" should be eliminated from the vector, as we accomplished in the sample above, to make this strategy more effective (Chen & Hsieh, 2006). Additionally, the same term should be viewed as existing in all variants. For instance, in the scenario above, "keywords" & "keyword" are regarded as one word instead of two different words. The ability to automatically derive KFVs from texts is crucial. Designing the architecture of this type of system is our design challenge.

Designs in Several Different Styles

The software program that derives a keyword vector from the text (input) is presently the subject of various architectural designs. The following architectural designs will be used:

- Shared data between the main program and its subroutines;

- Abstract information type;
- Pipe-and-filter;
- Event-driven.

Design 1: Subroutine/Main Program with Shared Data

Starting with a subroutine/main program architectural design—possibly the one we are most accustomed to is how we proceed. In this architectural design, all system components can retrieve information held in memory or on a system file. Subroutines, which are often processes or functions in a programming language, are used to separate the functionality into various parts. The main program serves as the control system and calls these functions and processes.

TIPS

An architectural style is characterized by the features that make a building or other structure notable and historically identifiable. A style may include such elements as form, method of construction, building materials, and regional character.

We break down the computation for this specific design problem into tasks, as shown below. Each task is a separate method or function, or subroutine. The order in which the jobs are executed is managed by a primary program (Jansen & Bosch, 2005).

- **Input:** The initial step is to obtain the input text from a certain device used for input or any other information source and to record it in the proper format in internal memory. Detailed design will dictate how the internal format is created.
- **Delete Small Words:** The text is now removed from the internal memory after the small words were deleted. It will examine each word in the text using a list of brief words.
- **Reduce Word to its Original Form:** The next step is to change every word in the text back to its original form, such as changing "architectures" to "architecture," "calculi" to "calculus," and "following" to "follow." Each word will be broken down into essential components using a dictionary (Aquilani et al., 2001).
- **Statistics of Frequency:** This list of pairings is not necessarily arranged in terms of occurrence; it might be arranged in accordance with keywords' alphabetical order. The outcome will be kept in a different memory storage.
- **Sort According to the Frequency:** A series of pairs containing a word and also its frequency is created by counting the number of times a word appears in the text.
- **Output:** To output the KFV to the device, the suitable output format must first be translated (Singh et al., 2011).

The two shared data formats (text and KFV) are used to convey information across the subroutines, illustrated in Figure 7.3. The architecture's shared data storages are both accessible and editorial by all of the components. The main program regulates access by sequentially calling subroutines (Garlan & Perry, 1995).

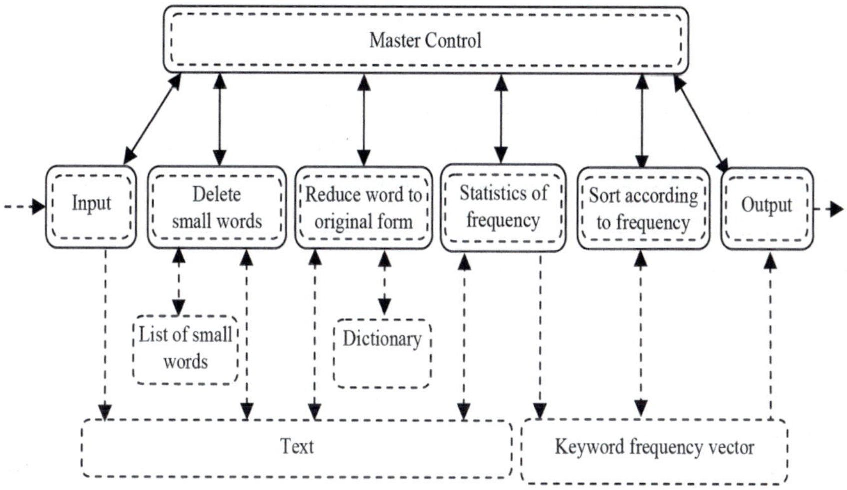

Figure 7.3. Keyword frequency vector in the architecture of shared information/ data storage.

Source: Image by MDPI.

Design 2: Abstract Data Type

The second design embodies abstract data type design principles. This approach encapsulates data queries and operations into abstract information types, which are computational entities that offer the interface for operations on the data while concealing the specifics of their implementation (Jouannaud & Okada, 1997). As a result, computations can be carried out by applying operations to the data, like how basic data types are used. The abstract information type, or the information structures and the procedures that must be performed on the data to accomplish the desired functionality, must be recognized to develop a software system in this manner.

Comparison and Analysis of Data

To contrast the design structures' advantages and disadvantages, we consider the following quality features (Dobrica & Niemela, 2002):

- **Modifiability:** How challenging it is to change the system after it has been put in place to satisfy the new requirements. The following potential modification patterns must be taken into account.

- **System Usage in a Proper Way:** For instance, the KFV can be extracted incrementally as the text is read from the input device, paragraph by paragraph, after each one has been read. It can also be extracted on command when the KFV is needed (Medvidovic & Taylor, 2000).
- **Description of Input/Output Data:** For instance, there are numerous methods for storing text, words, and symbols. The KFV can also be explicitly or implicitly stored, for example, as pairings of the frequency with the index.
- **Function of a System:** For instance, alter the system so that synonyms are treated as the same term, make it interactive, and enable the user to remove and add words from the actual text (Hofmeister et al., 2007).
    - **Performance:** System's efficiency regarding the amount of room required and time required to run the application.
    - **Reusability:** How many components may be reused over and over again? (Sibenik & Kovacic, 2020).

It will be challenging to change the data representation in a system with a shared data structure. If the way text is displayed in the system changes, you will need to update the code in at minimum four places: input, small-word deletion, word reduction to its original form, and frequency statistics. You will be forced to edit a minimum of three components, comprising statistics of frequency, order according to frequency, and output, if you change how the KFV is represented. Additionally, adapting to the changing usage requirements is exceedingly challenging (Immonen & Niemelä, 2008). As an illustration, if the system is designed to analyze a text after reading it all, it should require additional elements and a change to the master control component to analyze the text paragraph by paragraph. Only the dictionary and the reduction component need to be altered to improve the functionality of a system and consider synonyms as identical words. However, the modification will necessitate the removal of the control component and short words if we wish to regard phrases as synonyms of a single word. Things get a lot more challenging (Losavio et al., 2003).

If the user is permitted to add and remove words from the text, it is also challenging to switch the program into interactive mode. The system performs well in terms of time and space—components' limited capacity to be reused results from the numerous environmental considerations they make. Since access to the information is restricted by utilizing the operations described by the abstract information type, it will be relatively simpler to modify the characterization of data in a system with an abstract data type design. The abstract data type will only see local changes. The system will be forced to adjust the controller unit component, as well as maybe the vector & text abstract data types, due to a change in usage. The word abstract data type will need to be modified to support the functionality improvement to regard synonyms as the same word. In this architecture, dealing with sentences is particularly challenging (Martini et al., 2018). Two key abstract data structures will need to be modified for the system to become interactive. The system will operate well in terms of space but less effectively than shared architectural data because many more procedural calls are required. Since abstract information types are more autonomous than shared data types, the constituents are much more reusable as compared to shared architectural data components. If the user requirements change, a system that uses an indirect invocation design is simple to adjust (Babar et al., 2008). Improvements to data modeling are local and generally simpler than shared data design architecture because the data can also be accessible through abstract data types. Although interactive insertion and deletion operations on text are significantly simpler to manage than for abstract data types, feature enhancement is the same. The indirect execution of the extraction makes it harder to control the system's performance. The constituents in this system are very reusable, much like the architecture in the abstract data type style (Barry, 1998).

By swapping out the input filters with newer models, it is simple to modify the operating algorithm in a pipe-and-filter design. A stream's data representation can only be altered by moving two neighboring filters. It shouldn't be too challenging. By making changes to the reduction word filter, the functionality to consider synonyms as the same term can be improved (Card & Agresti, 1988). According to some other architectures, interacting with phrases is more challenging and may require changing the sequence of the filters and their parameters. Making the system interactive so the user can add and remove words from the text is also quite complicated. Since each filter has its internal area to hold the stream, the system's performance is less than ideal in terms of both space & time. Since each filter is very autonomous, the architecture has the benefit of being reusable (Song & Osterweil, 1994).

ACTIVITY 7.1.

Generally speaking, the scalability of a software system refers to the property that the system can be scaled up to a large-scale system, for example to handle a large number of users simultaneously or to store and process a large volume of data.

- Discuss various kinds of specific scalabilities;
- For each kind of scalability, discuss which architectural style will support it.

SUMMARY

The inherent nature of the computations within a certain design challenge and the quality considerations must be taken into account when deciding whether to utilize an architectural design. This chapter presents a set of criteria for an appropriate architectural design to help readers make informed selections. To create a better design, making numerous ideas in various styles and carefully comparing them is a smart idea (Goševa-Popstojanova & Trivedi, 2001).

An architectural design can be created by combining various architectural styles. Heterogeneous styles can take one of three different shapes. A component's hierarchical heterogeneity refers to its architectural style, which differs from the traditional architecture of the entire system. When a system may be viewed from two different architectural perspectives at the same time, this is referred to as simultaneous heterogeneity. When a system's components can be seen as belonging to distinct styles, this is known as locational heterogeneity. In software design techniques, combining architectural styles in one design is important. But when it comes, locational variability might lead to poor intellectual integrity if not used appropriately (Perry & Wolf, 1992).

REVIEW QUESTIONS

1. Explain the choices of styles briefly.
2. Explain the keyword frequency vector.

MULTIPLE CHOICE QUESTIONS

1. Which architectural style goal is to achieve Integrability?

a. Data Flow Architecture

b. Call and Return Architecture

c. Data Centered Architectures

d. None of the mentioned

2. Which architectural style goal is to achieve Modifiability with Scalability?

a. Data Flow Architecture

b. Call and Return Architecture

c. Virtual Machine Architecture

d. None of the mentioned

3. Which architectural style goal is to achieve Portability?

a. Data Flow Architecture

b. Call and Return Architecture

c. Virtual Machine Architecture

   d. None of the mentioned

4. **Data Centered architecture is subdivided into which of the following subtypes?**
   a. Repository and Blackboard
   b. Batch Sequential, Pipes and Filters
   c. All of the mentioned
   d. None of the mentioned
5. **Which of the following type has the main goal to achieve Modifiability?**
   a. Main program and subroutine Architecture
   b. Remote Procedure Call system
   c. Object Oriented or abstract data type system
   d. Main program and subroutine Architecture, Object Oriented or abstract data type system

Answers to Multiple Choice Questions

1. (c) 2. (b) 3. (c) 4. (a) 5. (d)

REFERENCES

1. Aquilani, F., Balsamo, S., & Inverardi, P., (2001). Performance analysis at the software architectural design level. *Performance Evaluation, 45*(2, 3), 147–178.
2. Babar, M. A., Kitchenham, B., & Jeffery, R., (2008). Comparing distributed and face-to-face meetings for software architecture evaluation: A controlled experiment. *Empirical Software Engineering, 13*(1), 39–62.
3. Barry, C. A., (1998). Choosing qualitative data analysis software: Atlas/ti and nudist compared. *Sociological Research Online, 3*(3), 16–28.
4. Card, D. N., & Agresti, W. W., (1988). Measuring software design complexity. *Journal of Systems and Software, 8*(3), 185–197.
5. Chen, R. C., & Hsieh, C. H., (2006). Web page classification based on a support vector machine using a weighted vote schema. *Expert Systems with Applications, 31*(2), 427–435.
6. Dobrica, L., & Niemela, E., (2002). A survey on software architecture analysis methods. *IEEE Transactions on Software Engineering, 28*(7), 638–653.
7. Faulkner, W., (2000). Dualisms, hierarchies and gender in engineering. *Social Studies of Science, 30*(5), 759–792.
8. Fritz, T., Begel, A., Müller, S. C., Yigit-Elliott, S., & Züger, M., (2014). Using psycho-physiological measures to assess task difficulty in software development. In: *Proceedings of the 36th International Conference on Software Engineering* (pp. 402–413).

9. Galster, M., Eberlein, A., & Moussavi, M., (2010). Systematic selection of software architecture styles. *IET Software, 4*(5), 349–360.
10. Garlan, D., & Perry, D. E., (1995). Introduction to the special issue on software architecture. *IEEE Trans. Software Eng., 21*(4), 269–274.
11. Goševa-Popstojanova, K., & Trivedi, K. S., (2001). Architecture-based approach to reliability assessment of software systems. *Performance Evaluation, 45*(2, 3), 179–204.
12. Hofmeister, C., Kruchten, P., Nord, R. L., Obbink, H., Ran, A., & America, P., (2007). A general model of software architecture design derived from five industrial approaches. *Journal of Systems and Software, 80*(1), 106–126.
13. Hossny, A. H., Moschuo, T., Osborne, G., Mitchell, L., & Lothian, N., (2018). Enhancing keyword correlation for event detection in social networks using SVD and k-means: Twitter case study. *Social Network Analysis and Mining, 8*(1), 1–10.
14. Hou, J. L., & Chan, C. A., (2003). A document content extraction model using keyword correlation analysis. *Int. J. Electron. Bus. Manag., 1*(1), 54–62.
15. Immonen, A., & Niemelä, E., (2008). Survey of reliability and availability prediction methods from the viewpoint of software architecture. *Software & Systems Modeling, 7*(1), 49–65.
16. Jansen, A., & Bosch, J., (2005). Software architecture as a set of architectural design decisions. In: *5th Working IEEE/IFIP Conference on Software Architecture (WICSA'05)* (pp. 109–120). IEEE.
17. Jouannaud, J. P., & Okada, M., (1997). Abstract data type systems. *Theoretical Computer Science, 173*(2), 349–391.
18. Le Métayer, D., (1996). Software architecture styles as graph grammars. In: *Proceedings of the 4th ACM SIGSOFT symposium on Foundations of Software Engineering* (pp. 15–23).
19. Le Métayer, D., (1998). Describing software architecture styles using graph grammars. *IEEE Transactions on Software Engineering, 24*(7), 521–533.
20. Lee, E. A., (2010). Disciplined heterogeneous modeling. In: *International Conference on Model Driven Engineering Languages and Systems* (pp. 273–287). Springer, Berlin, Heidelberg.
21. Losavio, F., Chirinos, L., Lévy, N., & Ramdane-Cherif, A., (2003). Quality characteristics for software architecture. *Journal of Object Technology, 2*(2), 133–150.
22. Martini, A., Sikander, E., & Madlani, N., (2018). A semi-automated framework for the identification and estimation of architectural technical debt: A comparative case-study on the modularization of a software component. *Information and Software Technology, 93*, 264–279.
23. Medvidovic, N., & Taylor, R. N., (2000). A classification and comparison framework for software architecture description languages. *IEEE Transactions on Software Engineering, 26*(1), 70–93. Mignolet, J. Y., Nollet, V., Coene, P., Verkest, D., Vernalde, S., & Lauwereins, R., (2003). Infrastructure for design and management of relocatable

tasks in a heterogeneous reconfigurable system-on-chip. In: *Design, Automation & Test in Europe Conference & Exhibition* (Vol. 2, pp. 10986–10986).

24. Monroe, R. T., Kompanek, A., Melton, R., & Garlan, D., (1997). Architectural styles, design patterns, and objects. *IEEE Software, 14*(1), 43–52.
25. Nunez-Yanez, J., Amiri, S., Hosseinabady, M., Rodríguez, A., Asenjo, R., Navarro, A., & Gran, R., (2019). Simultaneous multiprocessing in a software-defined heterogeneous FPGA. *The Journal of Supercomputing, 75*(8), 4078–4095.
26. Perry, D. E., & Wolf, A. L., (1992). Foundations for the study of software architecture. *ACM SIGSOFT Software Engineering Notes, 17*(4), 40–52.
27. Pu, J., Bell, S., Yang, X., Setter, J., Richardson, S., Ragan-Kelley, J., & Horowitz, M., (2017). Programming heterogeneous systems from an image processing DSL. *ACM Transactions on Architecture and Code Optimization (TACO), 14*(3), 1–25.
28. Shaw, M., & Clements, P., (1997). A field guide to boxology: Preliminary classification of architectural styles for software systems. In: *Proceedings Twenty-First Annual International Computer Software and Applications Conference (COMPSAC'97)* (pp. 6–13). IEEE.
29. Shaw, M., (1995). Making choices: A comparison of styles for software architecture. *IEEE Software, 12*(6), 27–41.
30. Sibenik, G., & Kovacic, I., (2020). Assessment of model-based data exchange between architectural design and structural analysis. *Journal of Building Engineering, 32*, 101589.
31. Singh, L. K., Tripathi, A. K., & Vinod, G., (2011). Software reliability early prediction in architectural design phase: Overview and limitations. *Journal of Software Engineering and Applications, 4*(3), 181.
32. Song, X., & Osterweil, L. J., (1994). Experience with an approach to comparing software design methodologies. *IEEE Transactions on Software Engineering, 20*(5), 364–384.
33. Verkest, D., Van, R. K., Bolsens, I., & De Man, H., (1996). CoWare—A design environment for heterogeneous hardware/software systems. *Design Automation for Embedded Systems, 1*(4), 357–386.
34. Zhu, H., (2005). *Software Design Methodology: From Principles to Architectural Styles*. Elsevier.

CHAPTER 8

ARCHITECTURAL DESIGN SPACE

UNIT INTRODUCTION

The majority of design challenges have solutions that reflect diversity. The design may be thought of as navigating the space of potential solutions to find the best one. What have been the structures of the design spaces, and how can we tell if we are heading in the right direction? We still have a long way to go before we can provide any reasonable answers to certain issues, which is regrettably not being conservative. As a comprehensive theory of design method and a foundation for creating software systems for computer-aided designs, design methodologists are building a theory of design spaces since the 1980s (Shahin & Chauhan, 2020).

- To comprehend the architecture of design space and how design spaces may be utilized to solve challenges involving design analysis and synthesis;
- To comprehend how distinct software architecture aspects vary from one another and how the range of such components creates a design space;
- By putting different styles into a design space, we can better grasp the different software styles of architecture (Ipek et al., 2008).

Learning Objective

At the end of this chapter students will be able to learn:

- To understand the structure of design space and how design spaces can be used to solve design synthesis and analysis problems;

- To understand the differences between various software architectural elements and how the variety of these elements form a design space;
- To deepen our understanding of software architectural styles by organizing various styles into a design space.

Key Terms

- Architectural design spaces
- Behavior features
- Static features
- Architectural styles

THEORY OF DESIGN SPACES

Structure of Design Spaces

Let's begin with an illustration. Let's say that our assignment was to create a chair. Think about the seats in Figure 8.1 (Goel & Pirolli, 1992).

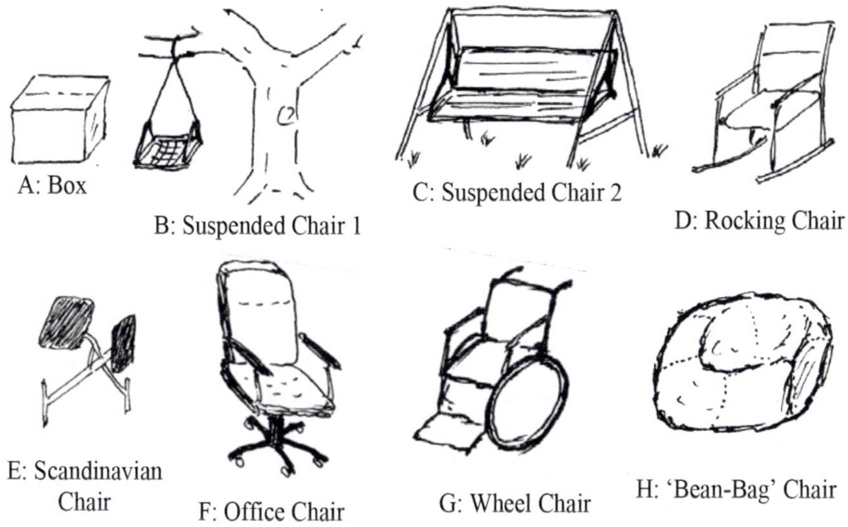

Figure 8.1. The domain of chairs. Source: Image by J. E. Mogensen.

Every chair in the illustration represents a piece of furniture in the area that our design assignment is focused on. An entity is any actual thing that has ever existed, is currently existing, or would someday exist. Every entity has a certain feature that is relevant to the design objective. Every chair, for instance, may fulfill the role of a seat. In other words, it stops the body from sloping downhill whenever a person sits upon that object. Additionally, several of the chairs offer additional features that are important to the design process. For instance, certain chairs can assist an upright posture by supporting the back. The rotation of the back may also be a restriction. These chairs could also have a range of other characteristics. For instance, they might be mobile, simple to produce, attractive, etc. Since they exhibit an object's behaviors whenever it is put in a context, such functionalities and qualities are known as functional properties. Grasp a design domain requires an understanding of its functional features. They specifically outline the functional features that can be realized as well as the design domain that has been focused on. The chairs shown in Figure 8.1 have several functional characteristics, which are listed in Table 8.1 (Radosavovic et al., 2020).

Table 8.1. Chairs' Functional Characteristics

Function	Chair							
	A	B	C	D	E	F	G	H
Seats: prevents a downward movement of the body	+	+	+	+	+	+	+	+
Supports back: supports an upright posture	+	+	+	+	+	+	+	+
Revolves: revolves around a vertical axis	+	+	–	+	+	+	+	+
Movable: can be easily moved	+	–	–	–	+	+	+	+
Constrains back: constrains backward movement of back	–	+	+	–	–	+	+	–
Easy to manufacture: has a simple design with standard components	+	–	–	–	–	+	–	+
Aesthetic	–	+	+	+	+	–	–	–

Did you Know?

Space is one of the elements of design of architecture, as space is continuously studied for its usage. Architectural designs are created by carving space out of space, creating space out of space, and designing spaces by dividing this space using various tools, such as geometry, colors, and shapes.

The things in the domain have additional types of characteristics in addition to such functional ones. For instance, a chair might be lightweight, have legs, or have a wheel. No matter what kind of property it is mechanical, physical, chemical, or any other it may be viewed or possibly measured with the aid of an instrument. Such characteristics are known as the entities' observable characteristics or attributes. The collection of qualities and their connections to the objects inside a design domain explains the range of design options. The entities depicted in Figure 8.1 have several qualities, which are displayed in Table 8.2 (Whitehead, 2001).

Table 8.2. Observable Properties of Chairs

Structure	Chair							
	A	B	C	D	E	F	G	H
Has a seat	+	+	+	+	–	+	+	–
Has a back support	–	+	+	+	–	+	+	–
Has legs	–	–	+	–	–	+	+	–
Has wheels	–	–	–	–	+	+	+	–
Has a vertical rotational degree of freedom	–	+	+	+	–	+	–	–
Is lightweight	+	+	–	–	+	+	+	+
Has a hanger	–	+	+	–	–	–	–	–
Has a brake	–	–	–	–	–	–	+	–

A nice way to formalize design understanding of particular domains is provided by the separation between functional characteristics and observable characteristics and the usage of a physical object to connect among such two categories of property. Such design knowledge representation has been empirical. The following characteristics of this empirical knowledge are important to note.

Remember

Space is the core of architecture. In order to design, it is necessary to conceive and think about architectural space surrounding us by decoding its nature and discovering messages in its built forms.

The structure or visible characteristics can be used to directly derive some functional characteristics. For instance, a chair with wheels can be moved. A chair with a level of freedom for vertical rotation may turn. The structure-function relationship, however, could not be exact. For instance, a chair's vertical level of freedom can't permit 360^0 rotation (Shaw, 2011).

Secondly, not all operational features can be derived from structure or other observable characteristics directly. For instance, a chair without physical back support may nonetheless provide some backsupport. For example, if the box chair (A) is placed close to a wall, it may support the back. Additionally, while lacking physical back support, the Scandinavian chair (E) supports the back.

Thirdly, functional qualities might not be constant or orthogonal. One role might fit another. For instance, the function "supports back" is qualified by the functional characteristic "constrains back." Similarly, to this, observable qualities might not always be orthogonal or independent (Albert et al., 1999).

Lastly, the entities that act as specimen objects for the domain implicitly codify the links between these 2 kinds of characteristics. The empirical understanding of the domain has been frequently used to support the connection of objects having particular qualities. The accuracy and value of the domain knowledge are influenced by three key criteria (Bernsen, 1993):

- **Entity Set:** If a good specimen of actual items was selected influences whether or not the design space's knowledge has been fully documented.
- **Observable and Functional Qualities:** The inclusion of design-related properties in the design space depends on whether a suitable collection of observable and functional attributes was selected.
- **Connection of Characteristics to Entities:** The accuracy of the domain knowledge that is expressed in design space is based on how well the properties are linked to the entities (Coley, 2021).

A set of topology-based axioms are provided by Yoshikawa's general design theory so that the domain knowledge may be mathematically analyzed. The scope of this work does not allow for a thorough examination of the mathematical theory (Rosen, 1996).

DESIGN SPACE OF ARCHITECTURAL ELEMENTS

Design is, in part, about "finding the correct element of a structure." Thus, it is crucial to comprehend the range of elements to choose and employ the appropriate component and also the variety of methods in that elements might be assembled. These kinds of structures provide a realm in which certain designs are components.

We consider many software architectural features in this section and employ the theory of design space to them. Therefore, we used the term "software architecture elements" to refer to both connectors and elements. As a design space, we methodically give information about software architectural components. To do this, we look at several observable characteristics of software architectural components (Philipp & Bletzinger, 2013).

It's important to note that software design differs fundamentally from the designs of many other physical artifacts. Software systems are unseen, as was discussed previously, thus the idea of observable attributes for physical artifacts doesn't make sense for software. However, behavior characteristics and static features may be used to categorize the characteristics of software artifacts. They resemble, accordingly, the functional aspects and the observable characteristics. As a result, we'll first look at the behavior characteristics of different software architectural pieces before talking about their static characteristics (White, 2011).

Behavior Features

Architectural elements' dynamic behavior throughout time is represented by their behavior characteristics. A set of continuous temporal "episodes" might be seen as the implementation of an architectural element. Each episode is a period during which the element has been continually active while being controlled by at least a single thread. Figure 8.2 shows the time perspective of one architectural component's implementation in one episode. The component is connected to 2 control threads. Beginning at moment *t1*, thread A ends at time *t*2. Beginning at moment *t'1*, thread B ends at time *t'*2. The illustration also depicts data moving into and out of thread A using the arrows designated *d1* and *d*2 and moving into and out of thread B using *d'1* and *d'*2, respectively. The beginning and end of the episode are indicated by the time's *ts* and *te*, correspondingly (Schoeppe et al., 2017).

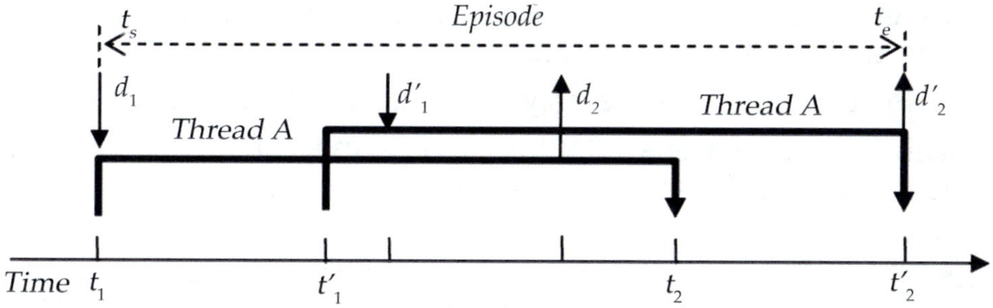

Figure 8.2. An example of how to examine architectural features in time.

Source: Image by khanacademy.org.

A software architecture component's behavior characteristics are associated with the temporal interactions between the components' run-time events. For instance, if or not the acceptance of data always occurs concurrently with the adoption of control whether or if it is impossible to accept the second thread of control? So forth. As a result, in, behavior features are referred to as temporal features (Casarrubea et al., 2018).

Static Features

The static characteristics have no connection to run-time events (Ngo & Nguyen, 2020). The component's code's semantics and syntax may be utilized to determine them. They mainly discuss how architectural components are structured and how those structures relate to other components. For instance, where does the information for the architectural components originate from and where do they go? Are there directions in the links to other components? The events that take place during run-time are unimportant to these characteristics. Static characteristics can be categorized into seven groups similarly to behavior characteristics (Ngo & Nguyen, 2020).

- **Ports:** This group's attributes are focused on the architectural element's connecting ports. How several ports, for instance, may a component have?

Are the ports pointed or not? If the ports are pointed, what are the orientations of the ports? The qualities are:

- **Several in-Ports:** Several in ports, or points wherein control and data enter the element, are possible.
- **One Person in Port:** Only a single component may be in port.

- **Several Out Ports:** The element may have several outports through which data and control may be the exit.
- **Singular Ports:** There can be only one outport per element.
- **Ports with Two Directions:** Control or data may enter and exit the components using ports that may operate in both directions (Islam et al., 2013).
- **Binding Time:** This characteristic relates to the connection of the component's ports to the data and control source and destination. The architectural component's port may occasionally be linked to another architectural element.

Generally, this binding may be decided upon at specification time, or before the software is executed. Whenever the architectural component is called, it may also be bound. Additionally, it may be decided as the element is being executed, and it might even alter. The following characteristics follow from these:

- **Binding at the Time of Specification:** At the time of description, the ports of the component may be connected to the destinations and sources of information and control.
- **Binding at the Time of Invocation:** At the time of invocation, or when the component is called upon and becomes active, the ports of the component may be bound to the destinations and sources of information or control.
- **Binding during Execution:** At execution time, or when the component becomes active, the ports may be tied to the destinations and sources of control and data (Shabtai et al., 2009).

DESIGN SPACE OF ARCHITECTURAL STYLES

Utilizing the theory of design spaces, we evaluate the software styles of architecture discussed in the earlier chapters in this part. We'll start by talking about the structural and behavioral characteristics of several software architectural designs that set them apart from one another. Next, we'll talk about how structural and behavioral characteristics might be used to categorize different architectural styles (Shahin & Chauhan, 2020).

Characteristic Features of Architectural Styles

An architectural style's structural element and the structure of its software systems have been related. These qualities consist of:

- **Constituent Components:** What are the permitted types of connectors and components for the design? For instance, in the pipe-and-filter design, connectors, and elements should both pipe.

- **Control Topology:** What geometric shape does the style's systems' control flow take? For instance, elements should be organized into a hierarchical structure for the main program-and-subroutine approach (Goel & Jawahar, 2012).
- **Data Topology:** What geometric shape does the data flow for systems in this manner take? For instance, elements are arranged in a linear sequence structure in batch sequential processing, which passes data from one component to the next.
- Is there a significant isomorphism between the control topology and the data topology in terms of their topological structures? As an illustration, the topological structure including all systems using batch sequential processing is the same from both a control- flow and a data-flow perspective. From a control perspective, the main-program-and-subroutine style's elements are arranged hierarchically. Furthermore, the system may have any structure from the perspective of dataflow because information may freely move between elements through shared information stores. As a result, there is no isomorphism between the data and control topologies (Blumenson, 1995).
- If the data and control topologies of the systems in the style are identical, does the route of the data/control interaction flow in the identical directions as the information flows, or in the other direction? Data is sent from one element to another in the batch sequential processing approach in the same way that control has been passed between the elements. Instead of passing data between elements in the same direction, control is shared between them in the server and client style. An architectural style's behavioral characteristics are traits connected to the systems' dynamic behavior. These are a few of them (Barz & Denzler, 2021).
- **Synchronicity:** To what extent are the behaviors of the elements controlled by one another? Each of the following may describe how two components are synchronized.
- **Lockstep:** The state of one element indicates the state of the other element. For instance, when using batch sequential processing, an element won't start running until its predecessor has finished (Dunlop, 2003).
- **Synchronous:** Elements synchronize at specific states to ensure they are in those states simultaneously to cooperate, but the links to other states are unpredictable. As an illustration, for synchronous communication to occur between components A and B, both A and B must be simultaneously in the condition of transmitting and receiving data. Element A should wait until B enters the receiving state if B is transmitting but A is receiving. A must wait for B if B is receiving

and A is not yet in the sending state. The components are free to do whatever they choose after the communication (Ali & Hassan, 2018).

- **Asynchronous:** Elements aren't synchronized at any point in time, although the behavior of one element can be influenced by the behavior of others. As an illustration, element C may communicate data to element D in an asynchronous communication scenario without having to wait for element D to be received. What element C sent would be received by element D once D is data-receiving (Shalunts & Sablatnig, 2012).
- **Opportunistic:** Two elements operate concurrently in total independence from one another.
- **Data Access Mode:** Why is data distributed among the system's components? It may be transmitted from one element to another, for instance, through the use of message passing. It may also be communicated by being placed in a location that is open to all sharers. The information access method is copy-out-copy-in if an element copies information from a general store, enhances it, and then puts it back into the general store. To certain recipients, information may be broadcast or multicast in certain styles (Wright, 1992).
- **Data Flow Consistency:** How consistently does data move through the system as a whole? In a system with continuous data flow, new data is constantly accessible. A system with sporadic data flow generates new data at specific intervals. In systems that require a lot of data or a lot of computation, data transfer among elements may be higher volume or lower volume, respectively.
- When names have been assigned to objects for data and control transfer, this is known as binding time. In other words, when a participant in control or data transmission has been identified. It could happen when the programmer is writing the source code, or at code-time. It could happen during compilation, and whenever source code has been turned into object code. It might happen at system invocation time, whenever the operating system first starts the system's execution. Additionally, it might happen while the system is being used at run-ti*me (Li, 2001).*

Classification of Styles

The defining characteristics mentioned above can be used to describe a software architecture style. Think about the pipe-and-filter design, for instance. Filters serve as the elements, which have been transducers, and pipes serve as the connections, which have been data streams, for structural features. Every directed graph may serve as the data topology, and any directed graph may serve as the control topology. Particularly, the system should be linear when it is executed in the Unix shell; that is, it should be made up of text output or input programs acting as filters that are linearly linked using the connector '|.'

The directions of the flow of information and the control flow are identical (Rasdi & Tajuddin, 2007).

When it comes to behavior characteristics, the elements may run concurrently and asynchronously. Instead of being copied or shared, data are transmitted from one element to another in the data access mode. Data transfers can be a large volume and intermittent. The operating system's initialization of the system is when the binding time may be as late as the invocation time. We may identify whether one style is a sub-style of another using a design space. We may state that style A is a sub-style of style B if style A's values for a distinctive feature are a subset or a special case of style B's values for the same characteristic. A sub-style of call-and-return style is, for instance, abstract data type (Khamparia & Pandey, 2020).

ACTIVITY 8.1.

What is a design synthesis problem? Describe the process of solving a design synthesis problem by using a design space.

SUMMARY

Generally, a design space shows a body of knowledge about the design of a group of artifacts that have similar primary functional properties but differ in several functional and structural aspects. Functional qualities and structural characteristics are the 2 categories into which the features associated with an artifact are often divided in a design space. This shows two different kinds of knowledge. Firstly, it gives information on the range of designs available in the field in terms of legal combinations of structural and functional qualities.

Secondly, it depicts the connections among structures and functions within the specified design domain. Designers can address the synthesis and evaluation of design issues using a design space that is depicted in this fashion. Finding the right structure for a system to satisfy specific functional needs is a synthesis design problem. Finding the qualities of a design whenever the design structure is supplied, at least partially, is the goal of an analytical design problem.

The analysis of the many software architectural components can be done using the generic theory of design space. A set of static characteristics and a set of behavior characteristics may be used to express and define the domain understanding of software architecture parts. Architectural elements are characterized by behavior attributes based on their run-time behaviors. They are explained in terms of the timings of different run-time occurrences, like the receipt and transmission of data and control. These characteristics resemble the practical characteristics of actual artifacts. Architectural elements' qualities that are unrelated to run-time events are represented by static attributes. They resemble the structural characteristics of actual artifacts. The range of software architectural designs also creates a design space wherein behavioral and static characteristics categorize the many software architectural styles.

REVIEW QUESTIONS

1. What do you understand from the theory of design spaces?
2. Differentiate between behavior features and static features.
2. Explain the design space of architectural styles in detail.

MULTIPLE CHOICE QUESTIONS

1. Which of them is the part of design space of architectural styles?

a. Behavior features

b. Static features

c. Both (a) and (b)

d. None of above

2. **In which of the following style new clients can be added easily?**
   a. Data Flow Architecture
   b. Call and Return Architecture
   c. Data Centered Architectures
   d. None of the mentioned
3. **What is correct about Data centered architecture?**
   a. It is modifiable with respect to changing the functionality of any particular client as other clients will not be affected
   b. It is non-modifiable with respect to changing the functionality of any particular client as other clients will be affected
   c. Coupling among the client will lessen the effect of data center architecture
   d. All of the mentioned
4. **What is pipes and filter style?**
   a. They emphasize on incremental transformation of data by successive components
   b. It is used in UNIX family of the system
   c. They return no state information
   c. All of the mentioned
5. **What is batch sequential style?**
   a. In batch sequential components are independent programs
   b. Assumptions is that each step runs to completion before the next step starts
   c. All of the mentioned
   d. None of the mentioned

Answer

1. (c) 2. (c) 3. (d) 4. (d) 5. (c)

REFERENCES

1. Albert, D., & Lukas, J., (1999). *Knowledge Spaces: Theories, Empirical Research, and Applications*. Psychology Press.
2. Ali, A., & Hassan, A. S., (2018). Influence of the Mughal architectural style on Malaysian mosques. *The Arab World Geographer, 21*(4), 318–330.
3. Balon, E. K., (1981). Additions and amendments to the classification of reproductive styles in fishes. *Environmental Biology of Fishes, 6*(3), 377–389.
4. Barz, B., & Denzler, J., (2021). *Wikichurches: A Fine-Grained Dataset of Architectural Styles with Real-World Challenges*. arXiv preprint arXiv:2108.06959.

5. Bernsen, N. O., (1993). Structuring design spaces. In: *INTERACT'93 and CHI'93 Conference Companion on Human Factors in Computing Systems* (pp. 211, 212).
6. Blumenson, J. J., (1995). *Identifying American Architecture: A Pictorial Guide to Styles and Terms, 1600–1945*. Rowman Altamira.
7. Casarrubea, M., Magnusson, M. S., Anguera, M. T., Jonsson, G. K., Castañer, M., Santangelo, A., & Crescimanno, G., (2018). T-pattern detection and analysis for the discovery of hidden features of behavior. *Journal of Neuroscience Methods, 310*, 24–32.
8. Coley, C. W., (2021). Defining and exploring chemical spaces. *Trends in Chemistry, 3*(2), 133–145. Dunlop, C., (2003). *Architectural Styles*. Dearborn Real Estate.
9. Goel, A., Juneja, M., & Jawahar, C. V., (2012). Are buildings only instances? Exploration in architectural style categories. In: *Proceedings of the Eighth Indian Conference on Computer Vision, Graphics and Image Processing* (pp. 1–8).
10. Goel, V., & Pirolli, P., (1992). The structure of design problem spaces. *Cognitive Science, 16*(3), 395– 429.
11. Ipek, E., McKee, S. A., Singh, K., Caruana, R., Supinski, B. R. D., & Schulz, M., (2008). Efficient architectural design space exploration via predictive modeling. *ACM Transactions on Architecture and Code Optimization (TACO), 4*(4), 1–34.
12. Islam, R., Tian, R., Batten, L. M., & Versteeg, S., (2013). Classification of malware based on integrated static and dynamic features. *Journal of Network and Computer Applications, 36*(2), 646–656.
13. Karsai, M., Kaski, K., Barabási, A. L., & Kertész, J., (2012). Universal features of correlated bursty behavior. *Scientific Reports, 2*(1), 1–7.
14. Khamparia, A., & Pandey, B., (2020). Association of learning styles with different e-learning problems: A systematic review and classification. *Education and Information Technologies, 25*(2), 1303– 1331.
15. Kim, J. S., & Garlan, D., (2010). Analyzing architectural styles. *Journal of Systems and Software, 83*(7), 1216–1235.
16. Li, A. I., (2001). *A Shape Grammar for Teaching the Architectural Style of the Yingzao Fashi*. Doctoral dissertation, Massachusetts Institute of Technology.
17. Marasco, E., & Sansone, C., (2012). Combining perspiration-and morphology-based static features for fingerprint liveness detection. *Pattern Recognition Letters, 33*(9), 1148–1156.
18. Mishra, P., Dutt, N., & Nicolau, A., (2001). Functional abstraction driven design space exploration of heterogeneous programmable architectures. In: *Proceedings of the 14th International Symposium on Systems synthesis* (pp. 256–261).
19. Ngo, Q. D., Nguyen, H. T., Le, V. H., & Nguyen, D. H., (2020). A survey of IoT malware and detection methods based on static features. *ICT Express, 6*(4), 280–286.
20. Obeso, A. M., Vázquez, M. S. G., Acosta, A. A. R., & Benois-Pineau, J., (2017). Connoisseur: Classification of styles of Mexican architectural heritage with deep

learning and visual attention prediction. In: *Proceedings of the 15th International Workshop on Content-Based Multimedia Indexing* (pp. 1–7).

21. Perreault, W. D., Darden, D. K., & Darden, W. R., (1977). A psychographic classification of vacation life styles. *Journal of Leisure Research, 9*(3), 208–224.
22. Philipp, B., & Bletzinger, K. U., (2013). Hybrid structures–Enlarging the design space of architectural membranes. *Journal of the International Association for Shell and Spatial Structures, 54*(4), 281–291.
23. Radosavovic, I., Kosaraju, R. P., Girshick, R., He, K., & Dollár, P., (2020). Designing network design spaces. In: *Proceedings of the IEEE/CVF Conference on Computer Vision and Pattern Recognition* (pp. 10428–10436).
24. Rasdi, M. T. M., & Tajuddin, M., (2007). Mosque architecture in Malaysia: Classification of styles and possible influence. *Journal Alam Bina, 9*(3), 1–37.
25. Rosen, D. W., (1996). Design of modular product architectures in discrete design spaces subject to life cycle issues. In: *International Design Engineering Technical Conferences and Computers and Information in Engineering Conference* (Vol. 97591, p. V003T03A008). American Society of Mechanical Engineers.
26. Schoeppe, S., Alley, S., Rebar, A. L., Hayman, M., Bray, N. A., Van, L. W., & Vandelanotte, C., (2017). Apps to improve diet, physical activity and sedentary behavior in children and adolescents: A review of quality, features and behavior change techniques. *International Journal of Behavioral Nutrition and Physical Activity, 14*(1), 1–10.
27. Shabtai, A., Moskovitch, R., Elovici, Y., & Glezer, C., (2009). Detection of malicious code by applying machine learning classifiers on static features: A state-of-the-art survey. *Information Security Technical Report, 14*(1), 16–29.
28. Shahin, M., Babar, M. A., & Chauhan, M. A., (2020). Architectural design space for modeling and simulation as a service: A review. *Journal of Systems and Software, 170*, 110752.
29. Shalunts, G., Haxhimusa, Y., & Sablatnig, R., (2011). Architectural style classification of building facade windows. In: *International Symposium on Visual Computing* (pp. 280–289). Springer, Berlin, Heidelberg.
30. Shalunts, G., Haxhimusa, Y., & Sablatnig, R., (2012). Architectural style classification of domes. In:
31. *International Symposium on Visual Computing* (pp. 420–429). Springer, Berlin, Heidelberg.
32. Shaw, M., & Clements, P., (1997). A field guide to boxology: Preliminary classification of architectural styles for software systems. In: *Proceedings Twenty-First Annual International Computer Software and Applications Conference (COMPSAC'97)* (pp. 6–13). IEEE.
33. Shaw, M., (2011). The role of design spaces. *IEEE Software, 29*(1), 46–50.
34. Shoaib, M., Jha, N. K., & Verma, N., (2012). Algorithm-driven architectural design

CHAPTER 8

space exploration of domain-specific medical-sensor processors. *IEEE Transactions on Very Large Scale Integration (VLSI) Systems, 21*(10), 1849–1862.

35. White, A. W., (2011). *The Elements of Graphic Design: Space, Unity, Page Architecture, and Type*.
36. Skyhorse Publishing, Inc.
37. Whitehead, Jr. E. J., (2001). Design spaces for link and structure versioning. In: *Proceedings of the 12th ACM conference on Hypertext and Hypermedia* (pp. 195–204).
38. Wright, G. R. H., (1992). Architectural details from the Asklepeion at balagrae (Beida). *Libyan Studies, 23*, 45–72.
39. Xie, Y., Loh, G. H., Black, B., & Bernstein, K., (2006). Design space exploration for 3D architectures.
40. *ACM Journal on Emerging Technologies in Computing Systems (JETC), 2*(2), 65–103.
41. Xie, Y., Zhu, J., Cao, Y., Zhang, Y., Feng, D., Zhang, Y., & Chen, M., (2020). Efficient video fire detection exploiting motion-flicker-based dynamic features and deep static features. *IEEE Access, 8*, 81904–81917.
42. Zdun, U., (2007). Systematic pattern selection using pattern language grammars and design space analysis. *Software: Practice and Experience, 37*(9), 983–1016.

INDEX

D

T

Printed in the United States
by Baker & Taylor Publisher Services